"This well-researched biography narrates the life story of a dedicated pioneer medical missionary, the fruits of whose labor lived on and still continue to flourish, as this book makes clear. Paul Balisky is to be highly commended for producing such a detailed and balanced biography of Thomas Lambie, missionary entrepreneur and servant of God. The book is a valuable resource for students of missiology in general and of the evangelical movement in Ethiopia, in particular."

—Debela Birri
former Director, Ethiopian Graduate School of Theology, Addis Ababa

"I well recall my mother Betty's unforgettable heroic stories about the Lambies' lives in Sudan and Ethiopia. While Grandma Charlotte's visits to us in England were rare, she was a great letter writer, binding our family together. Both my mother Betty and Grandma Charlotte excelled as mothers and homemakers in places far from home, raising their children, cultivating gardens, and welcoming anybody who dropped by. It gives me great satisfaction to know that their story has now been published."

—Margaret Mary Hall
granddaughter of Dr. Thomas and Mrs. Charlotte Lambie

"What might an ordinary person who unreservedly yields his life to God look like? Paul Balisky's biography of Dr. Thomas Lambie reveals human vulnerability, on the one hand, but celebrates God's love, providence, guidance, and unfailing presence for those who trust in him, on the other hand. This book is of profound importance for those who desire to respond to the call of God to serve cross-culturally. I highly recommend it to local churches, parachurch ministries, and theological schools."

—Shiferaw Wolde Michael
former President of the Ethiopian Kale Heywet Church,
National Director of Compassion International,
Founder of the Ethiopian Child Development Training and Research Centre

Thomas A. Lambie

Dr. Thomas A. Lambie
missionary statesman, medical doctor, friend to all,
builder of hospitals, author, and popular speaker
(Courtesy of Margaret Hall Special Collection)

Thomas A. Lambie

Missionary Doctor and Entrepreneur

E. PAUL BALISKY

Foreword by Darrell L. Whiteman

WIPF & STOCK · Eugene, Oregon

THOMAS A. LAMBIE
Missionary Doctor and Entrepreneur

Wipf & Stock
An Imprint of Wipf and Stock Publishers
199 W. 8th Ave., Suite 3
Eugene, OR 97401

www.wipfandstock.com

PAPERBACK ISBN: 978-1-7252-5764-1
HARDCOVER ISBN: 978-1-7252-5765-8
EBOOK ISBN: 978-1-7252-5766-5

Manufactured in the U.S.A.   FEBRUARY 20, 2020

To
Lila Willard Balisky
My beloved wife, helpmeet, scholar,
and mother of our three able sons,
Allen, Loren, and Kevin

"Christ the Chief Corner Stone"
–/–/–/–/–
In 1932 this motto of
Dr. Thomas A. Lambie's missionary career
was chiseled into the cornerstone
of the ALERT Leprosarium,
Addis Ababa, Abyssinia/Ethiopia.

Contents

Sidebars

Maps

Images

Foreword

WHAT CAN WE LEARN from the lives and ministries of missionaries from the United States who served in the heyday of twentieth-century colonialism? In today's mission world, greatly impacted by globalization, urbanization, and the growth of Christianity in the Global South, I have observed through personal experience that a growing number of cross-cultural witnesses emerging from the Majority World would greatly benefit from the story of Dr. Thomas Lambie. His life was one of struggle, failure, and yet fruitfulness in three diverse countries: Anglo-Egyptian Sudan, Abyssinia/Ethiopia, and Palestine. Missionaries no longer go from just the West to the rest, but from everywhere to everywhere. So, other than adding to the historical record, what missiological value might there be in the biography of another Western missionary?

Perhaps a hagiography would not be so helpful, but this biography of Thomas Lambie is far from hagiography. Based on careful archival research and the examination of hundreds of letters and reports, this book holds many relevant missiological and spiritual lessons from which we may learn and profit.

First, God uses imperfect people. This is not new information, but there are still some of us who are driven by unrealistic expectations formed by the Christian public image of a missionary as a saint who never sins, a hardy pioneer who without flinching suffers great deprivations and loss, an outstanding preacher or medical doctor or personal worker who is creative, sensitive, always triumphant, and willing to "stomp through the steaming jungles to reach the teeming millions of lost souls." Lambie had no such illusions about himself, as this unvarnished story makes clear. Self-awareness and humility, both of which Lambie had, are important assets for cross-cultural ministry.

Second, interpersonal conflicts with other cross-cultural witnesses almost always crop up. Two areas that reduce cross-cultural effectiveness are the inability to adapt when placed in new cultural contexts and inter-personal conflicts with mission colleagues. Lambie seems to have had little trouble with cross-cultural adaptation and, in fact, he flourished in new settings. He mastered several Sudanese languages, Amharic, and Arabic. Further, he had that indispensable characteristic of curiosity. He was eager to learn something new, whether it was medical knowledge or geographical discovery. At times early in his career referred to by missionary colleagues as a "loose cannon," Lambie exuded enthusiasm and confidence (but not arrogance) to the point of occasionally arousing strife, conflict, and misunderstanding with his colleagues.

A third missiological lesson we can learn from the life of Thomas Lambie is the *sine qua non* of establishing relationships across a broad spectrum of people, personalities, and positions. He had a large capacity for friendship and was able to connect with people from the lowest to the highest rungs of the social ladder, whether it was as personal physician to Haile Sellassie in Abyssinia or sharing what meager food he had with an indigenous helper. Too frequently, missionaries prioritize programs over people and become task-oriented rather than person-oriented in their ministry. In this biography we learn how Lambie balanced the two. In addition to developing a wide spectrum of public relationships, he never allowed them to crowd out his devotion and personal relationship to his wife Charlotte.

Fourth, the burgeoning field of missionary member care has underscored the importance resilience has for longer-lasting and more effective cross-cultural ministry. Like the Apostle Paul who rose above tremendous difficulties and was not deterred from "preaching" Christ (2 Cor. 4:8–9), Thomas Lambie exhibited enormous resilience and was always looking for ways to live out the Great Commission and enact the Great Commandment. Resilient cross-cultural witnesses, while acknowledging their own culpability, are able to rise above misfortune and tragedy and move beyond misunderstanding. Clarence Duff, one of Lambie's missionary colleagues, noted about him, "If sometimes his judgement or his actions proved to be unwise, he rose above his faults, outlived them and the criticisms incurred, and went on to fresh achievements."[1]

Fifth, another missiological lesson for today is the necessity of spiritual depth and deep commitment to the kingdom of God. Lambie was a man of prayer and the Word. He often read through the Bible every two years, and despite his strong individualism he seemed always to return to a fundamental awareness of his total dependence on God in the most difficult and trying of times.

---

1. Duff, *Cords of Love*, 334.

God continues to invite all of us to join Jesus in his mission in the world. In this engaging biography of Dr. Thomas Lambie we are presented with an opportunity to learn and be inspired by a saint who has gone before us.

Darrell L. Whiteman

Former Professor of Anthropology and Dean,
E. Stanley Jones School of World Mission and Evangelism,
Asbury Theological Seminary, Wilmore, Kentucky,
and former editor, *Missiology: An International Review*

Preface

ONLY AFTER I DECIDED to write this biography did I begin to realize the many ways in which my own life interconnected with the life of Thomas A. Lambie. The most salient, of course, is that my wife, Lila, and I served in Ethiopia under the Sudan Interior Mission (SIM) for forty years. When we first arrived in Ethiopia in 1967, we knew very little about Lambie, the pioneer missionary entrepreneur.

Over the years we began to discover interlinkings, and the Lambie story continues to come to life for us, even now. For example, Lila's parents were closely linked to the New Jersey Keswick movement, and she has found a photograph in her mother's old album entitled "Claneys at The Meadows." The Claneys were Charlotte Lambie's parents, Albert and Elizabeth, and their home, called The Meadows, was a special destination for many Christians from the Philadelphia area during the 1930s and 1940s. Several relatives on my wife's side of the family were also connected to the various Presbyterian missions of that era. Not least, Lila's family, on their way back to Kenya from a furlough in 1953, happened to be in London for the coronation of Queen Elizabeth II. The Lambies were also in London for that royal occasion.

There were Wheaton College connections. In 1962, I was one of twenty-two archaeology students who, under the direction of Dr. Joseph Free, spent three months on a dig near the biblical city of Dothan. At one point we were entertained by Mrs. Irma Lambie, Dr. Lambie's widow, at the Lambie Guest House located at Ain Arroub, just south of Bethlehem. Lila and I also knew Mrs. Winifred Hockman, who worked at Wheaton and who would tell intriguing tales of how her husband, Dr. Robert Hockman, had been killed by an Italian bomb in Ethiopia in 1936. On our first furlough from Ethiopia, while I was doing further studies at Fuller Theological Seminary, in Pasadena, California, we attended Glendale Presbyterian Church, where Lambie had preached.

Several Ethiopia connections come to mind. While we resided in Addis Ababa (1979–83), the Dutch ambassador, the Honorable Wieger Hellema, invited us to his home on several occasions for dinners and concerts. The Dutch Embassy residence happened to be the former SIM headquarters, a sturdy stone structure built by Lambie in 1932.

When Lila was hospitalized for a broken wrist in 2002, she was rushed to the ALERT Hospital (the former SIM Leprosarium at Furi) on the outskirts of Addis Ababa. Throughout the years we have taken many a visitor to view the cornerstone of the old hospital building, which proclaims, "Christ is the Chief Corner Stone." Lambie laid that cornerstone in 1932.

More recently, in 2013, we had the privilege of meeting Lambie's only granddaughter, Margaret Rees Hall, in Wales. Since then we have had the pleasure of hosting Margaret and her daughter, Teresa, in our home in Grande Prairie, Alberta. Together, we enjoyed a scenic holiday drive through the Canadian Rocky Mountains.

Little did I know many years ago that the itinerating I was doing by mule—from 1972 to 1975—in southern Ethiopia was in the tradition of SIM Ethiopia's founder. I was reaching out in Christian witness along with Ethiopian evangelists in the same spirit and mode as Lambie. My territory, however, covered a mere fraction of the vast areas of Ethiopia's mountains and valleys that Lambie previously traveled through. Last, but not least, Lila's faithful packing of my ancient but well-supplied army food box was reminiscent of Charlotte Lambie's faithful packing of food for the road, though Charlotte often packed for up to eight trekkers.

Today in Addis Ababa, one can still find a good cup of Ethiopian coffee at the colorful little Lambie Café that is located near the former George Memorial Hospital, built by Lambie in 1924. On the wall of the cafe is a black and white framed photograph of Dr. Lambie doing hospital rounds.

The interconnections with Lambie's history continue to live on.

Acknowledgments

FOR THOSE WHO HAVE assisted in bringing this work to completion, I am indeed grateful. I initially presented "Dr. Thomas Lambie in Ethiopia" as a lecture at the International Conference on SIM History in Africa convened in Addis Ababa, Ethiopia, July 9–11, 2013.[1] Dr. Gary Corwin and Dr. Tim Geysbeek, colleagues at SIM International, encouraged me to develop Dr. Lambie's story into a full biography.

My thanks to Mrs. Susan McGinney, Mrs. Evie Bowers, and Dr. Geysbeek for tracking down documents related to Lambie that are tucked away in the SIM International Archives located in Charlotte, North Carolina. Rev. Keith Coleman, executive director of the Independent Board for Presbyterian Foreign Missions, provided significant archival information and photographs of Dr. Lambie's medical ministry in Jordan.

I am grateful to my wife, Dr. Lila Balisky, and our son Allen, both of whom are gifted with eagle eyes when it comes to words. Lila also deserves special thanks for her assistance in making the Lambie story flow. To Mr. Stephen Plant, with his computer savvy in producing the final copies of maps and pictures, I give thanks.

Mrs. Margaret Mary Hall, granddaughter of Thomas and Charlotte Lambie, generously shared stories of her grandparents' visits to England in the 1940s and 1950s. When Lila and I visited her in Wales, Margaret displayed for us her treasures of exotic Lambie memorabilia which she has preserved in her home. One very special item is a distinguished royal blue cloak given to Dr. Lambie by Haile Sellassie, emperor of Ethiopia. She also generously shared her own personal archives, which hold dozens of documents pertaining to mission business plus invaluable pictures and precious family letters.

Dr. Paul Bowers, a former SIM colleague, is another Lambie relative who encouraged me throughout this writing project. Related to Dr. Lambie

---

1. See archives.sim.org/uploads/History%20Conference%20announcement.pdf.

through the McQuilkins of Columbia International University, Columbia, South Carolina, Paul is a professional historian in his own right. He pointed me to significant historical sources that shed light on the Lambie period of mission history.

I am grateful to Dr. Dwight Baker for his professional skill as copyeditor. My connection with him began in 2006 at the Overseas Ministries Study Center in New Haven, Connecticut. His work has enhanced the readability and accuracy of the Lambie account. A very special thanks goes to him for patiently serving as a "hound of heaven."

Support received through SIM Canada was vital to the project. The trust and confidence that Mr. John Rose of SIM Canada expressed that I would duly complete what I promised to accomplish was an ongoing encouragement. And thanks to the many generous donors, one of whom was Dr. Dieter Schmoll, formerly a missionary doctor in Ethiopia. In 1953 he was a student at Bibelheim, Beatenberg, Germany, when Dr. Lambie challenged the students for missionary service.

Readers should be aware that various spellings can be found online and in publications about Ethiopia for the names of persons, locations, and Ethiopian institutions that are referred to throughout the book. These variations commonly reflect differences in transliteration of Amharic and other Ethiopian languages. Again, my thanks to Dwight Baker for assistance with this challenge.

Several persons and archives have kindly provided photographs, maps, and illustrations. Credit for each is given where it appears in the text.

For the privilege of immersing myself in the missionary legacy of Dr. Thomas Lambie, I am indeed grateful to God. May all who read this book be blessed and challenged by the life of this extraordinary missionary entrepreneur.

E. Paul Balisky
Grande Prairie
Alberta, Canada
April 2019

1

Family, Early Life, and Education

Our Lord desires you to have swift feet to do His will.

THOMAS A. LAMBIE, *A BRUISED REED*, 91

THE FAMILY BACKGROUND OF Thomas Alexander Lambie is known back to the beginning of the nineteenth century. France, Scotland, and Holland each contributed to his lineage as his forebears made their way to the United States.

Jean Pierre Sioussat, one of Lambie's great-grandfathers, was born in Paris in 1781 and lived through the Reign of Terror there and the eventual beheading of Louis XVI in 1793. In order to escape the tyranny of the French revolution, Sioussat went to sea in a French merchant vessel at a young age. In 1805 he jumped ship in New York and traveled directly to Washington, DC, where he later was employed by President Madison as doorkeeper to the White House. Dolly Madison, the president's wife, took a fancy to Jean Sioussat (by then nicknamed "French John"), and retained him as her private assistant for the various elaborate state functions hosted at the White House. During the burning of Washington in 1814, Sioussat performed a heroic deed. "John Sioussa [*sic*] cut the [Gilbert] Stuart portrait of Washington from its frame with his penknife, and carried it to a place of safety. He warned those who would have rolled it up to keep it straight."[1] He died in 1864 at the age of 83 having been married three times.[2]

One of Thomas Lambie's great-grandmothers, Charlotte Julia De Graff, was born in 1799 in Holland.[3] Because of political upheaval in Holland, around 1818 she and her husband sailed for the New World. Their ship was wrecked in a stormy sea off the American coast; only Charlotte and two of the sailors survived. Now without her husband, Charlotte and the two sailors were picked up by a passing ship and taken to the New York harbor. Rather than seeking help from compatriots in New York, Charlotte began walking to Washington, DC, the country's capital. "At Bladensburg she sank, exhausted, by a tree to die, overcome by physical fatigue and the sorrows that had so early beset her life."[4] Charlotte was found in that exhausted state by a Mrs. King and was eventually placed in various Episcopalian homes in Washington where she was shown kindness. In 1820 she married John Sioussa (the "t" had been dropped from the family name), a widower with four children. Charlotte and John had ten children, four of whom died in infancy.[5]

One of Charlotte and John's daughters, Aimee, married William Lambie. They became Thomas Lambie's paternal grandparents. With roots in Paisley, Scotland, William Lambie was a stonemason who found employment in Washington, DC. The couple had five sons and two daughters.[6] Sadly, father William died soon after their last child was born. Mother Aimee and the seven children eventually moved to Pittsburgh, Pennsylvania, where jobs were more readily available.[7]

---

1. This statement, by a certain "E.M.G.," appears on page 9 of "Jean Pierre Sioussat and Charlotte Julia De Graff," a 42-page document dated 1887. (The document is now in the personal archives of Margaret Rees Hall, who resides in Kerry [near Newtown], Wales.) Lambie's account differs. He writes of Sioussat "cutting the painting from the frame and wrapping it around his body under his greatcoat"; see Lambie, *Doctor without a Country*, 13. The discrepancy between accounts becomes greater when, more recently, Peter Snow reports that "according to Marion Meckenburg, the conservator, there is no evidence that the canvas of the Washington portrait was ever cut to remove it from its frame"; see Snow, *When Britain Burned the White House*, 108.

2. E.M.G., "Jean Pierre Sioussat and Charlotte Julia De Graff," 18, Margaret Hall Special Collection (hereinafter MHSC).

3. E.M.G., "Jean Pierre Sioussat and Charlotte Julia De Graff," 21.

4. E.M.G., "Jean Pierre Sioussat and Charlotte Julia De Graff," 24.

5. E.M.G., "Jean Pierre Sioussat and Charlotte Julia De Graff," 26.

6. Lambie, *Doctor without a Country*, 13.

7. The information for Aimee Sioussa found at www.ancestry.com does not correlate exactly with the account provided by Lambie, *Doctor without a Country*, 13.

Thomas A. Lambie: Early years in eastern United States

The oldest son of William and Aimee Lambie, John S. Lambie, was an aggressive and able young workman, who attempted to fill the role of his deceased father and to provide for the material needs of the household. He was also an eager student and graduated in first place from the recently established Pittsburgh High School. Following that he went on to study law. John S. Lambie was also a sincere Christian and was noted as one of the founders of the Eighth United Presbyterian Church of Pittsburgh. He served as a church trustee, as treasurer, and for many years as the superintendent of the Bible Class. He was also a leader in political affairs in the city of Pittsburgh. A gifted speaker, he made many speeches for the Republican Party, seeking the election of noteworthy candidates from President Lincoln's time in office until 1903. His political friends included President McKinley. As a follower of Christ, John had a heart to help the poor. He enjoyed good literature and art and, with a keen eye for flowers, was a well-known figure among the horticulturists of Pittsburgh. Soon after the termination of the Civil War in 1865, he married Nancy Cunningham, who gave birth to one daughter, Bessie, born in 1866. But Nancy passed away soon after Bessie's birth; John married again, to Annie Robertson, around 1870.

Annie Robertson Lambie also had Scottish roots; her father had come from near Glasgow and migrated to western Pennsylvania. Annie's mother was from high-bred Virginia stock. John S. and Annie had eight children, five girls and three boys. Counting Bessie, their seventh child (and third son) was Thomas Alexander Lambie, born in Pittsburgh in 1885, the subject of this biography. Of his parents, Lambie wrote in *A Doctor without a Country*, "Into their happy home nine children were born: six girls, three boys."[8] See accompanying table.[9]

Children of John S. and Annie (Robertson) Lambie		
Name	*Born*	*Married*
Elizabeth (Bessie)	1866	Ed Wiggins
		(daughter of first wife Nancy)
Jean	1872	Louis Ross
Aimee	1875	David Beggs
Annette	1877	Died of typhoid in 1900
Charles	1880	Margaret McCandless
John	1882	Mary Harmon
Thomas	1885	Charlotte Claney
Marguerite	1887	Robert McQuilkin
Agnes	1891	Died 1894

Because John S. was overly involved with civic activities and allowed his law practice to suffer neglect, the Lambie family struggled financially.

8. Lambie, *Doctor without a Country*, 14.

9. Margaret Hall provided the information in this table on July 19, 2016, in the Balisky home, Grande Prairie, AB, Canada.

Mother Annie, however, was a frugal manager and gave wise direction to the management of the household finances. She was also the spiritual nurturer of the nine children, especially after their father died in 1903 following a protracted illness. It is a lasting testimony to Annie's courage and steadfast faith in God that she was able to manage the family's modest estate and was concerned that her children were well educated and raised in a godly manner.

Another significant person in the life of young Thomas was the saintly James M. Wallace, pastor of the Eighth United Presbyterian Church of Pittsburgh, who provided him with kind and loving counsel. At an early age Thomas believed in Jesus Christ as Savior and Lord and began to walk a disciplined Christian life. Two years before his death in 1954, he wrote about his spiritual pilgrimage,

> When I was eleven years old I had a dream or a vision that I have never told to anyone but it brought to me sure conviction that I was Christ's. I have never wavered from that belief. I joined the church and then when Father and Mother walked to the communicants' benches, I, with six or eight brothers and sisters, walked with them and the psalm we always sang while doing so was Psalm 128: "How blest and happy is the man that walketh not astray . . ." and then "like olive plants thy children compassing thy table round." I rejoice that even today I am one of those olive plants around my Heavenly Father's table.[10]

This sure belief gave Thomas the spiritual and moral courage to retain his Christian commitment in an elementary school environment where the majority of the students were non-evangelical. His experience at Pittsburgh High School was uplifting, with a number of stalwart teachers who challenged him intellectually.

When Thomas enrolled in Western Pennsylvania Medical College, located in Pittsburgh, he endured a number of trying experiences. Incoming students found the curriculum to be very difficult, and many dropped out. The students themselves were unruly, fistfights were common, and profanity and obscene language were used in the hallways. The environment made it difficult for a Christian to "stay the course." That the equipment in the laboratories was below standard added to students' difficulties. But with determination, discipline, and the benefit of summer jobs to pay school fees, he graduated from medical school in 1907. His summer employment

10. Lambie, *A Bride for His Son*, 130.

included doing land surveying and engaging in house-to-house sales of various goods.[11]

Thomas Lambie was regular in attending the Eighth United Presbyterian Church in Pittsburgh, an evangelical church in which the Lambie family had historical roots. As mentioned, his father, John S., was an elder and taught Sunday school there. While Thomas was in medical school, he heard about various worldwide doors for missionary service with the denomination's Foreign Missions Board. For example, China was open for missionaries to enter, and Korea also was asking for more recruits. Following the colonial powers' Berlin Conference of 1884–85, mission societies such as the Foreign Missions Board of the United Presbyterian Church of North America (FMBUPC) gained access to place missionaries in the Anglo-Egyptian Sudan under the aegis of the British colonial administration. Methodist John R. Mott (1865–1955), the long-serving leader of the Young Men's Christian Association (YMCA) as well as of the World Student Christian Federation, challenged young Christians with the slogan "The Evangelization of the World in This Generation."[12] Conferences in churches and mission conventions—such as the New Wilmington Missionary Conference, in western Pennsylvania, and others along the eastern seaboard of the United States—challenged many young people to serve as missionaries.[13]

It was at the first New Wilmington Missionary Conference that Thomas and his younger sister Marguerite (often referred to as Marg) committed their lives to wholeheartedly serve Jesus Christ.[14] The Eighth United Presbyterian Church of Pittsburgh heartily endorsed Lambie's call to missions. So, as a young man he applied on January 22, 1906, to serve as a missionary with the Foreign Missions Board of the United Presbyterian Church of North America, completing all thirty-eight of the board's application questions.[15] When asked what his motive was for missionary service, he responded, "I earnestly hope that it is my love for God and my desire to bring Christ's Kingdom upon earth that impels me."[16] Asked why his preference

11. See Lambie, *Doctor without a Country*, 13–15.

12. Norman E. Thomas, "John R. Mott," in Anderson, *Biographical Dictionary of Christian Missions*, 476–77.

13. Lambie, *A Doctor Carries On*, 14.

14. William B. Anderson, "Thomas A. Lambie: Missionary Pioneer in Sudan and Ethiopia, 1907–1942," in Pierli, Ratti, and Wheeler, *Gateway to the Heart of Africa*, 127–45.

15. Lambie, "Application for Appointment as a Missionary," Foreign Missions Board of the United Presbyterian Church of North America, Presbyterian Historical Society: National Archives of the PC(USA), Philadelphia.

16. Lambie, Response to question 18, "Application for Appointment as a Missionary."

was to serve in Sudan or in India, he responded, "It seems to me that the need for medical service at least is greater in these two fields."[17] The Eighth Presbyterian Church readily affirmed their young member with full financial support. He was assigned by the Foreign Missions Board to serve in the Anglo-Egyptian Sudan, a region with great physical and spiritual needs.

Under the leading of God's providence, inexperienced Dr. Thomas A. Lambie, only twenty-two years of age but full of enthusiasm and energy, set sail from the United States for Sudan, via Egypt, in September, 1907. For the uninitiated medical doctor an exciting new career was opening up.

17. Lambie, Response to question 22, "Application for Appointment as a Missionary."

2

Missionary Service in the Sudan, 1907–1917

Suffering is not for punishment,
but it is necessary to make us fit for service.

THOMAS A. LAMBIE, *A BRUISED REED*, 30

THOMAS LAMBIE ARRIVED IN the Anglo-Egyptian Sudan in 1907. Senior missionary colleagues soon dubbed the twenty-two-year-old upstart medical doctor "the most famous loose cannon on the deck of the American [Presbyterian] Mission ship in Africa during these years."[1] He was eager to tackle the evangelization of Sudan, in accord with the Student Volunteer Movement watchword, in his generation. The sea voyage terminated at Egypt's port of Alexandria. He found Alexandria as modern a city as any in Europe. While there he was introduced to several long-time stalwarts of the American Mission to Sudan, including Rev. and Mrs. J. Kelly (Grace) Giffen—men and women of determination with a passion to launch the mission in the Sudan. It was also in Alexandria that he first met another newly arrived Presbyterian missionary, Miss Charlotte Claney, a school-teacher. Lambie described her as "bright and vivacious; somehow I found her attractive."[2] Within two years they were married. Following their wed-

---

1. Partee, *The Story of Don McClure*, 445n38.

2. Lambie, *Doctor without a Country*, 16.

8

ding, also in Alexandria, on April 6, 1909, the Lambies boarded a train to the metropolis of Cairo. Before heading further south, they also viewed the majestic pyramids, monuments that had overlooked the desert for thousands of years.

But in 1907, while still single, Lambie traveled south through the desert, first by train, then by steamboat up the Nile as far as the first cataract, and then again by train, finally arriving at Khartoum North, on the Egyptian side. Khartoum is located at the confluence of two large rivers, the White Nile, flowing north from the deep south, and the Blue Nile, which tumbled down the mountain escarpments of Abyssinia (now called Ethiopia) to the east. Khartoum South was the hub of the American Presbyterian Mission for the entire Anglo-Egyptian Sudan. The city of Omdurman is located across the White Nile from Khartoum. It was a significant city. In the late nineteenth century, General Gordon estimated that with a population of 34,000 and with the Mahdi and his successor, Khalifa, present in it, Omdurman was one of the larger cities of Africa.[3]

Soon after Lambie arrived in Khartoum in 1907, Grace Giffen asked him to cross the river to Omdurman. She wished for him to temporarily carry on the medical clinic of Dr. H. T. McLaughlin, who was away at a mission association meeting being held at Doleib Hill, just south of Malakal (now in South Sudan). Since he lacked knowledge of Arabic, Lambie experienced considerable frustration in Omdurman as he attempted to oversee his first medical clinic there. Eventually he was supplied with a young translator. (Dr. McLaughlin, he came to learn, was an avid hunter of the Sudan bushbuck and was known as one of the mission's Nimrods.) He soon developed a high respect for both Dr. McLaughlin and Rev. Giffen, two mature mission leaders who had made an extensive survey up the White Nile some four years previously. Both the McLaughlins and the Giffens were passionate in extending the kingdom of God to the various Sudanese ethnic groups. Lambie wrote:

> Words can never express the high regard I have always had for Dr. and Mrs. Giffen. They were all that missionaries should be. Already veterans before leaving Egypt, they spent the last thirty years of their lives in the inhospitable Sudan. Ever kind-hearted and cheery, always unselfish, always willing by every way to

---

3. For a description of the Mahdi (formerly known as Mohammed Ahmed) and his military exploits in Khartoum, see Kwarteng, *Ghosts of Empire*, 218–23.

make Christ known, there was nothing sanctimonious about them—just pure goodness that shone out of every word and act.[4]

Lambie's first assignment with the American Mission in Southern Sudan, prior to his marriage to Charlotte, was at the mission station named Doleib Hill, a slight mound several hundred feet above the Sobat River which flowed on west into the White Nile. The station, situated some thirty miles south of Malakal, lay among the Shilluk. The McLaughlins and Giffens had pioneered the establishment of the Doleib Hill outreach among the Shilluk people in 1903. When Lambie arrived at Doleib Hill, Rev. Ralph Carson, his wife, and their two small daughters were stationed there along with Mr. Ralph W. Tidrick, a trained agriculturalist. Malarial attacks were rampant among the newly assigned missionaries, and this portion of Sudan was known as "the white man's grave." Some years earlier the Roman Catholic mission serving among the Shilluk along the White Nile had counted thirteen missionary deaths by malaria.[5] One may ask how the native Shilluk were able to survive in this inhospitable environment. Apparently through generation after generation the Shilluk had developed an immunity to malarial attacks. Through advice they received and practical know-how, the personnel of the American Mission began taking systematic doses of quinine and constructing mosquito proof dwellings. These steps nearly eliminated the debilitating malarial attacks on their personnel.

Lambie felt that "for the missionary doctor, prayer is at least equal in importance to sterile equipment. . . . I would as soon operate without prayer as I would without boiling my instruments or putting on rubber gloves."[6] Initially while at Doleib Hill, Lambie's medical practice did not place heavy demands on his time, for the majority of the Shilluk believed their traditional medicine was adequate. Because he had time on his hands, he decided to begin learning the Shilluk language in earnest. His station associate, Ralph Carson, a linguist, located an old man who knew Shilluk folklore well. With Carson's initial assistance, Lambie slowly began to catch the drift of these stories and began building a Shilluk vocabulary list. Before long he was able to converse in a limited manner with his Shilluk patients. Some six months after Lambie's arrival, the Carson family left for home assignment. The two remaining men missed the hospitality of Mrs. Carson. During this period of loneliness, letters sent by steamer and train to the young American lady

---

4. Lambie, *Doctor without a Country*, 22. See also Michael Parker, "J. Kelly Giffen: Launching the American Mission to Sudan, 1898–1903," in Pierli, Ratti, and Wheeler, *Gateway to the Heart of Africa*, 86–101.

5. Lambie, *Doctor without a Country*, 28.

6. Lambie. *Doctor without a Country*, 33.

in Alexandria, Miss Charlotte Claney, grew frequent. And Lambie eagerly awaited letters of response from her.

When Rev. Elbert McCreery came to join Lambie and Tidrick, they were quickly dubbed "the three monks of Doleib Hill" by their American Mission colleagues. Lambie comments,

> In some ways, that description applied; circumstances forced asceticism and the deprivation of feminine society upon us. Monks took vows of chastity, poverty, and obedience, and this was our manner of life. . . . Obedience to rules of the Mission, to the Association, or to the Mission leader—especially to God— is necessary for effective work to be done. Without chastity of heart, thought, and life, no spiritual work is ever really done.[7]

Missionary life at Doleib Hill presented challenges. Lambie was a keen observer of various insects, some helpful and others destructive. Ants belonged to the destructive category, especially in the rainy season. Precautions such as placing water in pans under the four bedposts had to be made before attempting to sleep. Ants attacked and devoured chickens, leaving only the bones. When beehives were invaded by ants, the honey was soon depleted and the bees were driven from their quarters. Termites, which looked like ants, did not attack man or animals, but they destroyed any dwelling made of wood. Even though the walls of a house might be made of brick, termites had the ability to make passageways up into the mahogany rafters and to destroy them completely. Lambie remarks, "Seldom have I seen a place where there were as many termites as at our station; the whole place was infested with them. A piece of wood left on the ground one night was always half devoured in the morning."[8]

As early as 1908, while at Doleib Hill, Lambie wrote to his mother in a prophetic manner, "Our mission should push on to Abyssinia some time I believe. Only a few Bibles there and they are in great demand."[9]

7. Lambie, *Doctor without a Country*, 36.
8. Lambie, *Doctor without a Country*, 38.
9. Lambie, letter to his mother, Annie Lambie, March 17, 1908, MHSC.

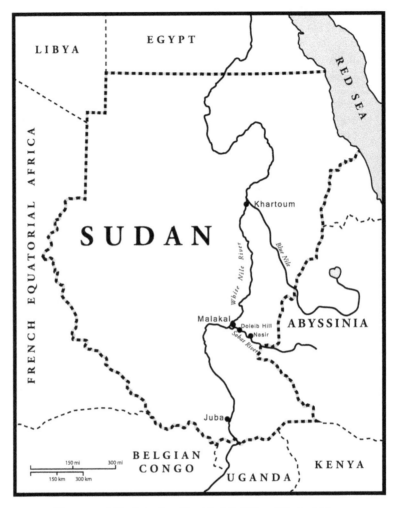

Thomas and Charlotte Lambie at Doleib Hill and Nasir stations

Adventurous experiences were never far from the young Doleib Hill doctor. One such occasion arrived at the end of 1908 when Yacoub Pasha Artin, a distinguished Egyptian official, was on an exploratory trip up the White Nile. Accompanied by the noted archeologist, A. H. Sayce, professor of Assyriology, University of Oxford, he was traveling on a new steamer. As the party neared Fashoda, just north of Malakal, the Egyptian Pasha became ill with minor cardiac arrest. Lambie was sent for at Doleib Hill and soon resuscitated him. Because the future health of the Pasha was questionable, the captain of the steamer proposed that Lambie accompany the expedition all the way to Central Africa and back so that he could care for the Pasha's medical needs. On the new steamer Lambie found there "were two or three British officers along and a European chef who served us marvelous food. Luxury such as we had—printed menus, uniformed servants—seemed too good to be true after months at my station eating 'Mrs. McDoddies' dehydrated cabbage."[10] After the month's cruise living in high style, Lambie found that his return to Doleib Hill to resume "plain living" required some adjustment. One could ask, "Was this an early indication of Lambie's itchy foot syndrome?"

A saving factor about residing at the Sobat River's inhospitable station of Doleib Hill was the dozens of lime trees and other fruit trees that the Giffens and McLaughlins had planted when they first were stationed there. These hardy fruit trees were bearing well and provided not only a healthy source of vitamin C but a cash crop as well that supplemented the missionaries' meager allowance. Missionary colleague, Ralph Tidrick, another mighty Nimrod, provided fresh wild meat of bushbuck, gazelle, and buffalo, as well as geese and ducks. Unfortunately, while Tidrick was hunting prey favored by lions, a large male that had been wounded attacked him and badly mauled him. Before Tidrick could reach medical help in Khartoum, he died.[11]

Skilled as a doctor, Thomas Lambie was also a passionate evangelist. Abdallah Nyidhok, a Shilluk from Doleib Hill, said of him: "I was taught by Mr. Carson [Scripture translator based at Doleib Hill] but the talk did not lodge in my head, or feelings. The talk of Dr. Lambie had no quarreling"— meaning that it completely convinced him.[12] In 1914 Abdallah was the first Shilluk to be baptized, and he credited Lambie as having a significant part in his conversion.

In 1911 the Lambies became implicated in a mission quarrel and were asked to leave Doleib Hill (Charlotte had arrived there shortly after their wedding in 1909). Lambie wrote:

> Oh the sadness of Mission quarrels and friction. . . . What harm they do—the wrong spirit engendered between missionaries, the un-Christlike tempers that develop, the damage done to the natives. Lest we judge the missionaries too severely, let us remember they are in a hard position. . . . Oh the heartache and the wounds, the discouragement and despair, the magnifying of

10. Lambie, *Doctor without a Country*, 42. See also Artin, *England in the Sudan*, esp. 200 and 207–8 for references to Lambie.

11. Lambie, *Doctor without a Country*, 52–53.

12. William B. Anderson, "Thomas A. Lambie: Missionary Pioneer in Sudan and Ethiopia, 1907–1942," in Pierli, Ratti, and Wheeler, *Gateway to the Heart of Africa*, 129.

trifles into mountains, and the brooding care that come from being misunderstood."[13]

Because of quarrels and cantankerous interpersonal relationships among the missionaries at Doleib Hill, the Lambies were assigned to Dr. McLaughlin's medical clinic in Khartoum North. Life in the urban setting of Khartoum was a happy time for the Lambies. A new house with red tile floors was constructed for them. The experienced and godly Kelly and Grace Giffen provided uplifting fellowship. The Lambies, with baby Wallace in tow, enjoyed walks along the shaded banks of the Blue Nile. Lambie found that he had become rather attached to Doleib Hill and longed to return, but this was not to be. Still, the Lambies' ministry in Khartoum North was short lived, for the mission leaders were keen on establishing a new outreach at Nasir, also on the Sobat River, among the Nuer people group. The new station was to be located some 200 miles upstream from Doleib Hill and about 100 miles to the west of the Abyssinian border.

> It had never occurred to us that we would be considered for the new station [Nasir]. In the first place, we were happily settled in Khartoum, and the work had been growing. I had none of the manual ability Mr. McCreery had, and having been raised in the city was unacquainted with house building and farm work, accomplishments necessary for pioneering. . . . Besides there was another young doctor who had not been located. . . . Surely they would appoint him, and not uproot us from our happy home. But that is what the Missionary Association decided to do, to our great dismay. We thought of resigning from the mission.[14]

The Lambies left in 1911 for the United States. After a six-month furlough, Lambie was ready and willing to pioneer the Nasir station on the Sobat. Leaving Charlotte with newborn Anne Elizabeth (called Betty) and toddler Wallace in Philadelphia, he returned to the Sudan. There, in 1912, he joined Rev. Elbert McCreery on a small houseboat some 35 feet long and 10 feet wide on a 700-mile journey from Khartoum, up the White Nile, then up the Sobat River to Nasir. Their houseboat was no match for the current of the White Nile, so McCreery and Lambie finally made arrangements to be towed to Nasir by a large steamer. The steamer was on its way farther upstream to load Abyssinian coffee at the Gambeila trading post on the Baro River. Upon reaching Nasir in June 1912, the two missionaries for the next six months made their home on the houseboat. During that period

---

13. Lambie, *Doctor without a Country*, 53–54.
14. Lambie, *Doctor without a Country*, 57–58.

they worked at building their houses using local materials—sticks and mud for the walls, straw for the roof.

Pok Jok, a former Nuer patient of Lambie's from Doleib Hill, and Ayik, a Nuer who was fluent in the Shilluk language, were a great help to them in building bridges to the Nuer tribe. Both had made a commitment to Jesus as their Savior and Lord. The two men, Lambie wrote, "stood shoulder to shoulder with us, and if at times they faltered and their lives were not in perfect harmony with Christian ideals, yet remember how far they had come and under what constant temptations, coming both from without and within, they groaned."[15] The conversion of an African, leading to holy living, was a thing to be marveled at—especially when there was not yet a local church among the Nuer to nurture and sustain Christian spirituality. Lambie's medical skills were put to use day after day in treating various kinds of illnesses, such as ulcers, tuberculosis, and a variety of stomach maladies. Providing meat for the half dozen boat hands who had joined the mission expedition from Khartoum was a challenge. Using a fishing hook and heavy line, they caught three-foot fish of the bullhead species. The flesh of these fish was muddy tasting but it did supplement their meagre diet. Launching the Nasir station took unusual sacrifice and commitment on the part of both Lambie and McCreery. Navigating the White Nile as well as the Sobat Rivers upstream in their small house boat had indicated their mettle, for initially it had taken ingenuity, muscle, and unsuccessful negotiations with several other larger steamers before locating one that would tow them.

During Lambie and McCreery's construction of a permanent house at Nasir for the Lambies, misfortune struck the family. By then Charlotte and the children had arrived from the United States and were staying temporarily at Doleib Hill with Mrs. Hannah McCreery. Three-year-old Wallace playfully struck a match that ignited a flammable mosquito net. Charlotte was in another room when she heard a shriek and rushed in to snatch both Betty and Wallace from the flames. The grass thatch on the roof ignited and at great speed their home along with all their clothing, cooking utensils, food stores, and office supplies was burned, leaving only smoking remains.[16]

In 1918, after six years at Nasir, Lambie could recount God's blessings and protection upon his family.

> The remarkable thing about the years at Nasir was that a person as poorly endowed and unfitted as I undoubtedly was for

15. Lambie, *Doctor without a Country*, 66.

16. William B. Anderson, "Thomas A. Lambie: Missionary Pioneer in Sudan and Ethiopia, 1907–1942," in Pierli, Ratti, and Wheeler, *Gateway to the Heart of Africa*, 132–33.

the work could yet be used by God to hew a Mission station
out of the jungle, learn a language, and, by the grace of a loving Heavenly Father, be the means of calling precious souls out
of heathen darkness. The only virtue I could claim was that I
tried to be obedient to Him at whatever personal cost. Often I
failed; but stumbling and falling, arising and then falling again,
staggered by adverse circumstances, and weakened by malaria
and dysentery and a hard climate, yet somehow we struggled on.
All praise to Him who always maketh us to triumph in Christ
Jesus.[17]

The strategy of the American Mission in establishing the station at Nasir was "that it might be a step in the direction of opening up Abyssinia, the
hermit kingdom of Africa."[18] Unexpectedly, in 1917 or so, three Abyssinian
surveyors dropped in at Nasir, asking for medicine and a Bible in their own
language. Neither Lambie nor McCreery had the correct Bible translation
available to offer them, but the Abyssinians left with a good supply of medicine and a promise of Bibles to come. These Abyssinians were assisting a
British survey party in fixing the Abyssinia/Sudan border. So Lambie advanced slowly toward Abyssinia, allowing God to lead him and Charlotte as
gently as a good shepherd.

We have no record of whether Lambie idealized Major-General Sir
Herbert Kitchener (1850–1916), but Kitchener's prowess and skill as a military leader would have been known to him. Kitchener embodied the highest
of Victorian traditions and ideals. His goal in Sudan was to leave behind
a system of government that would benefit the ruled, not the rulers. "In
contrast to the devilish rule that plundered and enslaved," he desired that
justice and kindly treatment for all Sudanese would now begin.[19] Lambie
admired the British for their prowess in leadership, and in turn, the British
administrators trusted Lambie.

In 1915 while the Lambies were in Alexandria for a brief holiday,
thousands of wounded British troops were sent there to recover. Lambie
volunteered his medical skills in service to the wounded soldiers. Never one
to lose an opportunity to share the "Good News," Lambie with his wife set
up a room at the Alexandria mission rest house where soldiers could read,
play games, and hear Gospel messages.[20]

17. Lambie, *Doctor without a Country*, 101.

18. Lambie, *Doctor without a Country*, 71.

19. Pollock, *Kitchener*, 162.

20. William B. Anderson, "Thomas A. Lambie: Missionary Pioneer in Sudan and
Ethiopia, 1907–1942," in Pierli, Ratti, and Wheeler, *Gateway to the Heart of Africa*,
132–33.

In launching their missionary service in the Sudan, the Lambies struggled with inhospitable environment, trying relationships with other missionaries, and the challenges of learning new languages and cultures. But they were obedient and labored faithfully. A new door of opportunity was about to open for Dr. Lambie.

3

Lambies Move from Nasir, Sudan, to Sayo, Abyssinia

I must be more willing to do whatever He demands,
for God's will is always the sweetest and best thing in the world.

THOMAS A. LAMBIE, *A DOCTOR WITHOUT A COUNTRY*, 100

IN 1917 THE LAMBIES were in the United States on furlough after a demanding and trying ministry, first at Doleib Hill and then at Nasir in southern Sudan. Thomas Lambie's brother-in-law, Dr. Edward Wiggins, urged him to remain in Philadelphia and share in a large and lucrative medical practice. The request went like this, "You have spent a long time in Africa. It is time for you to think about yourself and your family. Betty and Wallace are ready for school. I need an assistant."[1] The idea was that the entire medical practice, from which he might have an ample and attractive living, would soon be turned over to Lambie. A few weeks later, Lambie was attending a missionary conference at Tarkio, Missouri. The meetings were taxing and he was tired.

> Either I dozed off and had a dream, or I actually had a waking
> vision. I have never known which. But this I saw vividly in that
> midnight hour: a map of Northeastern Africa, from the centre
> of which came a hand and an arm. It was stretched out toward

1. Lambie, *Doctor without a Country*, 108.

me, pleading, beckoning, a hideous leper arm. What! Must I clasp that hand in mine? I sought to evade it, but compelled by some power beyond my comprehending, at last I reluctantly took it in mine. To my intense surprise I found it was not the hand of a leper but the hand of Christ, the beautiful hand of my Saviour—the imprint of nails in the palm.[2]

This vision of Christ settled the question for Lambie. The idea of remaining in Philadelphia lost all charm. He would not remain in the United States while another section of Africa needed Christ. After making that decision, both Lambie and his wife, Charlotte, were filled with great peace, joy, and love.

By 1918 the four Lambies were back at Nasir, renewed in body and soul. Their fruit trees such as guava and bananas were bearing well, and they harvested over twenty bushels of peanuts. Their Abyssinian worker, Desta, shot a big black African goose every Saturday, which made for delicious Sunday dinners. Looking east on clear days, the Lambies would catch a glimpse of the distant mountain peaks of Abyssinia. He would look and wonder "if the providence of God would ever lead us there."[3] He recalled that back in 1893 the United Presbyterian Mission had applied to Emperor Menelik II for permission to begin missionary work in Abyssinia. This had been denied because the Abyssinian Orthodox leadership were wary of outside Christian influences. In the summer of 1918 the Lambie family took an excursion from Nasir to Gambeila, a small Abyssinian town leased to the Sudanese government for trade purposes. From Gambeila large barges of coffee, hides, and some teff (a fine grain prized for making a flat bread much enjoyed by Abyssinians) were sent down the Baro, Sobat, and White Nile Rivers to Khartoum and eventually to Alexandria and world markets.

The Lambies were settled into their service at Nasir, but the end of 1918 opened up the possibility of a great change for the family. James McEnery, a British major posted in Gambeila, stopped at Nasir while on his way to Malakal. He posed the question, "If I can get a place for you in Abyssinia will you come up?"[4] It appears that Lambie, on a previous visit to Gambeila, had been discussing with McEnery his dream of one day serving in Abyssinia. Events quickly began to move in a positive direction, opening the opportunity for the Lambies to serve in Wellega, Western Ethiopia.

---

2. Lambie, *Doctor without a Country*, 109.

3. Lambie, *Doctor without a Country*, 116.

4. Lambie, *Doctor without a Country*, 122. From 1907 to 1919, during his assignment in Sudan, Lambie enjoyed cordial relations with British officials. See Debela, "History of the Evangelical Church Bethel," 119.

In 1933 Lambie reflected on the family's 1919 advance into the high-lands of Ethiopia. "Permission must first be secured from the Missionary Board [United Presbyterian Church] and from the Sudan Government. The latter required an interview at Khartoum which turned out to be very satis-factory, even the Governor General, the greatly esteemed late Sir Lee Stack favoured the project and at a specially arranged tea-party in the beautiful palace grounds in Khartoum, wished the writer and his wife God-speed on the new undertaking."[5]

Dejazmatch Birru, who was governor not of the entire province of Wellega but of the Qellem Awraja only, contacted Major McEnery in Gam-beila, soliciting the medical assistance of expatriate missionaries laboring in the Sudan for curbing the epidemic.[6] A part of the worldwide pandemic of 1918–19, the spread of influenza was devastating the Abyssinian popula-tion. Ethiopian historian Richard Pankhurst indicates the disease's severity:

> It may be said . . . that the late summer and autumn of 1918 was a critical moment in Ethiopian history. The influenza of that time was so intense, and evoked such terror, that the politi-cal, the economic, and social life of the capital, and indeed of the country as a whole, virtually came to a halt, and there was even talk of foreign interference. Whether as a result of divine intervention, as many Ethiopians thought at the time, or from natural causes, the epidemic subsided so rapidly that normal life soon resumed.[7]

Dejazmatch Birru offered to construct accommodations for medi-cal personnel who might come. As noted, if the Lambies were to be based in Abyssinia, they would need clearance from both the British officials in Khartoum and the Foreign Missions Board of the United Presbyterian Church in Philadelphia. Eventually both bodies agreed for a preliminary investigatory trip to be taken via Gambeila; the journey was slated for June 1919.[8] Veteran American mission personnel Kelly and Grace Giffen of Khartoum and Rev. Ralph McGill of Cairo were assigned to accompany

5. Lambie, "Medical Missions in Ethiopia," presentation to Medical Missionary As-sociation, SIM International Archives, Charlotte, North Carolina (hereinafter SIMIA), EA-1-82, File 12.

6. The title "*Dejazmatch*" indicated a high official with the rank of lead military commander.

7. Pankhurst, "The Hedar Beshita of 1918," 131.

8. Debela, "History of the Evangelical Church Bethel," 16n6, notes that the distance from Khartoum to Gambeila was 1,360 km (about 850 miles) or 11 days by steamer.

the Lambies up the Abyssinian escarpment.[9] Charlotte Lambie, the children Wallace and Betty, and Grace Giffen remained at Gambeila, lodged in the British guest house provided by Major McEnery. Lambie later wrote, "Gambeila was a beautiful place. Great spreading trees on the [Baro] river front gave it a parklike appearance. But it was very unhealthy."[10] From there the Lambie, Giffen, and McGill party departed on mule for Sayo, a small town on the Abyssinian escarpment, some forty-five miles distant.[11] As the group set out, Lambie was not sure having left his wife Charlotte and their two children in Gambeila for two weeks was wise, infested as that area was with malaria and conditions leading to heat exhaustion. He later commented, "If ever there was a pestilential spot in the world that spot was Gambeila. . . . Malarial mosquitoes and tsetse flies abounded, as well as dysentery and other tropical diseases. The high plateau, on the contrary, was singularly free from every kind of disease."[12] All three of the men were impressed about the potential for opening a ministry at Sayo. The Greek community in Sayo received them kindly. The Abyssinian officials sent gifts of food such as eggs, chickens, sheep, and the large flat *injera* bread, plus honey and beer; the beer they returned.

> As I left Sayo that morning, my heart was full of praise and song, for Abyssinia had proved beautiful beyond my dreams, and what impressed me most was the possibility of a home in a climate a little less like an oven than that hot Sudan plain, a multitude of needy people, a healthful environment, and, not least of all, the red roses blooming in the utmost profusion. . . . Roses over the fences, roses over the verandas, roses blooming and smelling in such wanton riot that everywhere one looked one seemed to see roses.[13]

Upon the party's return to Gambeila, the Giffens and McGill made their way by steamer downriver to Khartoum. Lambie hired head-carriers and four riding mules for the two-day ascent back up the escarpment. The goods they transported up the escarpment consisted of warm blankets and quality cavalry equipment such as saddles, bridles, tents, and cots purchased

9. Debela, "History of the Evangelical Church Bethel," 49. The mandate given to Lambie and the investigating committee by the Foreign Missions Board was: "Proceed to field, investigate, report conditions fully for sanction of Board before permanent establishment."

10. Lambie, *Doctor without a Country*, 124.

11. Debela, "History of the Evangelical Church Bethel," 47, states, "The name 'Sayo' is derived from the Sayo clan of the Matcha group who inhabited the area."

12. Lambie, *Boot and Saddle*, 24.

13. Lambie, *Boot and Saddle*, 28.

in Alexandria at post-war bargain prices. Charlotte described their entourage as a "queer procession, some carrying boxes, some chairs with many queer things tied to them to make up weight."[14] It was a grueling trip for the four Lambies—especially for the children; Wallace was nine and Betty only eight. When the weary family completed their ascent to the plateau, a grand surprise awaited them.

> When about five miles from our destination, we came to a band of two or three hundred Abyssinians dressed in all their finery, with gaily caparisoned horses and mules drawn up in a double line to receive us. They had been sent by the Governor to do us honor. We dismounted and gravely shook hands with the leader, who wore a velvet cartridge belt over his other clothes and a long curved sword that stuck out behind him like a monkey's tail. Then we mounted, and, followed by our guard, wended our way onward, the number of guards and hangers-on increasing as we went, so that we must have had at least five hundred when we finally reached Sayo town, with the rain still falling and the cold mist enveloping the hills.[15]

The Lambie family eventually settled on a rounded hilltop, a short distance from Sayo. The site, selected by Charlotte, "who had an eye for beauty and practicality, [was one] where there would be ample space for garden and grazing as well as ordinary Mission activities."[16] Before many months, Charlotte had planted hundreds of banana, fig, peach, mango, and assorted other fruit trees. The site was approved by Dejazmatch Birru. An adopted son of the former Emperor Menelik II, he had recently been appointed governor of Wellega Province.[17] He had recently traveled in Europe and was cognizant of the value of modernization. The center of his administration was located at Aussa at the foot of Tullu Walal, a day's walk northeast of Sayo.[18] Influenza, the main reason Dr. Lambie was recruited to Qellem

14. Charlotte Lambie, "An Account of the Lambie Expedition to Sayo, Abyssinia," ca. 1919, MS, p. 26, MHSC.

15. Lambie, *Doctor without a Country*, 127. See also Debela, *Divine Plan Unfolding*, 98.

16. Lambie, *Doctor without a Country*, 131.

17. Debela, "History of the Evangelical Church Bethel," 50. Debela quotes Lambie's assessment: "Sayo is as far as I have seen one of the most thickly populated districts of western Abyssinia. As you stand on a little hill just outside Sayo and look around there are little hamlets in all directions as far as you can see."

18. See Debela, *Divine Plan Unfolding*, 67.

Awraja, sub-province of Wellega, had taken many lives in Abyssinia the previous year, but by July 1919, the epidemic had abated.[19]

Lambies relocate from Nasir, Sudan, to Sayo, Abyssinia

Shortly after Lambie settled his family on their idyllic hilltop, he observed that the Amhara overlords ruled the local Oromo population with an iron rod. Feeling it was a rotten system that imposed a kind of slavery, he wrote to William B. Anderson, who was general secretary of the Foreign Missions Board of the United Presbyterian Church of North America and located in Philadelphia:

> These rulers and high ones all profess the greatest love and re-
> spect for us and shower presents on us that they have filched

19. Pankhurst, "The Hedar Beshita of 1918," 103–31, reports that on August 27, 1918, Regent Ras Tafari Makonnen was struck down with influenza and was gravely ill for nearly three weeks, causing great concern among foreign diplomats.

from the poor without doubt. . . . We are determined not to enter into politics. We are not here for that purpose but how can one keep silent about these wrongs? I will, however, try to keep silent until at least the mission is established here on a firm basis.[20]

Two events that transpired in Qellem Awaraja had a significant impact on the future of the evangelical cause.[21] The first was the conversion of blind Gidada Solon, a young man who had been born in 1901 near Sayo.[22] When he was a young lad of four, a smallpox epidemic spread throughout much of Abyssinia and many people died. Gidada survived but was blinded by the dread disease. Because he was incapacitated to do any kind of physical work, his lot was to beg. He found that begging at the entrance of the newly constructed Orthodox Church at Aussa was rather remunerative. When he was about twenty years of age, he was encouraged to beg from the newly arrived *ferenj* (foreigner) who was the doctor at Sayo. Led to Lambie, Gidada extended his empty hand and called out, "*Santim, santim*" (Ethiopia's smallest coin). Lambie placed a coin in his hand and said to Gidada in the Oromo language, "My gift is small, but believe on the Lord Jesus Christ and you will be saved. He will give you much."[23] Gidada had tired of visiting local soothsayers, whom he thought represented his gods for healing and other needs. He believed in Jesus Christ and experienced a deep happiness.

A newly appointed missionary to Sayo, Rev. Fred Russell, began discipling Gidada. Soon Gidada was able to share his faith with other beggars as well. Lambie wrote, "One of the early converts was blind Gidada, a poor beggar who was wonderfully converted at a beggars' meeting we organized for the poor, halt, maimed and blind. What a change it made in his life."[24] Eventually Gidada had an effective ministry to the carriers of coffee and hides to Gambeila, the Baro River port. He learned to read the Bible in Braille, which greatly enhanced his ministry and extended it to a wider

---

20. Lambie, letter to William B. Anderson, August 10, 1919, cited from Debela, "History of the Evangelical Church Bethel," 72.

21. Birru was governor, not of the entire Wellega Province but of Qellem Awaraja, the territory previously governed by the indigenous ruler Jote Tulu; information from Debela, *Divine Plan Unfolding*, 67.

22. The information that follows is drawn from Gidada, *Other Side of Darkness*.

23. Gidada, *Other Side of Darkness*, 12.

24. Lambie, *Doctor without a Country*, 133.

community. His ministry extended for some fifty years and was the impetus behind the evangelical work in Wellega Province.[25]

The other significant event that had long-lasting results was Dr. Lambie's medical treatment of the Gorei governor, Ras Nadew, in 1922. The treatment occurred at the same time Lambie was engaged in negotiations for the purchase of some property, for he had learned that a large coffee warehouse and residence, owned by a Greek, were for sale. The American Mission officials in Cairo authorized him to negotiate the purchase of these premises, together with some two acres enclosed by a high secure stone wall.[26] The intention was that the property, located at Gorei, would eventually serve as a second mission outreach center in the densely populated Illu Abba Bor Awaraja, under the governorship of Ras Nadew. In the course of his treatment of the governor for a chronic disease, which took nearly two weeks, Lambie had time to carry to completion his negotiations on the Greek coffee warehouse and residence.[27] But at one point while he sleeping on the upstairs veranda of the residence the mission was in the process of purchasing, Lambie was awakened from sound slumber by loud knocking at the outside gate. Immediately Ras Nadew was ushered up the stairs by fifty of his armed men.

Lambie later reported:

> It was at Gorei that occurred the incident which put me in favor with the governor, and eventually with Haile Selassie himself. It was a little thing, in fact a very little thing—a little beetle, to be exact, that had crawled into the gubernatorial ear and was causing intense pain. I was able to remove the beetle, to the satisfaction of *Ras* Nadew, the governor. When shown the offending insect, the great man's followers solemnly assured him that it was a wood-boring beetle that would have bored its way through his head and killed him. Nothing I could say would shake from him the conviction that his life had been saved. He

25. Lambie, letter to Anderson, March 6, 1919, affirms that the focus of the Presbyterian Mission outreach would be the Oromo people, formerly known as Gallas. He writes, "Most of our work will be with the Gallas" (cited in Debela, "History of the Evangelical Church Bethel," 109). Gidada Solon's son Negasso Gidada became president of Ethiopia in 1995 and served until 2001. In 2002, while I was lecturing at the Ethiopian Graduate School of Theology, I invited President Negasso to present a lecture titled "A Christian's Role in Politics."

26. In *Doctor without a Country*, 136, Lambie notes that Mr. C. H. Walker, the British consul for Western Abyssinia, resided in Gorei. Walker's book, *The Abyssinian at Home*, is a gold mine of Amarinya Orthodox vocabulary.

27. Lambie, *Doctor without a Country*, 137.

wrote a commendatory letter to the Regent of Abyssinia, *Ras*
Tefere, telling him of the circumstances.[28]

This incident served to remind Lambie that often God uses the small
things of life to shape destiny. He commented that the incident "makes me
value the seemingly trivial events, the little things of life that add up to a
great sum."[29]

The Lambie entourage now began wending its way by horse and mule
from Gorei to Addis Ababa, some 400 miles to the east. They finally arrived
in Addis Ababa in 1922 and took a room at the Taitu Hotel, named after the
deceased empress. The Lambies intended to soon take the train from Addis
Ababa to Djibouti and then sail to New York. But there was business to be
done with Ras Tafari Makonnen, for Ras Nadew's letter had preceded the
family to Addis Ababa. Lambie made an appointment to meet Ras Tafari
Makonnen. He recounts:

> The new suit was donned for the occasion, as I wanted to look
> my best, and mounting the big white horse, I set out for the pal-
> ace a mile away. The horse was feeling quite fresh, and bucked
> me into a stone wall in a narrow place, tearing my fine new trou-
> sers in a disgraceful fashion; but as there was no time to go back
> for repairs, I decided to go forward and trust the tear would not
> be noticed. It was common at this time to see diplomats dressed
> in formal morning coats and silk toppers riding in Addis Ababa
> on their way to some function, for there were no automobiles.[30]

Upon his arrival at the palace, Lambie was not kept waiting more
than ten minutes. When he was ushered into the large room, who should
he see but Dejazmatch Birru from Aussa (Dembi Dollo) seated beside Ras
Tafari Makonnen. After hearing from Dr. Lambie about the Sayo hospital,

---

28. Lambie, *Boot and Saddle*, 58. Until his death in 1926, Gorei governor Ras
Nadew Abba Wollo was a significant government official during the latter years of
Emperor Menelik II (1844–1913) and initial years of the reign of Ras Tafari Makonnen (1892–1974). He attended the 1918 Versailles Peace Conference and, along with a
small cadre of delegates, was sent to England and the United States in 1919 to establish
friendly relations. While in the United States, he visited Detroit in order to see where
Ford automobiles were manufactured. In 1923, in the company of three Ethiopian officials, he officially received acceptance of Ethiopia as a member of the League of Nations
in Geneva. See Haile Sellassie, *My Life and Ethiopia's Progress*, 60, 77.

29. Lambie, *Doctor without a Country*, 138. See also Tibebe, "SIM in Ethiopia." According to Tibebe, p. 7, Lambie always felt that his initial relationships with Dejazmatch
Birru and Ras Nadew were pivotal in establishing SIM in southwest Ethiopia.

30. Lambie, *Doctor Without a Country*, 144–45.

Ras Tafari shared his desire to have a hospital built in Addis Ababa.[31] During the following month, prior to the Lambies' departure for the United States, a tentative agreement was drawn up and signed in Amharic. "He promised land and financial assistance for the hospital," Lambie states, "and we undertook to supply the personnel, always provided that our Board of Foreign Missions smiled upon our proposals and gave the money and men needed."[32]

Once in Philadelphia the Lambies were well received by leaders such as William Anderson, general secretary of the Foreign Missions Board. As Lambie related Ras Tafari Makonnen's desire to have a modern hospital built in Addis Ababa and his commitment to provide land as well as some finances, the members of the board gave their sympathetic attention. The Foreign Missions Board, however, had just entered into a "Five-Year Plan," which meant that "no new projects were to be introduced during this time. The proposed hospital in Addis Ababa was distinctly a new project, and therefore they could not permit me to bring it before our churches in America as an object for their gifts. . . . This seemed a discouraging condition."[33]

But Dr. and Mrs. Lambie had been reading an account of the life of George Müller of Bristol, England, and were learning how he had been led to build orphanages near Bristol without a church or mission agency to back him. He prayed and God answered his prayer. The Lambies also read about J. Hudson Taylor and the story of the expansion of the China Inland Mission (CIM). Hundreds of CIM missionaries were sent to China without a fixed income of any kind. The Lambies believed that God could answer earnest, faithful prayer to meet the capital cost of the proposed Addis Ababa hospital. During the following weeks, funds slowly began to come in for the hospital. A woman in the congregation at the Shadyside United Presbyterian Church in Pittsburgh, Pennsylvania, handed Dr. Lambie an envelope which contained $100. Then a Young People's Christian Union meeting conducted by Dr. Theophilus Mills Taylor (who was later ordained and became the presiding officer and titular head of the United Presbyterian Church in the United States of America) brought $7,000 into a Special Object Fund. Other

---

31. J. Spenser Trimingham writes that Ras Tafari Makonnen attempted to reform the Ethiopian Orthodox Church in three spheres: finances, training of the clergy, and the teaching of the church. He did not view it as merely an encumbered social heritage. See Trimingham, *Christian Church and Missions*, 23.

32. Lambie, *Doctor without a Country*, 146. See also Debela, "History of the Evangelical Church Bethel," 143, where Debela refers to the signed document of February 25, 1922, presently housed in the archives of the Bethel Synod office, Addis Ababa.

33. Lambie, *Doctor without a Country*, 155.

small gifts continued to come in—but not nearly enough for such an expansive project as the proposed Addis Ababa hospital.

> One eventful day, while riding on the train, I was lifting up my heart to God about the whole matter, and it seemed to me that He spoke to me, telling me that my prayer was heard, that the hospital would be to His glory, and that He would provide the money needed. My heart welled up in praise to Him, for now I felt I knew it was His will and what He promised He would do.[34]

At the New Wilmington Missionary Conference, held yearly near Pittsburgh, a man by the name of William Shaw George, from East Palestine, Ohio, came up to Lambie and asked if he could talk about the hospital project for Addis Ababa. He did not appear to be a person of means, so Lambie asked if he might be interested in building the women's ward and possibly equipping it. Mr. George's response was, "No, that does not interest me. If I am going to build a hospital, I will build it. How much do you want?"[35] Mr. George channeled $70,000 (roughly equal to $1,000,000 in 2018 US dollars) through the Presbyterian Women's General Missionary Society for the Addis Ababa hospital.[36]

In May 1923, soon after the Lambies returned to Addis Ababa, a site in the Guleili area was selected for the hospital and approved by His Highness, Ras Tafari Makonnen. After the legal papers were in hand, building commenced sometime in October, following the end of the rainy season. Two families with professional building experience, Mr. Phil and Mrs. Effie West and Mr. and Mrs. Douglas, were recruited by the Foreign Missions Board. The proposed building proved to be, at the time, one of the largest structures in Addis Ababa. Lambie commented that "the architect had made it much larger than I had contemplated."[37] To guarantee that the walls would not crack, the foundations were dug fifteen to twenty feet deep, with concrete footings reinforced with rebar. Even as plastering of the walls in one wing remained to be completed, the medical staff began treating patients because

---

34. Lambie, *Doctor without a Country*, 156.

35. Lambie. *Doctor without a Country*, 157.

36. Initially it was agreed that the hospital would be named Tafari Makonnen and American Mission Hospital. Internally the mission called it the George Memorial Hospital, after the godly mother of William Shaw George. At present the two-story facility stands strong and functions as the Ethiopia Ministry of Health, Central Laboratory. Local Guleili residents continue to call the edifice *Ye'Dr. Lambie Hospital*. Information on William Shaw George can be found at https://en.wikipedia.org/wiki/W._S._George_Pottery_Company and also www.salem.lib.oh.us/SalemHistory/YesteryearsSearch/1998/Vol8No5Jul7op.pdf.

37. Lambie, *Doctor without a Country*, 159.

of the demand for medical attention. Dr. Lambie appreciated the frequent visits of Ras Tafari, who came to see how the building was progressing and offered many encouraging comments.

The hospital soon filled with patients, including many with gunshot wounds and skull fractures from falls from horses. Two of Dr. Lambie's patients were rather influential—the Coptic archbishop from Egypt and the old war minister, Fitaurari Hapte-Giorgis.[38] Together with Empress Zauditu, the daughter of the former Emperor Menelik, these three held unusual power in both state and church. "The Tafari Makonnen Hospital was erected at a cost considerably exceeding twenty-five thousand pounds and [was] designed to accommodate a hundred to a hundred and twenty-five patients, in a modern building . . . with three operating theatres, X-ray, electric lighting plant, sewerage disposal plant and laundry."[39]

On December 21, 1925, a special function was held at the Ras Tafari Makonnen Hospital in connection with the sale of Christmas dolls, offered as a fundraising event for the benefit of the hospital. Besides the prince regent, Ras Tafari, a number of high-ranking Ethiopians as well as Europeans of prominence were present, including Mr. Charles Bentinck, the British minister, and missionaries from Sayo and Gorei. Following a tour of the well-equipped hospital, some seventy dolls were auctioned off. One doll brought in US$90. The proceeds of the auction totaled nearly US$4,000. In a brief speech Lambie expressed "deep gratitude to the regent, 'our kind friend and benefactor,' for his kind love and sympathy for the work that bears his name."[40]

Various tensions, however, developed as the Addis Ababa hospital was being launched. The first of these related to strict accounting of the finances. The newly formed missionary administration in Abyssinia had elected Lambie as treasurer. William Anderson, secretary of the Foreign Missions Board in Philadelphia, strongly advised Lambie to resign from that position because of many inaccuracies in accounting. It was felt that Dr. Lambie was severely overworked as the chief surgeon in the newly opened hospital and that he needed to spend his energy on the medical work.[41] A second trial for the Lambies concerned incompatibility with Dr. Clifford Lee Wilmoth and his wife Helen. Dr. Lambie asked the Foreign Missions Board to withdraw Dr. and Mrs. Wilmoth from the hospital and recall them to the United States. In a four-page letter to Anderson, Lambie quoted 1 Peter

---

38. The title "*Fitaurari*" signified an eminent military leader.
39. Lambie, "Medical Missions in Ethiopia," 1933, MS, 7 pp., SIMIA, EA-1-82, File 12.
40. Aren, *Envoys of the Gospel*, 386–87.
41. Anderson, letter to Lambie, July 15, 1924, MHSC.

3:9, "Not rendering evil for evil . . . but contrariwise blessing."[42] The third trial for Lambie was that he felt that the Foreign Missions Board failed to understand the Lambies' situation regarding the Wilmoths' insubordinate spirit. Lambie deeply wished that he could have a face-to-face discussion with the board in Philadelphia to make the matter clear.[43] His letter of April 25, 1925, contains a hint that he and Mrs. Lambie might eventually sever their relationship with the Foreign Missions Board. The stress and strains at the Addis Ababa hospital were becoming unbearable.

The medical work in Addis Ababa was a significant project that served a wide clientele with a variety of medical needs. Still, Lambie felt that his vision for evangelizing southern Abyssinia would not be fulfilled if he were to be overly involved in a medical ministry based in Addis Ababa.

> When we first entered Abyssinia [in 1919] it was with the vision of reaching its southern and western sections that were either pagan or Mohamedan and for those people no Christian work had been done. Sayo was an opening wedge, and Gorei followed soon after. We had gone to Addis Ababa with no real thought of opening mission work there, but had been drawn into it by the kindness of His Majesty in promising to help with the hospital project as well as the evident need. . . . In a sense we had been surprised into building a hospital.[44]

Lambie was truly an "entrepreneur for Christ" who continued looking for new opportunities.[45] In 1927 he withdrew from the Foreign Missions Board of the United Presbyterian Church because their financial policy did not encourage "advance into new territory."[46]

> It was not easy to leave the fine new hospital which had enjoyed the favour of His Majesty and had done much for Ethiopia. Other physicians, however, came to take over the work of the hospital. The United Presbyterians felt unable to undertake any new work as receipts had so greatly decreased and retrenchment was the order of the day rather than forward movement."[47]

---

42. Lambie, letters to Anderson, December 24, 1924, and January 27, 1925, MHSC.

43. Lambie, letter to Anderson, April 25, 1925, MHSC.

44. Lambie, *Doctor without a Country*, 162.

45. I am indebted to Donham, *Marxist Modern*, 85, for this phrase.

46. Lambie, *Doctor's Great Commission*, 162.

47. Lambie, "Medical Missions in Ethiopia," 1933, MS, SIMIA, EA-1-82, File 12. Lambie expresses similar sentiments in *Doctor without a Country*, 165.

The way was now prepared for a new phase of Dr. Lambie's entrepreneurial missionary career in Abyssinia.

4

Establishing the George Memorial Hospital in Addis Ababa

*I have always felt that for the missionary doctor
prayer is at least equal in importance to sterile equipment.*

THOMAS A. LAMBIE, *A DOCTOR'S GREAT COMMISSION*, 33

AS THE PREVIOUS CHAPTER intimated, establishing and directing the George Memorial Hospital in Addis Ababa was a mixture of glory and agony for Dr. Lambie.[1] This chapter, with some overlap, tells that story much more fully.

On leaving Sayo in western Wellega in early 1922, Lambie later wrote, "My heart was full of praise and song, for Abyssinia had proved beautiful beyond my dreams, and what impressed me most was the possibility of a home in a climate a little less like an oven than that hot Sudan plain, a multitude of needy people, a healthy environment, and not least of all, the red roses blooming in the utmost profusion."[2] Lambie now began envisioning the potential for mission work in broader Abyssinia.

The initial contact had come from the provincial governor, Dejazmatch Birru, who was based at Sayo in the cool temperate highlands of western Wellega. He invited Lambie, a medical doctor, to relocate from Sudan to Abyssinia to provide medical assistance in stemming the 1918 influenza plague that was devastating much of Abyssinia. Now, several years later, as

---

1. The hospital was later officially designated "Tafari Makonnen Hospital."

2. Lambie, *Boot and Saddle*, 28.

Lambie reflected on what had transpired at Sayo, he began dreaming about what might take place when the Gospel would impact many communities throughout southern Abyssinia. He writes,

> The mission at Sayo had been established on firm foundations, school, small clinic/hospital, and church were all functioning well, and best of all, many friends had been made for the mission. . . . Other missionaries had come and took our places and it seemed that God was calling us to 'fresh fields and pastures.' The pioneer task, at least at Sayo, was finished and another phase of work was to begin.[3]

The Lambie family's journey by mule caravan from Sayo to Addis Ababa, going via Gorei, took three months. Following their arrival in Addis Ababa in 1922, Lambie made an appointment to see Ras Tafari Makonnen in his palace. He knew that Ras Nadew, governor at Gorei, had already written ahead about his medical exploits.[4] Lambie describes his first meeting with the regent:

> We got our appointment for Thursday afternoon, but as that hour approached I got more nervous about it. We knelt beside the ornate bedstead that had once belonged to the Empress [Taitu] and confessed to our Heavenly Father our weaknesses and fears and asked for Heaven's blessing upon the interview. Thus, having first met Heaven's King, we were no longer afraid of meeting any earthly ruler.[5]

During that first interview, Ras Tafari indicated that he desired to have a first-rate hospital constructed in Addis Ababa and that he would like Dr. Lambie to raise funds in America for the project. An earlier existing hospital, built and staffed by Russians, was now old and understaffed. Ras Tafari promised land and some financial assistance for the project. Lambie's mission agency was to provide funds, architects, and builders for the construction of the hospital as well as the necessary professional medical staff. After drawing up a proposal, which went through several drafts, for a hospital that satisfied both the regent and Dr. Lambie, the Lambies in 1922 boarded a train in Addis Ababa which was bound for Djibouti and a ship that would take them to the United States. Accompanying the Lambie family of four were three Ethiopian potential scholars, Bashawarad, Workou, and Malaku. These young men were to be enrolled in Muskingum College in New

---

3. Lambie, *Boot and Saddle in Africa*, 54. See also Lambie, letter to Medical Missionary Association, London, December 1932, SIMIA, EA-1-82, File 12. This seven-page letter reviews the initiation of Lambie's several medical ministries in Abyssinia.

4. Lambie, *Boot and Saddle*, 58.

5. Lambie, *Doctor without a Country*, 144.

Concord, Ohio. Malaku Beyene eventually, in 1935, returned to Ethiopia as a medical doctor trained in India and gave assistance within the Ethiopian Red Cross.[6]

When Lambie met with the FMBUPC in Philadelphia, he was given a warm and gracious welcome. The board members were sympathetic to the Addis Ababa hospital proposal. But then an unexpected bombshell exploded. Because of a decrease in giving, the board was currently in debt and had agreed to a "Five Year Plan." No new projects were to be undertaken during this period of time. Because the proposed Addis Ababa hospital would be a "New Project," it did not meet with the mission board's approval. Lambie was further informed that the board "could not permit [him] to bring it [the proposed hospital] before the [Presbyterian] churches in America as an object for gifts. If the money needed could be provided by individuals without any public appeal for funds, they would approve."[7] In spite of these setbacks, Lambie was convinced, after much prayer, that the project was of God and that the needed funds would be provided.

While riding on a train in Pennsylvania, he began praying for the medical project that he felt was so badly needed in Abyssinia. Suddenly, he later wrote, "I seemed to hear God say, 'Your prayer is heard.' God would provide the money needed. My heart welled up in praise to Him, for I knew it was His will and what He had promised He would do."[8] Lambie then began to thank God for what he was going to do. Three weeks later, at the New Wilmington Missionary Conference in a small town in western Pennsylvania, a man came up to Lambie and asked, "Are you Dr. Lambie? I hear that you are hoping to build a hospital in Abyssinia."[9] Thus began a conversation between Lambie and businessman William S. George. Initially Mr. George gave US$50,000 which was deposited in the account of the Presbyterian Women's General Missionary Society headed by Mrs. Elizabeth M. Campbell.[10] She was a gifted, able, and efficient secretary of the women's society and agreed to raise additional funds to equip the hospital. Even to complete construction of the hospital would require more funds. Later, in October 1924, Mr. George willingly donated an additional sum of US$20,000.[11]

---

6. Baudendistel, *Between Bombs and Good Intentions*, 52, 96, 97n3.

7. Lambie, *Doctor without a Country*, 155.

8. Lambie, *Doctor without a Country*, 156.

9. Lambie, "The Story of the Tafari Makonen Hospital and the George Memorial Building," ca. 1933, 1 p., MHSC.

10. Elizabeth M. Campbell was the wife of Hugh C. Campbell; in correspondence her signature is often given as Mrs. H. C. Campbell.

11. Campbell, letter to Lambie, October 28, 1924, MHSC.

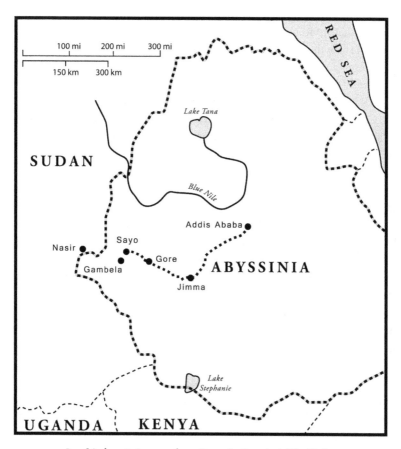

Lambies' route in 1922 from Sayo via Gore to Addis Ababa

John Lewis Beatty of Philadelphia was the building's architect. Two Americans, Phil West (with his wife, Effie) and William H. Douglass, went to Addis Ababa to do the building. "The foundations were fifteen and twenty feet deep, with cement footings. While nearly every other building in Addis Ababa has cracked, due to the poor soil, the George Memorial Hospital has stood staunch and true, its grey stones affording a pleasant contrast to the background of eucalyptus and black wattle [*acacia mearnsii*] trees."[12] After completion of construction in April 1924, George Memorial Hospital, with over 100 beds, was said to be one of the finest buildings in Addis Ababa. When completion of the building had neared, architect Beatty had advised

---

12. Lambie, *Doctor without a Country*, 159. In his letters, Lambie usually refers to the hospital as the "George Memorial Hospital," named after the mother of William George.

regarding additional artistic touches: "Now about the balustrade on the front porch, whether to use wood rail and wood balustrades or make it stone. If the cost is anything near the same I would by all means use the stone. It will look better and save in upkeep."[13] Lambie commended the builders Douglas and West "for their fine supervision" of the hospital's construction.[14]

With Tafari Makonnen Hospital now receiving patients, in May 1924 Dr. Clifford Wilmoth, a gifted surgeon, arrived along with his wife, Helen, to assist Dr. Lambie with the growing patient load. For unknown reasons serious friction developed between Dr. Wilmoth and Dr. Lambie. The conflict led to a lengthy conversation by mail between Lambie and William Anderson, secretary of the FMBUPC. Elizabeth Campbell, secretary of the Presbyterian Women's General Missionary Society, also offered wise counsel. Numerous "round robin" letters attempted to build understanding between Anderson, Campbell, Wilmoth, and Lambie.

The first issue Lambie faced with his young apprentice surgeon was a letter that Dr. Wilmoth wrote to the church in Philadelphia containing a serious accusation against a Mr. Williamson, director of the Abyssinian Corporation, a British importing and exporting pharmaceutical company based in Addis Ababa. Dr. Wilmoth's letter accused Williamson of ineptness and failing to provide the correct medicines that were ordered. Unfortunately, Wilmoth's letter reached not only the head office of the London-based Abyssinian Corporation but also the FMBUPC in Philadelphia. Apparently in his accusatory letter Dr. Wilmoth identified himself as the head of the Presbyterian Mission in Addis Ababa. Lambie was at a loss as how best to resolve the situation.[15]

A second issue arose because of Dr. Lambie's special relationship with Ras Tafari Makonnen. Various outsiders took advantage of Lambie's good graces and skills in obtaining an audience with the regent. In 1924 two British delegates representing the Phelps-Stokes Commission were invited to attend a function at the palace and present the purpose of their visit to Addis Ababa. They explained that the newly established Phelps-Stokes Commission was an attempt to wed government and mission initiatives in fostering education in developing countries. Apparently the Commission had matching funds behind it. Lambie lamented to Anderson, "The two representatives of the Commission were an embarrassing disaster in Addis Ababa. The men attended a function at the palace but were inappropriately

13. John Lewis Beatty, letter to Lambie, October 9, 1924, MHSC.

14. Lambie, letter to William S. George, April 16, 1924, inviting him to see the nearly completed hospital edifice, MHSC.

15. Lambie, letters to Anderson, June 24 and December 6, 1924, MHSC. See also Lambie, letter to Phil West, May 20, 1925, MHSC.

attired—they came in shorts, stole two pieces of gold cutlery from the Ras's table, and then vacated their Addis Ababa hotel without paying their bills! I was left to tidy up the mess! I feel that Dr. Jones, who arranged for their visit is somehow responsible!"[16]

A third issue occupying Lambie appears in correspondence with a Mr. J. Loder Park, US vice consul in Aden, regarding the affairs of the Anglo-American Oil Company. The company desired to obtain a concession to drill for oil in Harar Province, Eastern Abyssinia. Lambie responded to the oil company officials conveying Ras Tafari's recommendation "that the Anglo-American Oil Company either send an agent to Abyssinia to complete the concession or that they appoint me to act as their agent for them. In the latter case, they would of course have to inform me very fully as to just what they desire."[17] It would appear that Lambie was overextending his good will and negotiating skills to affairs beyond the sphere of the Tafari Makonnen Hospital.

But not all was gloom and doom at the hospital. Elizabeth Campbell mentions that the June 1925 issue of *National Geographic* magazine featured Dr. Lambie as head surgeon and carried a picture of the three-story Addis Ababa hospital in process of being completed. Apparently the reporter for *National Geographic* became rather ill while in Addis Ababa and was treated professionally by Lambie. Campbell comments, "So your fame is becoming world-wide, and we think you deserve it." Then she concludes with consoling words for the rift between him and Dr. Wilmoth, "You have our sympathy, our confidence and our love."[18]

In 1924 Ras Tafari Makonnen and Dr. Lambie decided that a special plaque should be placed in the foyer of the now completed building. It read:

TAFARI MAKONNEN HOSPITAL
GEORGE MEMORIAL BUILDING
GIVEN BY W. S. GEORGE OF
EAST PALESTINE OHIO U.S.A.
IN LOVING REMEMBRANCE OF HIS
MOTHER AND WIFE

16. Lambie, letter to Anderson, April 5, 1924, MHSC. Dr. Thomas Jesse Jones served as chairman of the Phelps-Stokes Commission which reported on the state of education in Africa.

17. Lambie, letter to J. Loder Park, November 29, 1925, MHSC.

18. Campbell, letter to Lambie, June 4, 1925, MHSC, citing *National Geographic* 47, no. 6 (June 1925).

Lambie noted that when Ras Tafari came to see the plaque he was rather pleased with it, and Lambie wrote to William George, "I do not think there is an institution of our church [United Presbyterian Church of North America] that looks better. It is by far the finest building in Addis Ababa."[19]

Some among the Addis Ababa hospital staff thought that sending Dr. and Mrs. Wilmoth to the Gorei hospital/clinic in Wellega Province of western Abyssinia might ease the friction between the two doctors. Lambie wrote to Anderson, "I want you all to understand that I have no personal thing against Dr. Wilmoth and I am quite willing to work with him. On the other hand, if I am so incompatible to him that no matter how hard I try to please him I do not please, possibly it might [be] wise for him to go somewhere else."[20] When Lambie approached Dr. Wilmoth about the possibility of serving in the Gorei hospital/clinic, Wilmoth flatly refused.[21]

A fourth issue reared its head. Apparently Dr. Wilmoth had written to Elizabeth Campbell complaining of Lambie's inability to handle finances well. Subsequently, William Anderson recommended that Lambie should resign from serving as treasurer of the Presbyterian Mission Abyssinia Association.[22] Lambie was willing to resign from this responsibility, but his five Presbyterian mission colleagues in far-off Sayo protested strongly against "any acceptance of my resignation."[23]

Compounding it all, in October 1924, Dr. Wilmoth wrote a negative letter to the Foreign Missions Board of the United Presbyterian Church complaining of Dr. Lambie's inability as a surgeon and his limited administrative skills. One month later, Campbell wrote to Dr. Lambie affirming her confidence in him: "We cannot believe there is such a feeling and wish to assure you that no matter what anybody says we still believe you to be an honest, upright, consecrated Christian."[24]

During this period of 1924 to 1926, various Ethiopian dignitaries were admitted to Tafari Makonnen Hospital for treatment. Empress Zauditu was treated for diabetes and other recurring ailments. Then Blattengeta Heroi Wolde Sellassie (a high court official), serving as the Secretary of the Pen to Ras Tafari, "was admitted to hospital . . . nigh unto death. *Ras* Tafari [was]

19. Lambie, letter to William S. George, October 3, 1924, MHSC.

20. Lambie, letter to Anderson, December 24, 1924, MHSC.

21. Lambie, letter to Anderson, November 1, 1924, MHSC.

22. Anderson, letter to Lambie, July 15, 1924, MHSC.

23. Lambie, letter to Anderson, November 1, 1924, MHSC. See also five missionaries resident at Sayo, letter to Lambie, September 20, 1924, confirming his role as association treasurer, MHSC.

24. Campbell, letter to Lambie, November 24, 1924, MHSC.

coming to visit [him] regularly."[25] After forty days of medical treatment and bed rest, the Secretary of the Pen recovered and returned to work. Ras Desta Demptew, son-in-law to Ras Tafari, came by the hospital and left a donation of US$200 showing his support and friendship.[26]

By December 1924, Lambie had reached his limit with Dr. and Mrs. Wilmoth. He unburdened his frustration in a letter to the secretary of the FMBUPC.

> At the present time Dr. Wilmoth and his wife have practically nothing to do with the other Presbyterian missionaries [on the Addis Ababa station]. They come to business meetings, but rarely to any religious meetings. . . . Charlotte and I have had them over to our house, but the Wilmoths have not reciprocated. And long-time British military friend from Sudan days, Colonel Sandford, had advised, "Do write to your people and have him [Dr. Wilmoth] recalled. He is doing your work a lot of harm here by the things he is telling out through the town." [But, Lambie concluded,] I am willing to have Dr. Wilmoth take charge of the hospital.[27]

Elizabeth Campbell sensed that Dr. Lambie was over-burdened with too many responsibilities. She affirmed that he should be released from the demanding load of being treasurer for the mission. "We do not think it is fair that you should be responsible for the operating of the hospital, for the erection of the buildings, for the evangelistic work, and at the same time act as treasurer for the whole country"—that is, for the mission work in Sayo, Gorei, and Addis Ababa.[28]

Lambie sent an urgent telegram to Secretary Anderson requesting that the Wilmoths be recalled immediately to the United States.[29] An immediate response came by telegram from Anderson: "It seems almost an unthinkable thing to call home a man who is professionally one of the most highly qualified we have sent to our fields."[30]

Concurrently Dr. Wilmoth resigned from the Tafari Makonnen Hospital without notifying Dr. Lambie as to where he was going. On May 27, 1925, Lambie wrote to Wilmoth,

25. Lambie, letter to Anderson, June 24, 1924, MHSC.

26. Florence White, letter to Lambie, July 6, 1926, MHSC.

27. Lambie, letter to Anderson, December 6, 1924, MHSC.

28. Campbell, letter to Lambie, December 16, 1924, MHSC.

29. Lambie, telegram to Anderson, January 27, 1925, MHSC.

30. Anderson, telegram to Lambie, January 27, 1925, MHSC.

I take it that you are soon leaving, although I have had no direct word from you. I wish to take this opportunity of saying how greatly I regret contretemps that caused your departure. Possibly neither you nor I are competent to judge on the merits of the case which concerns us both so intimately, but must leave that to God. But if I have in any way unthinkingly injured either one or the other of you, I sincerely regret it and ask your pardon. I believe that I can truthfully say that what I have said or done, I have done merely in order to protect myself and the work from injury at your hands. I wish you every good wish for the future and hope that in your new field of work wherever that may be, that there will be no more Lambies to make life miserable for you, and that perhaps you may realize that he was sometimes feeling quite miserable himself.[31]

The Lambie correspondence within the SIM International Archives shows no further letters between these two men of unusual medical skills. It appears that no tears were shed by either Lambie or Wilmoth when they finally parted ways.

Elizabeth Campbell had attempted to be courteous but firm when she chided Lambie for several of his shortcomings in a six-page letter dated March 16, 1925.[32] The significant issues she raised were:

1. It appears that there is no missionary "technic" [administrative protocol] in the hospital. Rather unusual that Nurse Ewing did not obey Dr. Wilmoth when ordered to leave the operating room.

2. The cost of the building of the hospital has doubled the initial projected cost of US$50,000.

3. Allowing mourning and wailing of relatives on the hospital premises does not seem appropriate.

4. Dr. Lambie has not been reporting "direct transfer of personal gifts."

5. Launching of the Mennen girls school without permission from the Philadelphia Missions Board.

6. Station business meetings held without inviting Dr. and Mrs. Wilmoth.

7. Additional mission property purchased in Dr. Lambie's personal name.

---

31. Lambie, letter to Wilmoth, May 27, 1925, MHSC.

32. Campbell, letter to Lambie, March 16, 1925, MHSC. See also Lambie, letter to Paul Gilmor, November 25, 1924, relating that Dr. Wilmoth refused to go to Gorei, MHSC.

And then, one month later the tenor of Campbell's letter to Lambie was somewhat softened. "I expect you to make some mistakes—we all do— but I know that your heart is faithful and true to your Lord and to the very important work He has entrusted you with. . . . I cannot understand why all this trouble has come into your life and work."[33]

In July 1925, Lambie requested by letter to the FMBUPC that he be granted a two- or three-month trip to the United States. He listed three reasons for such a trip.

1. There appears to be a growing misunderstanding between the Foreign Missions Board and Lambie.

2. Ras Tafari desires that Lambie lay a wreath at the tomb of Mr. George (who died in April 1925), in East Palestine, Ohio. Ras Tafari is willing to pay Lambie's transportation.

3. Lambie needs a rest.

His letter continues,

> The most important reason that I feel I should come home is: that I feel that neither you nor the Board have understood our conditions and understood these in their true light. Perhaps I have misinterpreted your letters and you have misinterpreted mine. But however this may be, it has seemed impossible for us to come to an understanding through letters: things seem to grow more obscure with each letter. I feel this work [here] is in a very critical period and it seems to me that the establishment of mutual understanding and confidence is the most important thing in the world for me at the present time. . . . I feel that a candid conversation with you and the Board would be the means of coming to such an understanding. Failing this, I should be led to believe that the Lord is seeking to guide me to some other field of similar work.[34]

The Foreign Missions Board of the United Presbyterian Church approved that the four Lambies return to the United States in June 1926, after Wallace and Betty would be out of school.[35] Miss Florence White, serving as secretary at the Tafari Makonnen Hospital, wrote to the Lambies of the recent staffing arrangement at the hospital:

---

33. Campbell, letter to Lambie, April 26, 1925, MHSC.

34. Lambie, letter to Anderson, July 11, 1925, MHSC.

35. Lambie, letter to McLellan, March 6, 1926, MHSC, confirmed that the Lambies would arrive in the United States in July 1926.

Dr. Pollock would replace Dr. Lambie as surgeon in the George
Memorial Hospital. Nurses Viola Bayne and Hazel Ewing were
to continue on as nurses. Fred Russell was appointed to serve
as Association Treasurer based in Addis Ababa. Miss Florence
White to continue on as corresponding secretary of the mission
in Addis Ababa.[36]

Florence White continued her letter to the Lambies, who were now in
Philadelphia awaiting their appointment with the Foreign Missions Board
and Elizabeth Campbell, "We at the George Memorial Hospital are praying
often that everything will turn out all right and with as little disturbance as
possible."[37] The Lambies met with officials of the FMBUPC board and Mrs.
Elizabeth Campbell on September 6, 1926. Just over six months following
that meeting, the Lambies resigned from the Foreign Missions Board, "with
as little disturbance as possible."[38]

Meanwhile, even as they arrived in the United States in 1926 a new
door of opportunity was already slowly beginning to open for the Lambies.
Dr. Lambie's growing vision for placing dozens of mission stations among
southern Abyssinian ethnic groups might be realized. Could it be that now
was the time to attempt a new mission initiative into the South?

36. Florence White, letter to Lambie, July 6, 1926, MHSC.

37. White, letter to Lambie, July 6, 1926, MHSC.

38. See the Lambies' rather curt certificate of resignation, March 6, 1927, archives of
the Foreign Missions Board of the Presbyterian Church of America, Philadelphia. Note
also that Lambie, letter to Phil West, May 20, 1925, had already stated that the Lambies
were "ready to give up and go home," MHSC.

Tafari Makonnen, who became Emperor Haile Sellassie I, was born in Harar in 1892. His father, Makonnen Walde-Mikael, a renowned general in the 1896 Battle of Adwa, was a member of the dynastic royalty of Shewa. As a young boy, Tafari was tutored by Catholic priests in Harar; he later attended the Menilek School in Addis Ababa. Tafari's father, Makonnen, groomed him in administrative skills as well as encouraging his inclination to learn about the outside world from foreigners. In 1918 Tafari was named regent (ras) of Abyssinia while Menelik's daughter, Zauditu, served as empress. In 1924, Ras Tafari together with an entourage of Abyssinian nobles traveled to Europe with the purpose of enlisting Abyssinia as a member of the League of Nations. After their extended tour of Europe, these nobles supported Ras Tafari in his ambition to modernize Abyssinia. His friendship and growing ties with foreign countries caused suspicion among Abyssinian traditionalists, and they accused him of becoming Roman Catholic. His close association with foreigners, however, stood him in good stead for it strengthened his political power and aided his efforts to usher in modern improvements. Ras Tafari befriended Dr. Thomas Lambie in 1922, and they cooperated closely in building the Tafari Makonnen Hospital (George Memorial Hospital) in Addis Ababa.

Ras Tafari was crowned king (*negus*) in 1928. On November 2, 1930, soon after the death of Empress Zauditu, he was installed as "king of kings" (*negus nagast*) and took the name Haile Sellassie I, meaning "power of the Trinity." His installation was a great national event with dignitaries from many foreign countries present. Missionaries Thomas and Charlotte Lambie also attended the gala event. Rowland Bingham, international director of the Sudan Interior Mission, published a complimentary article titled "Long Live the King of Kings." The newly installed emperor strove to introduce modern institutions, acting on the belief that they added to his imperial power and the authority of the central government. Haile Sellassie was supportive of missionary institutions of education and medicine, and he enabled SIM to establish sixteen mission stations in various parts of Abyssinia.

When Italy invaded Abyssinia in 1935, the emperor led the resistance and appointed Dr. Lambie, his trusted friend and advisor, as secretary general of the Ethiopian Red Cross. After the Italian Fascists defeated the Abyssinian military, on May 2, 1936, Haile Sellassie was forced into exile in England. With the advent of WWII, the British came to the aid of the emperor. British troops, together with Abyssinians, led in the attack against the Italians from several strategic positions in British Sudan. SIM personnel such as Glen Cain, Alan Webb, and Laurie Davison assisted the British military with language interpretation and logistics as they advanced into Abyssinia. Thomas Lambie also assisted the Abyssinian military operation by conducting covert intelligence work based in Malakal, Sudan.

In 1941 when Haile Sellassie was restored to his throne in Addis Ababa, he selected Ethiopia as the new name for the country, and he again moved forward, implementing social, economic, and education reforms. Protestant missions served willingly under the emperor's jurisdiction as they were assured of his friendship toward Christianity. Political stagnation and devastating famine conditions in northern Ethiopia led to Haile Sellassie's deposition from office in 1974. In 1936, George Steer, a war correspondent and a previous confidant of the emperor, described him as a bundle of contradictions: "Courageous but cowardly, suspicious yet trusting, loyal but jealous" (*Caesar in Abyssinia*, 367). Yet, in God's providence, Emperor Haile Sellassie was instrumental, even if unknowingly, in launching the evangelical movement in Ethiopia.

5

Launching the Abyssinian
Frontiers Mission

Fear keeps us back from many things. . . .
Many, even of God's children,
suffer under the bondage of fear.

THOMAS A. LAMBIE, *A BRUISED REED*, 71

IN 1939 THOMAS LAMBIE wrote regarding George Memorial Hospital, "We never regarded it as a final objective. In fact, even before the hospital was built but when the money was in hand, I had said to the home secretary of the mission [the Foreign Missions Board of the United Presbyterian Church], 'Now that we have the money for the hospital, I regard it as a *fait accompli*, and we ought to be thinking of advancing into these southern areas.'"[1] By 1926, five years in which he had been thoroughly immersed in medical work had flown by since the Lambies had first become based in Addis Ababa. He felt that with qualified medical personnel the hospital ministry was now capable of standing on its own. Lambie, of a pioneer and entrepreneurial nature, felt it was time to expand the outreach of the Presbyterian mission by opening new mission stations in the south. But he commented, "Our Church was not ready to advance into new territory."[2]

1. Lambie, *Doctor without a Country*, 162.
2. Lambie, *Doctor without a Country*, 162.

45

In reality Lambie had been frustrated for several years over a personnel issue with another doctor at the George Memorial Hospital and was ready to leave that ministry. He felt the mission secretary of the FMBUPC in the United States was reluctant to settle the personnel issue that was gnawing at his spirit. By 1926, Lambie was neither happy nor fulfilled in the role of director of the George Memorial Hospital in Guleile, Addis Ababa.

Lambie's story now moves to the steps that lay behind the founding of Abyssinian Frontiers Mission (AFM). A small group of evangelicals in New York, burdened for the lost in Africa, was to play a significant role in the launch of the new mission. Led by Miss Constance Brandon, a spunky and talented British lady, the group was on the lookout for some virgin field in which to establish a mission. Members of the New York group were aware of Heart of Africa Mission that had been founded by the famous cricketeer, C. T. Studd. At this point Alfred Buxton, son-in-law to Studd, was back in England from mission work in Congo and was recovering from ill health.[3] Members of the Constance Brandon prayer group in New York knew of Buxton and contacted him by letter with a suggestion of a needy field in Africa. Soon after Buxton received the group's letter, he happened to see Lambie's article "The Importance of Abyssinia," published in *World Dominion*, a mission magazine.[4] Lambie's article in turn, through various circumstances, brought together Mr. Alfred and Mrs. Edith Buxton and Rev. George W. and Mrs. Nellie Rhoad, missionaries who had served with the Africa Inland Mission in Kenya for a number of years. The couples met together in the recently acquired home of Dr. and Mrs. Lambie—a handsome property called "The Meadows"—near Baltimore, Maryland. Lambie relates that they "spent many happy days in earnest prayer that God would show [them] what His will was."[5] The three men and their wives had been reading *Daily Light*, a small booklet that assembled Bible verses on a certain theme for each day of the year. The reading for March 3, 1927, quoted Exodus 33:15, "If thy presence go not with me, carry us not up thence." Based on this verse,

---

3. For a full account of the missionary activity of Buxton, see Grubb, *Alfred Buxton*.

4. Lambie, "The Importance of Abyssinia," 192–98.

5. Lambie, *Doctor without a Country*, 163.

the three men had each independently made the decision that they should boldly make plans for entering Abyssinia.[6]

Lambie faced a great personal struggle about joining this nascent mission endeavor. He did not want to give up his nearly twenty-year appointment with the Foreign Missions Board of the United Presbyterian Church.

> They had been good to me. I had an assured salary, with liberal educational allowances for our two children. I had an annual holiday, if I chose to take it, and expenses paid. I had a generous freight allowance, and other extras; when old age came I was assured of a pension for declining years. Against all this, what could the new organization offer? Practically nothing. . . . The decision involved not only myself, but my wife and our two children.[7]

After full consideration, Lambie submitted his resignation to the Foreign Missions Board of the United Presbyterian Church on March 6, 1927. His comment, "Resigned," with no further explanation, was terse if not curt. The newly formed Abyssinian Frontiers Mission (the name suggested by Charlotte Lambie) was now launched.[8] The three founding fathers, Lambie, Rhoad, and Buxton, soon began a tour of speaking engagements in the New England area. Lambie wrote to his mother "that this new mission seems like a 'leap in the dark,' in some ways and yet we feel it is of God and it is better to work for Him in the dark than to walk alone in the light. If I did not believe it was His will for me I would not do it, but I believe and feel sure it is."[9]

To spell out the rationale for launching the new mission, Lambie penned a twelve-page document, "A New Mission to Abyssinia's Unknown Frontiers." Its introduction states,

> The [work of missions] must be done by Christian churches of the world and the nationality most acceptable by Abyssinians is the American as the other great powers have African colonies or protectorates that border on Abyssinian territory and are frequently in dispute with the Abyssinian Government on political

6. Donham, *Marxist Modern*, 95, quotes SIM missionary Brian Fargher: "[The SIM missionaries] felt duty-bound to have a bible text for every religious statement they made." Of another SIM missionary dependent on one Scripture verse for guidance, SIM missionary Alfred Roke comments, "This kind of theology seems to need a lot of luck" (Roke, *They Went Forth*, 180). Lambie himself asserted: "We do not believe in blindly opening the Bible, shutting one's eyes and putting one's fingers on a verse at random" (*Doctor without a Country*, 177).

7. Lambie, *Doctor without a Country*, 164.

8. Lambie, *Doctor without a Country*, 168.

9. Lambie, letter to his mother, Annie Lambie, March 6, 1927, MHSC.

questions arising from borderline troubles. . . . The Abyssinian Government well knows that America has no design upon their country and missionary work is therefore not subject to the same suspicious scrutiny."[10]

Lambie also carefully stated that the goal of this "New Mission to Abyssinia" differed from that of other mission agencies such as the Church Missionary Society, which sought to revive the ancient Orthodox Church. Abyssinian Frontiers Mission would view with favor "the reviving of this old Church if it is possible," but its focus would be directed to the large population of unevangelized people groups of southern, western, and eastern Abyssinia.[11]

Bolstered by the example of forerunners such as Hudson Taylor of the China Inland Mission and Adoniram Judson of Burma, Lambie, the Rhoads, and Buxton had now charted their course in mission. They began sharing their vision of a new faith mission to Abyssinia in various churches along the East Coast of the United States, but they met with limited success. For the newly formed board of trustees for AFM, in 1927 Lambie attempted to enumerate the goals of the newly founded mission. He listed five points:

1. This is not an experimental expedition. Much is known about the countries mentioned and their tremendous needs, enough to warrant the sending out of hundreds of missionaries without ever crowding the greatest unreached areas, but,

2. The most strategic points for commencing a missionary campaign are not certainly known and require a greater definition before a great number of missionaries are sent out so as to avoid any over-lapping, and that accessibility, receptivity by the native peoples, densely populated areas, Mohamedan [sic] advances and other compeling [sic] factors be thoroughly weighed.

3. Information can only be obtained by observation and study on the part of the members of this first group of missionaries as there are no reliable sources of information.

4. That this first expedition should not only be for the purpose of information by travel and study but should be definitely committed to beginning one or two mission stations so that the work might gain

10. Lambie, "A New Mission to Abyssinia's Unknown Frontiers," 1927, 6, SIMIA, EA-1-82, File 13.

11. Lambie, "A New Mission to Abyssinia's Unknown Frontiers," 3, SIMIA, EA-1-82, File 13.

continuity and by practical beginning give a real evidence to the Abyssinian Government that we intend to carry on.

5. That due to the lack of any means of transportation beyond Addis Ababa, caused by lack of wagons or auto roads and the rough description of much of the country that mule transport will have to be relied upon for the purpose of getting the information indicated above and for the conveying of missionaries to their locations beyond Addis Ababa. That this transportation element will until roads be built, be a matter of great importance to the mission and will mean that for a time at least the location of mission stations should not be too widely separated as this would tremendously isolate the missionaries from each other and make extremely difficult the missions [sic] providing such conveyance of person and goods as would seem incumbent.[12]

Lambie concluded by affirming that the objective of the new faith venture was to penetrate the "regions beyond," going to territory where Christ had never been preached. This meant that AFM would be directed to the many unreached tribes in southern Abyssinia and Muslim areas of Jimma. The placement of AFM missionary stations would not be directed toward reviving the ancient Orthodox Christians of the north.

At a notable "faith missions" conference held at Stony Brook, New York, on July 16, 1927, the three founding couples of the new AFM met with Rowland Bingham, director of the Sudan Interior Mission (SIM). He had just returned from New Zealand and Australia, where an increasing number of candidates were applying to SIM. But for those candidates, the distance to serve in SIM's field in Nigeria seemed to be an insurmountable problem. For New Zealand missionaries, ocean travel to Nigeria meant purchasing passage all the way to Liverpool, then transshipping back five thousand miles to Lagos. Such passage was a great expense. Might the two missions benefit by joining forces? Bingham cited an additional positive result to be gained by melding the two organizations. He wrote rather enthusiastically:

The gain was immediate. All the machinery of the Sudan Interior Mission at the home end was immediately available, and a constituency of praying people already prepared to take the new work upon their hearts. This was best evidenced in that during the summer, funds had been very short, but the fall announcement of an advance into a new field instead of creating greater financial difficulties immediately drew forth the strongest cooperation from our praying friends; so that by November the

12. Lambie, "Goals of the First Missionary Party of the AFM to Enter Ethiopia," June 27, 1927, SIMIA, EA-1-82, File 17.

full amount was on hand for the launching of the new party into Ethiopia."[13]

The Lambies, together with the Rhoads and Buxtons, readily endorsed Bingham's proposal. Lambie wrote:

> Dr. Bingham felt that if we could join our forces, it would make a stronger organization than the two could be separately. To join with the Sudan Interior Mission seemed to be distinctly to our advantage, especially when it meant to have the guidance of such a veteran missionary leader as Doctor Bingham. . . . Passing years have confirmed the belief that the union of the Abyssinian Frontiers Mission with the Sudan Interior Mission was indeed of God; and they have also confirmed the high opinion we formed of the character of our beloved Doctor Bingham.[14]

Rowland Bingham had been praying that SIM would be able to establish a mission "beach-head" somewhere in East Africa. Therefore, he thoroughly endorsed the marriage of the nascent AFM to the previously established Sudan Interior Mission. The union of SIM with AFM brought the new venture synergism with experienced East Africa missionaries. In an editorial for *Evangelical Christian*, Bingham wrote:

> We want to commend to our readers for prayer Dr. T. A. Lambie, who has spent some eighteen years in the Egyptian Sudan and Abyssinia, and his fellow worker, Mr. George Rhoad, who has given over twenty years of service in Kenya Colony, East Africa. These two brethren will be leading a party in October to establish our first station in that section of Africa. They will need divine guidance and we trust they will have God's richest blessing in the presence of One whose "Lo I am with you always" still holds good. Mr. Alfred B. Buxton, M.A., who has been jointly responsible for the launching of the new enterprise, has undertaken to serve with us in the promoting of the work at the home end [England], as his health will not permit the consideration of further field work at present.[15]

The first party of the Abyssinian Frontiers Mission/Sudan Interior Mission consisted of Dr. and Mrs. Lambie with daughter Betty (son Wallace remained in the United States with relatives), Rev. and Mrs. George (Nellie)

---

13. Bingham, "Entering into Ethiopia," 226. Also see the memo documenting the merger of the Abyssinian Frontiers Mission with SIM, ca. July or August 1927, 3 pp., SIMIA, MM-1-158a.

14. Lambie, *Doctor without a Country*, 168.

15. Bingham, "A New Call to a New Land," 399.

Rhoad with son George Jr., Rev. Walter Ohman, Mr. Clarence Duff, Mr. and Mrs. Carl Rasmussen (scheduled to meet the party in Liverpool), and Mr. Glen Cain from Australia who would wait for the missionary band in Aden. They arrived in Addis Ababa on December 26, 1927. Peter Cotterell comments, "They enjoyed a deferred Christmas dinner on Ethiopian [Abyssinia] soil."[16] Now the SIM missionary band faced the challenging task of gaining official permission from Abyssinian officialdom to launch mission stations in southern Abyssinia.

16. Cotterell, *Born at Midnight*, 21.

The persons below are listed according to the year in which Lambie had significant interaction with them.

Dejazmatch Birru Walda Gabriel invited Dr. Lambie in 1919 to come from Sudan to Sayo, Wellega, to aid in staving off the devastating influenza epidemic. After replacing former Governor Dejazmatch Balcha, based in Agere Selam, Birru warmly welcomed Lambie's establishment of a mission station at Homacho, Sidamo. In 1932 Birru was promoted to war minister. In 1934—prior to his exile to Europe by train on May 2, 1936—Birru entrusted his infant daughter and her nurse to the Lambies in Addis Ababa.

Ras Nadew Abba Wollo, governor of Illubabor, had Lambie remove a boring beetle from inside his ear. This unusual incident occurred in Gorei in 1920. It opened the door for Lambie to meet with Ras Tafari Makonnen in 1921. Nadew attended the 1919 Versailles Peace Conference.

Dejazmatch Mosheshe had been a patient of Lambie's in Sayo, Wellega. In 1929 he was serving as governor at Hosanna and, with his wife, acquired the land contract for SIM at Lambuda.

Dejazmatch Yigezu Bahabté, governor of Wolaitta (formerly known as "Wolamo"), was stationed at Soddo. In 1929 he was very helpful to Lambie in selecting the site for the Otona mission near Soddo.

Dejazmatch Makonnen Habta-Wald in 1930 replaced Yigezu as governor of Soddo. During the political unrest of 1936, he escorted SIM personnel from Dubancho to Soddo and provided for their needs.

Blattangeta Hiruy Wolde Sellassie, proficient in several international languages, was a noted author. A trusted person, he became Secretary of the Pen to Ras Tafari in 1928 and held the post of Minister of Foreign Affairs, 1931–36. In August 1935, Hiruy was appointed as president and Dr. Lambie as secretary general of the Ethiopian Red Cross Society. Mission societies claimed Hiruy as "their man" as he proved to be helpful in many situations. He often served as a trusted middleman between Lambie and Ras Tafari.

Dejazmatch Beyenne Merid married Li'ilt Romanewerq, daughter of Haile Sellassie. As governor of Gofa province, in 1931 he invited SIM officials to establish a mission near Bulqi, Gofa, where the Ohmans were the first to serve.

Ras Dasta Damtaw married Li'ilt Tenayewerq, daughter of Haile Sellassie. He selected Yirga Alem at a lower altitude as the capital and asked Lambie to provide an engineer (Cliff Mitchell) to lay out the new town. Dasta willingly granted Lambie's request to establish the Tutitti station, about thirty miles south of Gedeo, where Cliff and Myrtle Mitchell would be based. In 1933 Dasta offered a mission station to SIM on the edge of Yerga Alem and assured Lambie, "Have no fear, you need us and we need you. Just leave everything in my hands" (Lambie, letter to Bingham, March 6, 1933). Lambie commented that Ras Dasta "has been one of my very best friends for about ten years." Dasta eventually died at the hands of the Fascists in February 1937 while taking refuge in the Sidamo forest.

Ras Kassa Haylu Dargé, governor of Lasta province, invited Lambie to open two SIM stations in the north, at Lalibela and Debra Markos. In order to investigate this northern option, on February 23, 1934, Thomas and Charlotte Lambie, traveling with Rowland Bingham, set out by mule for the north country. In his invitation Kassa said to Lambie, "Do for my people in the north what you have done for the people in the south."

Ras Emeru Hayla-Sellase, governor of Gojam, was a cousin of the emperor. In 1934 he offered two sites for SIM mission activity in the province of Gojam. Lambie said of Emeru, "He was, in my opinion, after the Emperor himself, the very finest man in Ethiopia. Honest and faithful to his friends, he never took a bribe or concealed a fault; he was generous and unselfish. In the war he proved himself the best general of all."

6

The Struggle with Abyssinian Orthodox Church Officials over Permission to Travel South

The real kings and priests are after all Christ's servants.

THOMAS A. LAMBIE, *A DOCTOR WITHOUT A COUNTRY*, 149

WHEN TAFARI MAKONNEN HOSPITAL opened its doors in 1924, many members of Abyssinian officialdom were successfully treated for various ailments. Dr. Lambie often treated Empress Zauditu in her official residence as well for her recurring liver ailment and diabetes. The Egyptian Archbishop Abba Mattewos, who served as the titular head of the Abyssinian Orthodox Church, developed a friendship with Dr. Lambie.[1] But he died in December 1926, while the Lambies were on furlough.

In December 1927, when the Lambies (now members of SIM) attempted to reestablish fraternal relationships with Abyssinian officialdom, especially with Ras Tafari Makonnen, they were kept at a distance. One reason for their rebuff was that Ras Tafari Makonnen had other concerns requiring his attention. When he along with his entourage of Abyssinian officials returned to Addis Ababa from Europe in 1925, his negotiations for Abyssinian access to a port on the Red Sea, at Assab, had been unsuccessful. Back in Addis Ababa, "rumours circulated that [Ras Tafari] was a Roman

1. Lambie, *Doctor without a Country*, 160.

Catholic, that he had embezzled state funds, and that his only objective in Europe was to display himself as a 'modern' statesman."[2] Another criticism leveled against Ras Tafari was that he purposely delayed appointing another Coptic Egyptian as titular head of the Abyssinian Orthodox Church, leaving the position vacant. The regent felt dejected and Lambie sensed that political tensions were brewing within Abyssinia's ruling class. In spite of the tensions, as a courtesy the newly arrived missionaries were invited for "afternoon tea with the Regent, Ras Tafari, and each of us was introduced to his Highness by Dr. Lambie." Several days later, "all of us also went to the Christmas party [January 6] at the palace, attended [by] a large part of the diplomatic, business and missionary population of the city."[3]

As a result of the tensions present, the regent was reluctant to issue travel permits for the newly arrived Sudan Interior Mission band to travel into the interior of the country. Pressure came from several sources. Empress Zauditu continued to resist the regent's modernization policies.[4] With the church now under the strict influence of the Ichege Gebre Menfes Qidus, the head of the Debra Libanos Monastery, the Abyssinian Orthodox Church authorities mounted strong opposition.[5] Prior to the missionaries' being granted permission to travel to the south, they were asked by the Ichege to present a written statement of their faith and practice to the Council of Priests.[6] When Lambie and George Rhoad met with this council of some fifty priests to explain their religious position, the Council of Priests "seemed determined to disagree with everything we said. We tried to placate them, but it was no use. The verdict was determined in advance. We were not permitted to go [to the interior]. We must not go."[7] And now the Lenten season was upon them, so further discussion with the Council of Priests was delayed.

Another unusual factor further delayed the missionary band from leaving Addis Ababa. In mid-February 1928, Ras Tafari summoned Dejazmatch Balcha Safo, governor of the coffee-rich Sidamo province, to come to Addis Ababa to respond to charges of misgovernment. When Dejazmatch Balcha arrived in Addis Ababa accompanied by an entourage of several hundred soldiers, he was officially deposed and his coffee-rich

2. Marcus, *Haile Sellassie I*, 73.

3. Duff, *Cords of Love*, 26.

4. Marcus, *Haile Sellassie I*, 20: "Zawditu was now empress; she had a reputation for being stubborn, deeply religious and conservative."

5. The Ichege is the second highest ecclesiastic of the Ethiopian Orthodox Church.

6. Lambie, *Doctor without a Country*, 170, incorrectly refers to this group of priests as "the Abyssinian Sanhedrin."

7. Lambie, *Doctor without a Country*, 171.

fiefdom was eventually handed over to Ras Birru, formerly governor based at Sayo.[8] Clarence Duff wrote on February 27, 1928, "The political situation seems very tense. There is some talk of civil war. There are rumours galore, and it isn't much wonder that Blattangeta Hiruy Wolde Sellassie, who really seems to be our friend, and the *Ras* himself, suggest quietly that we just take it slow.... It is a most critical situation indeed.... We have been absolutely thrown upon God for help."[9]

Eventually the missionaries were given written permission, couched in vague and indefinite terms, to travel to the hinterland. Ras Tafari had many detractors who were resistant to change, so permission, when it was granted, included the understanding that no schools or churches would be built prior to further discussion with Addis Ababa officialdom. When it came, the permission was for Lambie and his associates to travel to the south *sila nefas*, literally, "for the air" or "for their health." Duff comments, "This was typical of the devious kind of permission by which much of our work was to be authorized."[10] Blattangeta Hiruy shared in confidence with Lambie that at the present time he should not ask for official permission. In their travels south the mission party could quietly visit a town. If conditions were right they might "slip in a mission station" without making a fuss and probably everything would be all right.[11] On March 7, 1928, the large entourage finally set off from Addis Ababa for their initial destination of Jimma. Some seventy-five muleteers and head carriers, about a dozen riding horses, plus sixty pack mules carried food supplies, personal goods, tents, camp equipment, medical supplies, and Bibles.[12] On the trail, George and Nellie Rhoad and their son George took the lead with the initial group. The second party consisted of Thomas and Charlotte Lambie with Betty. They were trailed by the final group of the entourage; it was composed of the three "COD boys"—Glen Cain, Walter Ohman, and Clarence Duff. Mr. and Mrs. Carl Rasmussen remained in Addis Ababa, living in the rental facility across from the Ras Makonnen Hospital at Guleile. This couple was to support the SIM team by forwarding mail and needed supplies down-country.

8. Bahru, *History of Modern Ethiopia*. For Ras Tafari's stratagem to overcome De-jazmatch Balcha and his soldiers in Addis Ababa, see pp. 132–33. Bahru's account of the upending of Dejazmatch Balcha is somewhat different from that of Cotterell, *Born at Midnight*, 23.

9. Duff, *Cords of Love*, 30.

10. Duff, *Cords of Love*, 33.

11. Lambie, *Doctor without a Country*, 171.

12. SIM missionaries could be called "Biblicists" because they "stressed the Bible text and they transferred this emphasis to the movement." See Fargher, *Origins of the New Churches*, 195.

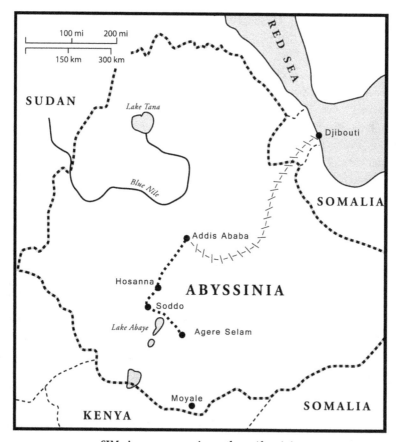

SIM pioneers survey in southern Abyssinia

Four days of easy riding brought the group to Marako, where Joseph Be-hesnilian, an Armenian entrepreneur, had a farm and a water-powered grain grinding mill. The missionaries were invited to launch a school on his property, but that project was deferred to a later time. The missionary caravan continued their journey, heading for Jimma. On the trail they met a Singer sewing machine salesman who advised them that a well-traveled road to Jimma via Hosanna town lay further to the south. He assured them that crossing the Gibe River would not prove to be difficult if they crossed before the rainy season began in earnest and that traveling on this western trail would take them swiftly to Jimma.

Before they reached Hosanna they were met by six armed men and later were joined by a larger escort of nearly three hundred men who cere-moniously guided the missionaries to the governor's well-secured residence in Hosanna. There Lambie was surprised to discover his former friend from

Wellega, Dejazmatch Mosheshe, now based in Hosanna as governor of the Kambatta region.[13] The governor, who happened to be the godfather of Ras Tafari, gave the group a most cordial welcome. "He insisted that we stay at least four days, assuring us that our stay would all be at his expense. That evening he sent thirty-four bundles of hay and teff straw for our mules, four hundred loaves (large, round flat cakes [*enjera*]) of one kind of bread and two hundred of another, twenty eggs, two chickens, milk . . . and the promise of ten sheep and two oxen in the morning."[14] The mission group was well taken care of during their four-day stay. As they were preparing to leave, Dejazmatch Mosheshe informed Lambie that another of his former patients from Wellega, Dejazmatch Yigezu, had been transferred to Soddo, Wolaitta (formerly known as "Wolamo"; Soddo was the capital of the region). The missionary entourage "put on hold" their plans to visit Jimma immediately, for they felt keenly that it was of God for them to continue south to Soddo instead of heading west to Jimma.[15]

After trekking south for another five days, the missionary band reached Soddo, where they were met in grand style by the governor, Dejazmatch Yigezu. He sent out "a large band of soldiers with minstrels making music on flutes and horns to escort us to a camp-site where the soldiers proceeded to clear weeds and grass."[16] The governor begged the missionaries to settle in his territory because of the great medical needs there. But the Lambies and Rhoads decided that the eastern section of Sidamo province should be explored first. The travelers continued south through the lowlands. Duff describes the terrain after they had crossed the Bilate River and headed to the southeast: "The country through which we travelled the last three days is most beautiful, with its broad grazing lands surrounded by forest, rolling hills and deep valleys with mountain ranges always towering in the distance in every direction."[17]

The Lambie party arrived on April 9, 1928, at Agere Selam, which at an altitude of over 9,000 feet occupied the high point of the plateau. The local population were anticipating the arrival of the newly appointed governor

---

13. The Kambatta and Gudeile ethnic groups were governed as one entity until after 1944.

14. Duff, *Cords of Love,* 45. Duff was assigned the task of keeping a detailed diary of this missionary excursion. Much of the data contained in *Cords of Love* is from Duff's diary.

15. It might well be said that this twentieth-century missionary band were kept temporarily by the Holy Spirit "from preaching the word in the province of [Jimma]" (Acts 16:6–7 NIV).

16. Duff, *Cords of Love,* 50.

17. Duff, *Cords of Love,* 52.

Dejazmatch Birru, the former official from Sayo, Wellega, who had invited Dr. Lambie to come from the Sudan some ten years earlier. While waiting for Birru, they observed Dejazmatch Birru's trusted associate, Fitaurari (that is, military commander) Atena Giorgis hard at work supervising the digging up of former Dejazmatch Balcha Safo's buried treasures and sending these off to Addis Ababa. "All his days were spent in counting Marie Teresa thalers. He could do about 50,000 a day, and as this was twenty-five mule loads of silver he thought he was doing pretty well."[18] Because of the cold and the clouds and wind of Agere Selam, the Lambie party relocated to the slightly lower altitude of Garbicho. On April 23, 1928, Dejazmatch Birru arrived by mule from Addis Ababa and greeted the missionaries warmly. Soon Lambie and Rhoad began laying out plans with the governor for mission work in Sidamo province. They prayed earnestly for guidance into the future. This was a crucial time for them; they could go no further without knowing God's specific direction. Duff wrote to his parents from Garbicho,

> We had seen the need in the provinces through which God led us and we felt the time had come when He must show us where we should begin our work. There seemed to be open doors in the Gurage country, in Kambatta, in Wolamo and almost certainly in Sidamo. Now questions arose as to the strategic centres at which to begin our work in the south country.[19]

It was now six weeks since the pioneer mission party had left Addis Ababa, and they were ready to put down roots. The decision was made that Charlotte Lambie and Betty together with Glen Cain should remain at Garbicho (near Agere Selam) and that Thomas Lambie, Clarence Duff, Walter Ohman, and the three Rhoads would return to Soddo, since George Rhoad felt the decision of choosing a site for the mission at Soddo should be made together with Lambie. Dejazmatch Yigezu in Soddo was also waiting for Dr. Lambie to begin treating what seemed like leprosy on his face. Therefore, Lambie joined the Rhoad, Duff, and Ohman contingent. After they had been two days on the trail, a messenger caught up to Lambie with a note from his wife saying that Betty was running a high fever. Because of this distressing news, Lambie began retracing his steps from Aletta posthaste. As he began climbing the escarpment towards Garbicho, a second messenger

---

18. Lambie, *Doctor without a Country*, 173. After these funds reached the crown, they were donated to the building of the Balcha Hospital in Addis Ababa. Dejazmatch Balcha Safo, appointed governor of coffee-rich Sidamo province by Menelik II, had acquired substantial wealth by exporting coffee through Kenya. Deposed and imprisoned in 1927 because of insubordination, Balcha was replaced by Dejazmatch Birru, formerly of Aussa, Wellega.

19. Duff, *Cords of Love*, 51.

intercepted him with another note saying that Betty had taken a turn for the better. With a grateful heart, Lambie turned his mule around and rode hard in an attempt to reach the Rhoad party, who had now crossed the Bilate River on their return to Soddo. By evening he had traveled ninety miles on his big black mule—this all in one day![20]

The two parties, one in Garbicho and the other in Soddo, began to construct houses made of local materials. After moving into their "new home" in Garbicho, Lambie wrote, "How happy we were; for bad as it was, it was better than the tent, and we were together again and in good health. It was a wonderful place for birds. At the first streak of dawn they began their glad chorus, which swelled in volume until the sun appeared. A little spring gave us cold water."[21] And from Soddo, Duff penned similar words, "We are planning our houses and the material is being brought in little by little. . . . We are building in the native *tukul* style, round hut with thatch roof. . . . There is beautifully clear water in springs at the base of the hill."[22]

As the missionaries were settling into their new environs, by mid-September 1928 they began learning the Sidamenya and Wolatenya languages. They also began trekking into the local communities and attempting to share the good news about Jesus. Then suddenly, "like a thunderclap out of a clear sky, we were told that we must leave it and return to Addis Ababa."[23] The missionaries were at a loss as to what to do. When Lambie and Rhoad queried Dejazmatch Birru at Agere Selam as to the reason for this sudden eviction notice, "Birru flew into a rage and would not listen to their pleas. Instead, he told them to leave at once."[24] It seems that the governor felt somewhat betrayed by Lambie, his trusted friend from Sayo days. What angered him was that Lambie and his cohorts had come into Sidamo without adequate official permission papers from Addis Ababa. Dejazmatch Birru made a concession by allowing Glen Cain and Clarence Duff to remain in Garbicho until official Addis Ababa papers were presented.

When the Lambies and the Rhoads arrived in Addis Ababa they discovered the reason for the sudden antagonism toward them. Apparently the Roman Catholic Mission in Kafa province had obtained six mission sites without adequate Abyssinian government permission. When challenged, the Catholics in Kafa had used their Vatican diplomatic avenues to counter the eviction notices and had made the whole matter into an international

20. Lambie, *Doctor without a Country*, 175.

21. Lambie, *Doctor without a Country*, 176.

22. Duff, *Cords of Love*, 58.

23. Lambie, *Doctor without a Country*, 176.

24. Duff, *Cords of Love*, 78.

affair. Charlotte Lambie wrote to her mother, "The Abyssinian Government has forbidden the opening of any new stations by any mission for a time."[25] Another issue was that the Orthodox priests were attempting to rein in Ras Tafari's moves towards liberalizing Abyssinia. In Addis Ababa Lambie's efforts to obtain official permission to remain in Sidamo or in Wolaitta were at a stalemate.

September 1928 saw a palace plot in which Ras Tafari's authority was challenged by Empress Zauditu. In spite of the political confusion, on October 7, 1928, Ras Tafari was proclaimed king of Abyssinia. An invited guest wrote that the event was "the most gorgeous and most imposing spectacle of a day. . . . It was a day of splendour."[26] In the midst of these developments, Lambie continued to be frustrated that he was not given an opportunity to meet personally with the regent, Ras Tafari, or with Prime Minister Blattangeta Hiruy. No doubt the regent continued to feel insecure in his position and could not openly support Dr. Lambie's mission in its advance into the south. A further complication for Lambie was that new SIM recruits were to arrive in Addis Ababa in November 1928, awaiting posting to a down country ministry. Where should they be assigned? The rented SIM facility in Addis Ababa had limited space. One option was to assign them to Marako, where the Armenians would be eager for them to open a school. Another option was for Clarence Duff to leave Garbicho and open a station near Hosanna. But Duff had no sooner arrived in Hosanna on January 10, 1929, than he too was evicted because he also had inadequate permission. And on March 4, 1929, Glen Cain and Eric Horn, a missionary from New Zealand who had arrived in 1929, were evicted from Garbicho. Duff commented, "The High Priest's party seemed to be winning that skirmish in the 'cold war.'"[27]

Adding further to the stress on Dr. Lambie, Charlotte was not well. She had developed a condition that needed surgery, and the decision was made that she should travel to the United States for the operation. Lambie accompanied Charlotte and Betty by train to Djibouti on April 2, 1929, so that his wife and daughter could board ship for home. As Lambie returned alone by train to Addis Ababa he experienced agony of soul and mental torture in the face of all the discouraging barriers that were hindering the advance of the mission. He wrote, "In times of adversity the heart looks upward in a peculiar way, and we sought guidance from God. Was this to be the end of

25. Charlotte Lambie, letter to her mother, Elizabeth Claney, February 18, 1929, MHSC.

26. Marcus, *Haile Sellassie I*, 92.

27. Duff, *Cords of Love*, 103.

the enterprise? So many times God gives us a word of cheer or encouragement, either in prayer or by bringing to mind a special verse from the Bible
that applies to the trying circumstance through which we are passing."[28] Was
any hope to be found for this nascent missionary enterprise?

28. Lambie, *Doctor without a Country,* 177.

Ethiopian Orthodox Church:
Impact for Change in the New Church Movement

The introduction of Christianity into northern Abyssinia (Ethiopia) began ca. 350 ad with Frumentius of Tyre, Syria. Patriarch Athanasius of Alexandria appointed Frumentius as the first bishop of Axum. Thus began the centuries-long connection between the Egyptian Coptic Church and the Ethiopian Orthodox Church (EOC) which lasted until the mid-1950s, when the Ethiopian Orthodox Church (EOC) became an independent entity with an indigenous patriarch. Christian Abyssinia (Ethiopia) zealously guarded the Orthodox faith and territory against Muslim invaders throughout the centuries. Dr. Lambie wrote in *Mission Review* (1928, p. 3), "The Abyssinian Church deserves great credit for keeping the name 'Christian' in the dark middle ages when cut off from all communication with the world outside. She struggled for her very life against the hordes of the false prophet of Arabia."

During the reign of Emperor Menelik (1844–1913), who was instrumental in extending the borders of Abyssinia far to the south, enclaves of northerners were positioned as government officials in much of the south. Menelik's political goal was to unify Abyssinia against the challenge of European imperialism. The enclaves of northerners were accompanied by EOC priests and deacons who provided Christian teaching and encouraged biblical ethical practice. When Dr. Lambie and his missionary cohorts arrived in Addis Ababa in 1927, their efforts to obtain permission to launch missionary activity in the southern provinces were initially blocked by conservative EOC officials. Eventually, through the good will of the emperor and previous friendships with governors now posted in the south, permission was granted for SIM to open educational and medical services in southern Abyssinia.

The EOC was a catalyst for social change in southern Abyssinia in several ways. First, EOC priests and deacons were purveyors of a literate society. The Bible and other holy writings read by EOC priests and laypersons conveyed a sense of power and mystery. The reading of the Bible in Ge'ez within the confines of the Ethiopian Orthodox Church compound impressed the southerners. The northerners based their religion on a book and the worship of one God who controlled the spirits. Following 1934, several years after SIM opened mission stations in the south, SIM missionaries prepared translations of the Gospels of Matthew, Mark, and John for speakers of Hadiya, Sidamo, and Wolaitta. Second, technology introduced by the northerners, such as the telegraph and telephone, began to change the worldview of the animistic southerners. The arrival of modern means of transport such as trucks and railroads also brought about change.

A third way the EOC influenced the societies of the south was through the newly appointed provincial governors. These adherents of the EOC showed themselves to be just, fair, and religious. For example, Dajazmach Makonnen, governor of Wolaitta from 1932 to 1937, attempted to curb thievery.

Dajazmach Balcha Abo Nafso, governor of Sidamo from 1918 to 1927, disciplined those who were unruly and was concerned about the spiritual development of the Amharas in his court. Fourth, the EOC built churches as centers of worship in the south. Most of the churches were unpretentious buildings constructed of local materials. These Orthodox churches no doubt served as an incentive to the growing church communities in the south to construct their own buildings of worship. Fifth, the Orthodox liturgical music aroused a desire for music among believers within the new church movement. The tunes of the new churches were often borrowed from work songs, but the lyrics were compositions of naturally gifted poets from the rank and file of new believers. The enclaves of northern EOC worshippers, however, failed to communicate meaningfully to the soul of the local indigenous population or to meet the southerners' spiritual needs. The southerners were left standing outside the gates of the Orthodox churches, alienated by language and unfamiliar forms of worship. Not until 1929 did Haile Sellassie and his officials open the door for Dr. Lambie and his missionary band to launch evangelistic activities within southern Abyssinia.

7

Expansion into Southern Abyssinia

The great things are often done by the most obscure people.

THOMAS A. LAMBIE, "A NEW MISSION TO ABYSSINIA'S UNKNOWN
FRONTIERS" (MS), 11

UPON RETURNING TO ADDIS Ababa in April 1929 after having escorted
Charlotte and Betty to Djibouti, Lambie encountered unexpected political
tensions. He felt unwelcome. Even earlier, at the end of March 1929, the
missionaries who had recently been located in Garbicho, Soddo, and
Hosanna were being evicted with strict orders to return to Addis Ababa. As
Clarence Duff and Reg Annan left Hosanna, they were insulted and jeered.[1]
The following days became particularly dark for Lambie. He began to question whether the missionary venture into southern Abyssinia would ever
succeed.

In Addis Ababa Ras Tafari avoided meeting with Lambie, as did other
officials of influence. Finally, through Foreign Minister Blattangeta Hiruy,
Lambie was able to have a private interview with Regent Ras Tafari. At the
conclusion of a congenial discussion, Lambie recalls the regent saying, "Do
not be angry with me nor think I am unwilling to help you. You do not know

1. Duff, *Cords of Love*, 120–22.

what enemies I have. Do not ask too much of me for a period of one year, after which I will be in a position to do more for you."[2]

Dejazmatch Yigezu, governor of Soddo, then visiting in Addis Ababa, cautiously indicated to Lambie that he was willing to allow SIM to initiate medical work in Wolaitta. A fifteen-point official document was formulated and was in the process of being ratified. But under point 13 the governor had inserted a subclause which startled Lambie. It read, "They promise that they will not teach religion."[3] Lambie questioned the reason for this insertion and firmly declared, "No, we will never sign that!"[4] The impasse entailed more discussion, and the debate ran late into the evening. But Lambie was firm, stressing that he would honor what he signed. When the scribe rewrote paragraph 13, he omitted the subclause about not teaching religion. George Rhoad was handed the permission letter signed and sealed by Dejazmatch Yigezu and cosigned by Lambie. With the precious document in hand, the Rhoads set off with their son George on the journey to Soddo.

During the 1929 struggles to obtain official permission to place missionaries in the three provinces of Kambatta, Wolaitta, and Sidamo, Mr. and Mrs. Orval Kirk together with Charles Barton quietly settled in Marako. The opportunity there was unique because in 1928, the Behesnilians, an Armenian family, had invited SIM to establish a school on their Marako property.[5] A private rental agreement was made and SIM opened a school for the Gurage people. The arrangement provoked no questions by the Addis Ababa government.[6]

The prospect for obtaining official permission for Clarence Duff and Reg Annan to begin their ministry among the Gudeilla people group based in Lambuda began to look brighter. On April 13 Lambie was able to acquire official permission (with a limiting caveat) for mission work in Kambatta Province. It read:

To His Excellency Dejazmatch Moshesha Walde:

2. Lambie, *Doctor without a Country*, 181. One year later, on April 2, 1930, the regent was proclaimed emperor of Ethiopia.

3. Lambie, *Doctor without a Country*, 179.

4. Lambie, *Doctor without a Country*, 179.

5. The Behesnilian family had a close relative in Addis Ababa who was sympathetic to the evangelistic outreach of the Lambie Mission (as the mission was at times called). See Lambie, *Doctor Without a Country*, 178.

6. Duff, *Cords of Love*, 255. Prior to 1916 expatriates such as the Armenians and Greeks had been allowed to purchase property, and they were allowed to rent out their property without official permission from Addis Ababa.

Dr. Lambie's association has been permitted to build a hospital with its own money in Kambatta to cure the sick. Therefore do not prevent them. Further, they intend to establish a school within the enclosure of the hospital to teach languages and trades. Therefore you have been ordered to examine them and watch them occasionally that they may not teach other religious knowledge.

Megabit 23, 1921 (April 1, 1929)

(Signed:) *Bilaten Geyta* Hiruy, W.S. H.D.S.

(Seal:) Empire of Ethiopia

Minister of Foreign Affairs.[7]

After receiving a copy of the official letter, Duff commented,

The permission to stay was not a disappointment, but the restrictions that were included were. I am sure that Mr. Rhoad and Dr. Lambie were both much disappointed that after all their interviews, and all their efforts to get recognition for our aims and organization, yet the paper gives specific permission only for medical work and teaching languages and manual work.[8]

Lambie responded to Duff, stating that the document was not signed by the mission agency. Therefore, this would not prevent anyone from doing personal work and bringing men and women to Christ. Rhoad commented further, "We have not agreed to refrain from preaching or teaching the gospel. Since that is the case, it seems to me that it is not a compromise for us to go as far as we can on the permission that has been given."[9]

Now, one more permission letter was still needed, and that was for Sidamo. Lambie boldly entreated Ras Tafari Makonnen, "Your Majesty, I have no desire to harass you by our requests, nor do I come seeking definite permission to enter Sidamo; but I thought perhaps you could give me a kindly personal letter to Biru [sic] the governor [of Sidamo] that would help us."[10] The king consented and agreed to send the promised official letter by runner to the Lambie caravan, which was already on its way to Sidamo. While on his journey to the south, Lambie received the "open" permission letter, which looked very impressive. But he was disappointed in the wording, for it said nothing definite about permission for the mission to serve in Sidamo. In faith, Lambie and Rhoad had taken Glen Cain and

---

7. Duff, *Cords of Love*, 129; translated from Amharic.

8. Duff, *Cords of Love*, 129–30, quotes Lambie's letter to Duff, ca. April 15, 1929.

9. Duff, *Cords of Love*, 130, quotes Rhoad's letter to Duff, ca. April 15, 1929.

10. Lambie, *Doctor without a Country*, 181.

Eric Horn with them in order to establish the Sidamo mission outreach. While they were on the way, some ten miles from Agere Selam, a small band of uniformed soldiers met the Lambie party and ushered them to Dejazmatch Birru's establishment. There they were generously entertained with much levity. On the third day Lambie presented the highly decorated letter stamped with the royal seal. As was customary, the Dejazmatch stood as he received the letter from Addis Ababa royalty. He read it rapidly and a smile spread over his face. "That is a very good letter," Birru commented. "It is all right now. Your missionaries can stay here. I never wanted to expel them; now it is all right. How many missionaries would you like to place in Sidamo? Would ten be enough?"[11]

Lambie and Rhoad, together with the two young missionaries, Glen Cain and Eric Horn, returned to their tents and fell on their knees with praise to God. Lambie wrote, "Too full for words I could only say, 'Thank You. Thank You.' Nearly a year's struggle was over. Sidamo was open. Also Wolamo, Kambatta and Marako. The two verses, 'He will not suffer thy foot to be moved' and 'Resist not the powers' coincided. God had answered!"[12] The initial struggles of launching SIM's mission in Abyssinia were now over. Clarence Duff, ever the optimist, wrote on July 30, 1929,

> In retrospect, though it had been a time of great trials, yet it can be seen as a beneficent providence that in those months we men were free from the rush of building, and were able to learn much about the people among whom we would be living, establish lasting friendships, and make a good beginning in the tribal language.[13]

The "Lambie Mission" had now been in Abyssinia for just two years, 1928 and 1929, with twenty-two missionaries based on four stations.[14] Besides the headquarters in Addis Ababa, the stations to the south were Marako in Gurageland, Lambuda among the Gudeile, Soddo among the Wolaitta, and Homatcho in the heart of Sidamo. The offices in Addis Ababa,

11. Lambie, *Doctor without a Country,* 183. It would appear that in the intervening time, Birru, in Agere Selam, had received a message by telegram or telephone from the regent in Addis Ababa affirming that Lambie's mission association had permission to begin mission activity. Emperor Menelik had pioneered entry of the country into the International Postal Union in 1908 and shortly afterward installed telegraph and telephone communications throughout Abyssinia to link each of the provincial governors with Addis Ababa. See Marcus, *Life and Times of Menelik II,* 200.

12. Lambie, *Doctor without a Country,* 183.

13. Duff, *Cords of Love,* 138.

14. "Lambie Mission" was the informal name used by officialdom in Addis Ababa; see Cotterell, *Born at Midnight,* 53fn1.

in the rented facilities of Mohamedellei, an Indian-owned import/export company, were staffed by three missionaries. During 1929 Dr. Lambie served as the resident doctor in Soddo. His medical work did not limit him from itinerant preaching in various districts of Wolaitta. Dr. Percy Roberts and his wife, Vi, who were later assigned to the Soddo hospital, followed Lambie's example in itinerant preaching: "Last Sunday we went out preaching and had such a good time. . . . An old lady took us to her place and gathered about eighty people to hear the Word."[15]

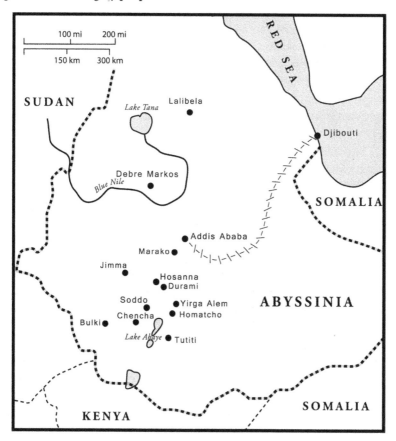

SIM stations in Abyssinia, 1928–36

For Abyssinia, 1930 was an eventful year. On April 2, the day after the death of Empress Zauditu, Ras Tafari Makonnen was proclaimed emperor and took his baptismal name of Haile Sellassie I. Empress Zauditu had

15. Percy and Vi Roberts, letter to family, November 1, 1935, SIMIA, EE-1-104, File 6.

eventually succumbed to complications of diabetes from which she had suffered for many years.[16] The daughter of Menelik II, she had staunchly opposed Ras Tafari and resisted his support for modernization. Her death weakened the influence of the Orthodox Church, as she was the church's main power broker. Ras Gugsa Wolle, a governor from the north, who was dedicated to the overthrow of the regent's government, had been killed in battle. These events transformed the political situation and defeated the designs of reactionaries who were resisting modernization. The death in December 1926 of Abba Mattewos, the former Coptic patriarch, had further diminished the Abyssinian ecclesiastical dominance. Following his death, Ras Tafari became subject to sharp criticism voiced by the Debre Libanos Ichege together with a host of Abyssinian Orthodox priests for the lengthy but inadvertent delay in replacing the patriarch. Finally, in early 1930, Cyril was brought from the Coptic Church in Egypt as the new patriarch of the Abyssinia Orthodox Church. His arrival blunted ecclesiastical criticism of the new king.

Two additional mission stations were opened in 1931. Dejazmatch Beyenne Merid, married to the emperor's daughter, Li'lt Romanewerq, requested SIM to establish a school near Bulqi, Gofa. A newly married couple, Walter and Marcella Ohman, were stationed there. Soon after they arrived, Walter Ohman wrote, "I wish I could describe the place to you. There are mountains on all sides and from the spot where the house is to be placed we can look down into the most beautiful valley. . . . We are about 8,000 or 8,200 feet above sea level . . . because of that we do not have to fear the fevers that the people do who live down in the plains."[17] When the Lambies had passed through Jimma in the 1920s during their journey from Sayo to Addis Ababa, they were struck with the thought that this Muslim area should be given priority for the gospel. Prior to 1930, Lambie had purchased an Armenian coffee merchant's property, located at Qochi on the outskirts of Jimma. That purchase prepared the way in 1931 for Mr. and Mrs. Rudolph and Grace Piepgrass together with Miss Irma Schneck and Miss Olive Sealy, trekking by mule, to establish the Jimma station.[18] This coffee-rich province

16. Marcus, *Haile Sellassie I*, 95–96.

17. Ohman, letter to "Dear Prayer-Helpers," May 6, 1931, SIMIA, EE-2-105, File 34.

18. The trip by mule was recorded by Rhoad in "'Wayside Jottings': Being a Personal Account of the Second Advance towards the Frontiers on the Southwesterly Route through Jimma Province, March–June 1931," MS, 45 pp., SIMIA, EE-1-104, File 5. Following Charlotte's death in 1946, Lambie married Irma Schneck, in 1947, in Palestine. From 1937 to 1947 Miss Schneck served with SIM in Nigeria.

was under the rule of Sultan Aba Djifar, a Muslim, who eagerly encouraged education in his domain.[19]

When Lambie left in 1931 to join Charlotte in the United States, one assignment left to George Rhoad as leader of the mission was to locate two properties adjacent to Addis Ababa, one for the proposed mission headquarters and the other as a site for a leprosarium.[20] While in the United States, Charlotte Lambie addressed the 1929 annual meeting of the American Mission to Lepers. As a result, that organization committed to give "five thousand dollars a year for five years to build a leprosarium there."[21] Securing two large properties suitable for the SIM headquarters and the leprosarium proved to be a challenge. "Mr. Rhoad had been several times, as he thought, on the point of signing an agreement, but always the Abyssinians drew back."[22] No doubt the reason for the hesitation was that Rhoad was not well known to Abyssinian officialdom. Several weeks after the Lambies returned to Abyssinia, two contracts were signed (in February 1932) and building commenced on the rather expansive sites, forty acres for the headquarters and 140 acres for the leprosarium.[23] By August 22, Dr. Hooper, who was slated to oversee the leprosarium, expressed concern about his own dwelling: "I suppose the erection of the other buildings in connection with the Leper Hospital should go on apace with the building of the Doctor's house."[24]

Several significant dignitaries were in attendance at the opening ceremony of the Leper Hospital, including the archbishop of the Abyssinian Orthodox Church. With upraised hands he blessed all the lepers seated before him and then commented to Drs. Lambie and Hooper, "I have never

19. Lambie, *Doctor without a Country*, 208.

20. SIM Soddu, "[Abyssinian] Field Council Minutes," May 16–18, 1932, SIMIA, EA-1-82, File 1: "Lambie said that 'Headquarters' [in Addis Ababa] is a new station in as true a sense as is any new station in the south, and should be so considered." For the leprosarium, see Pankhurst, *Medical History of Ethiopia*, 208.

21. Lambie, *Doctor without a Country*, 209. On the need for the leprosarium in Addis Ababa, see also Lambie, letter from Soddo to Charlotte Lambie, August 4, 1929, MHSC.

22. Lambie, *Doctor without a Country*, 209.

23. Lambie, letter to Bingham, February 1932, SIMIA, EE-2-92, File 1. The headquarters site overlooked the Akaki River. The Netherlands Embassy has refurbished the original SIM building for its own use. The original 1932 leprosarium building has been converted into a storeroom and continues to serve the ALERT (formerly All Africa Leprosy Rehabilitation and Training Center) program.

24. Hooper, letter from Soddo to Lambie, August 22, 1932, SIMIA, EB-2-92, File 2. See also article about Dr. Ralph Hooper's ministry at the Addis Ababa Leprosy Hospital, *Toronto Evening Telegram*, September 13, 1935.

in all my life seen a work so Christ-like."[25] On December 23 Lambie wrote concerning progress on the SIM headquarters building at Akaki: "The whole thing is coming out very well. Our chief need is for doors upstairs. . . . We will be using every bit of headquarters now with the new [missionary] reinforcements."[26]

Up until 1932 SIM had been expanding rapidly in Abyssinia. During this period of rapid growth, however, the directors, Lambie and Rhoad, developed major personal differences. Rowland Bingham wrote a seven-page letter to Lambie in an attempt to address several of the issues. He began, "No man has come into my heart in a sweeter way than you have. I have loved you and do love you dearly, Doctor, and at the same time Mrs. Lambie as a sister has been to me in a similar way." One issue focused on financial accounting. When Lambie departed for furlough on May 25, 1930, the SIM finances for which Rhoad became responsible were in a tangle left behind by mission treasurer Carl Rasmussen, who had previously resigned from SIM. (As official SIM treasurer in Abyssinia, Rasmussen should have stood up to Lambie, but did not.) Another issue of contention arose from Lambie's longstanding relationship with Abyssinian officialdom. Lacking Lambie's personal connections, Rhoad was unable to finalize agreements with appropriate officials regarding the sites for the proposed leprosarium and SIM headquarters.

For his part, Bingham was no doubt aware of the financial difficulties and accusations that Lambie had faced while with the Presbyterian Mission. Bingham upbraided Lambie for carelessly misdirecting funds from one account to another. In the same letter, Bingham chided Lambie for recruiting a housekeeper for the Addis Ababa guest house without having her go through regular SIM channels. Near the end of his letter, Bingham's comment was rather sharp: "I must beg you, Doctor, just to be constitutional in your actions, and don't let your heart run away with judgement in this matter. You have this danger." Bingham concludes with a fatherly comment, "I beg of you, Doctor, to accept George Rhoad's confession as one of the tremendous things wrought by the Spirit, and then accept that as an accomplished fact."[27] At the May 1932 Field Council held at Soddo, a letter

25. Bingham, *Seven Sevens of Years*, 83.

26. Lambie, letter to Rhoad, December 23, 1932, SIMIA, EB-2-92, File 1. See Mesele, *Leprosy, Leprosaria, and Society in Ethiopia*, 57–70, for a brief account of Dr. Thomas Lambie.

27. Bingham, letter to Lambie, October 17, 1932, SIMIA, EB-2-92, File 3. George Rhoad, Lambie's deputy, appeared to be jealous of Lambie and he often spoke sharply to both Thomas and Charlotte Lambie over minor issues. Rhoad confessed this spirit of jealousy to Lambie.

from Bingham's office announced, "Mr. Rhoad to act as Deputy General Director [of SIM International] in view of his [Bingham's] absence from the homeland during his Sabbatical Year."[28] Apparently Bingham felt that the most honorable solution to Lambie and Rhoad's incompatibility was to separate their spheres of activity.

In 1932 the baptism of new believers was another major issue of discussion within the fledgling mission enterprise; that topic will be discussed in a subsequent chapter. The years 1932–33 saw four additional SIM stations opened, all located in the south, and the SIM headquarters was moved from Soddo to Addis Ababa. In Sidamo, Ras Desta Damtaw (married to L'elt Tanayewerq, daughter of the emperor) replaced Ras Birru as governor of Sidamo. He transferred the capital from Agere Selam to the lower altitude of Yirga Alem. SIM had a keen desire to establish a station some sixty miles south of Homatcho at Tutitti. Ras Desta was willing to grant permission, but as a tradeoff desired that skilled builder Cliff Mitchell assist in developing a master plan for the new government center at Yirga Alem and begin construction of the governor's residence.[29] SIM was also asked to establish a school at the new center. Ras Desta concluded, "Have no fear, you need us and we need you. Just leave everything in my hands."[30] Lambie and Glen Cain visited the proposed mission site at Tutitti, the southernmost station east of the two large lakes, Marghareta (Abaya) and Chamo. Lambie describes the station's location:

> [It] is built on what might have been formerly the entrance of a heathen temple in ancient times as there are dozens of curiously shaped stones of phallic origin which we have read somewhere were universally used in the religion of the Greek God Priapus. . . . There is a little [small] carving on them at the base of a design something like a butterfly. . . . There are literally hundreds if not thousands of them and no one knows where they have been quarried.[31]

28. SIM Abyssinian Field Council Minutes, Soddo, Wolamo, May 16–18, 1932, SIMIA, ME-1/A-155, File 2.

29. Lambie, report to Bingham, March 6, 1933, SIMIA, EB-2-92, File 1, discusses the opening of new stations in southern Abyssinia. The final sheet of this 8-page report describes the launching of SIM's Yerga Alem station in Sidamo, where on February 4, 1932, Miss Leona MacGregor and Miss Win Robertson had been assigned.

30. Lambie, report to Bingham, March 6, 1933, p. 8, SIMIA, EB-2-93, File 3.

31. Lambie, letter to Bingham, December 14, 1933, SIMIA, EB-2-92, File 1; written while on trek in the south. In 1992 the author and his wife, Lila, visited Tutitti and saw about 50 of these 20- to 30-foot-tall phallic stones still standing.

Cliff and Myrtle Mitchell were appointed to Tutitti but were delayed in their posting because his gifts in building were in demand at various other SIM sites.

Clarence Duff, relocated from Lambuda, pioneered the new SIM location at Duramei among the Kambatta people group.

> We have a great mountain, Ambericho, more than 8,000 feet above sea level. Several times since we have come here there have been great thunder storms up among the peaks of the mountain. One could watch the clouds racing through the clefts of the mountain, then almost the whole mountain would be hid by the rain."[32]

Duff selected and negotiated for the station site at Duramei among the Kambatta. Subsequently he assisted in building the first houses for the missionary couple, John and Peggy Philips, and Zillah Walsh, the schoolteacher.[33]

Lambie was met at Chencha by Dejazmatch Ababa Damtaw, the brother of Ras Desta Damtaw of Sidamo. The governor had an unusual welcome for special guests—five half grown lions escorted by young boys met the Lambie party at the entrance to Chencha. "The mule caravan nearly stampeded" in fright.[34] The Chencha station was situated 9,200 feet above sea level and was staffed by Ruth Bray, RN, and Selma Bergsten. That two ladies should be sent alone to launch a mission station was a new departure for the mission, but "these two were such exceptional young ladies and Miss Bray being of mature years, it was felt that with God's blessing everything would come out for the best, especially as the Governor was kindness itself and promised to do everything in his power to assist us."[35]

During this period of expansion, portions of Scripture were translated by the original "C.O.D. Boys." Glen Cain translated the Gospel of Mark into the Sidamenya language and had it printed by the British and Foreign Bible Society. Walter Ohman's translation of the Gospel of John into the Gofenya language received high compliments from Thomas Percival Bevan, resident secretary of the BFBS, who said "it was the most beautiful he had ever seen, and it arrived . . . in perfect condition, thanks to having been wrapped in

32. Duff, *Cords of Love*, 245–46. Duramei continues to be a strong Kale Heywet Church center. The national missionary training school is located there.

33. Lambie, *Doctor without a Country*, 212–13. See Lambie, report to Bingham, March 6, 1933, SIMIA, EB-2-92, File 194

34. Lambie, *Doctor without a Country*, 212.

35. Lambie, report to Bingham, March 6, 1933, p. 5, SIMIA, EB-2-92, File 1.

cardboard and oiled silk."[36] The Gospel of Matthew was translated into Hadinya by Clarence Duff and printed by the BFBS for distribution in 1935. The little booklet *God Hath Spoken* was published by the Scripture Gift Mission of London. It consisted of a compilation of verses and was widely used by the Wolaitta believers during the dark years of the Italian occupation.[37] On the great value of the translated Scriptures, meager though they were, Duff comments: "Thus in spite of many difficulties the Word was in one way or another preached and taught and read; and it proved a powerful means of grace to the young churches."[38]

In summing up the gains of 1932 and 1933, Lambie wrote, "Four new places are now open to the Gospel; four new centres are now waiting for the glorious message committed to us. An entrance has been made and now the work needs to be commenced. Much prayer, much effort, much money, and much faithfulness are needed. We are unable but He is able."[39] At the end of 1933 the ministry of SIM in Abyssinia was achieving stability and was staffed by fifty-eight young and energetic missionaries serving on thirteen SIM stations.

---

36. Lambie, letter to SIM Abyssinia missionaries, June 1933, in Duff, *Cords of Love*, 265. See also Ohman, letter to "Prayer Helpers," September 17, 1943, SIMIA, EE-2-105, File 34. Thomas Percival Bevan and his wife, Ane Marie Bevan, served with the British and Foreign Bible Society in Abyssinia from 1927 to 1938 (information courtesy of Onesimus Ngundu, Cambridge University Library, England).

37. Duff, *Cords of Love*, 266. See also Lambie, letter to Earl Lewis, November 7, 1932, SIMIA, EB-2-92, File 1.

38. Duff, *Cords of Love*, 267. See Donham, *Marxist Modern*, 95, where Donham critically assesses SIM's view of the Bible: "Consider for example the Biblicism that the missionaries brought to southern Ethiopia, their emphasis on the Bible as the 'inerrant' word of God. . . . Whatever science professed to know, all that anyone really needed to know was the Bible."

39. Lambie, report to Bingham, March 6, 1933, p. 8, SIMIA, EB-2-92, File 1.

Rowland V. Bingham, 1872–1942

Rowland V. Bingham was the cofounder and long-serving director of the Sudan Interior Mission (SIM). Born in England, Bingham, following his conversion as a lad, first served Christ in that country with the Salvation Army. At the age of sixteen he migrated to Canada and became connected with a Toronto missionary group. In 1893 he sailed to West Africa with two other volunteers, intending to launch a mission enterprise in Nigeria. Unfortunately, his missionary companions, Walter Gowan and Thomas Kent, both died of malaria and were buried in Nigeria. Despite these setbacks, Bingham was not to be defeated. Under his leadership, the first SIM mission station was established in 1902 at Patigi, Nigeria. Eventually, SIM grew to be the largest "faith mission" agency in Africa with some 400 missionaries spread across the continent from Niger in the west to Abyssinia and Somalia in the east.

In 1927 Bingham invited the fledgling Abyssinian Frontiers Mission to amalgamate with SIM. Bingham's journey for his first of three visits to Abyssinia was rather arduous. He first traveled across the continent from Jos, Nigeria, to Nairobi, Kenya, by Ford station wagon. From there he obtained passage aboard a Kenyan lorry—through rain and mud—eventually arriving at the Kenya/Abyssinia border town of Moyale in early 1930. At Moyale, Bingham was met by Thomas Lambie and the George Rhoad family. In Abyssinia Dr. Bingham visited the four SIM stations in south Abyssinia, sharing counsel and Bible meditations. In May 1930, Bingham and Lambie traveled together by train from Addis Ababa to Djibouti and across the Mediterranean Sea by ship, eventually arriving in England by plane.

When Lambie was invited by trusted Abyssinian officials in 1934 to launch SIM ministry in northern Abyssinia among Ethiopian Orthodox Church adherents, he felt he needed Bingham's sagacious advice. Bingham accompanied Thomas and Charlotte Lambie on a trip by muleback to survey northern Abyssinia. The trek over mountainous terrain to Lalibela involved three weeks' travel. Enduring the heat in the valleys and cold on the mountain heights was somewhat alleviated by Bingham's bass singing around the campfire each evening, during which he accompanied himself on his harpsichord. Bingham encouraged SIM to open new mission stations in the north: "As we scatter, we will increase," he stated, referring to Proverbs 11:24. The fruit of this exploratory venture was that one year later, five SIM personnel were stationed in Lalibela and Debra Markos.

The fledgling SIM missionary enterprise in Abyssinia was naturally fraught with interpersonal challenges between members of different nationalities as well as diverse denominational leanings. Though not trained as a professional counselor, theologian, or missiologist, through his wide reading and continual study of Scripture, Bingham became a knowledgeable mission leader and missiologist in his own right. He encouraged a holistic approach to mission, melding the Great Commission and the Great Command. He launched the widely read *Evangelical Christian* in 1904 and retained editorship of it until his death in 1942. This periodical proved to be an able mouthpiece for missions during both WWI and WWII. At Bingham's invitation, Thomas Lambie contributed a number of well-written articles to the *Evangelical Christian*.

In his long tenure as the international director of SIM, Rowland Bingham skillfully guided the process of discipling and equipping believers in churches across much of Africa. In 1932 Wheaton College honored him with a D.D. degree in recognition of the exemplary quality of his labors as a missionary statesman. A definitive biography of Bingham can be found in J. H. Hunter, *A Flame of Fire* (Toronto: Sudan Interior Mission, 1961).

8

SIM's Basic Principles of Church Planting

We have a weapon—the sword of the Spirit
which is the Word of God.

THOMAS A. LAMBIE, *A BRUISED REED*, 55

WE HAVE LITTLE EVIDENCE regarding churches that may have been planted in Sudan during Dr. Lambie's missionary service there (1907–18) under the Foreign Missions Board of the United Presbyterian Church (FMBUPC). Several Sudanese are known to have come to faith in Christ while the Lambies served on the two Presbyterian stations at Doleib Hill and Nasir on the banks of the Sobat River. One bit of information comes from Dr. Ried Frampton Shields of the Presbyterian Mission in Sudan, who stated in a January 16, 1942, prayer meeting in Khartoum "that an encouraging word of growth had come from their [the Lambies'] work in Sayo and Gorei." He was referring to the 1919–22 church planting ministry of Thomas and Charlotte Lambie in the Abyssinian province of Wellega.[1]

During Dr. Lambie's service as the chief surgeon and director of the George Memorial Hospital in Addis Ababa (1924–26), he felt, "We surely ought to get on with our work and open new stations in the south [of

---

1. Lambie, *A Doctor Carries On*, 173. Dr. Shields served in Sudan, 1917–23; in Abyssinia, 1923–26; and again in Sudan, 1927–58 (information courtesy of Jennifer Barr, reference archivist, Presbyterian Historical Society). See Debela, *Divine Plan Unfolding*, 87–123, for further elaboration of the growth of the American Presbyterian Mission ministry in the Sayo and Gorei districts.

Abyssinia]. But our [Presbyterian] Church was not ready to advance into new territory."[2] Lambie's passion was to reach the large population of primal religionists in southern Abyssinia as well as Muslims located in the Jimma area. His vision for evangelism led Lambie, together with George Rhoads and Alfred Buxton, to establish the Abyssinian Frontiers Mission. In 1927, the fledgling mission united with the established Sudan Interior Mission (SIM).

Lambie acknowledged his debt to the experienced and sagacious leadership of Rowland Bingham, general director of SIM who had spent years pioneering in Nigeria. Bingham acknowledged that Bishop Tucker's experience in Uganda, as well as careful reading of Roland Allen's book *Missionary Methods: St Paul's or Ours*, had shaped his thinking along indigenous church principles. Subsequently, Lambie and his younger missionary colleagues "were so thoroughly convinced that these were the right lines that from the very beginning the greatest emphasis was placed upon the necessity for a truly indigenous church. The Holy Spirit seems to have used this method in a marvelous way."[3]

One might well ask why Lambie was so keen, actually driven, to establish sixteen SIM outreach centers in Abyssinia despite limited finances and personnel. The following gives a succinct rationale for his missiology:

> Missionaries go [are sent] to a place where Christ is not known. They study the language, translate some of the Bible, and preach Christ crucified as the only way of salvation. In time they gather, or rather the Holy Spirit gathers out a little group of true believers. They baptize these believers and form them into a church, ordaining elders. They give them all that the Bible says about church organization as outlined in the Epistles of Timothy and Titus. Then the missionaries take their hands off and let the believers carry on. The missionaries do not build any churches or pay native evangelists, but from the very beginning they encourage the native believers to do all these things for themselves.[4]

Lambie was willing and eager to learn missiological concepts and practices from his mentor, Rowland Bingham, who visited Abyssinia in 1930 and 1934 at two crucial points during the development of the indigenous church. The SIM ministry in Nigeria, which Bingham had pioneered, preceded that in Abyssinia by nearly thirty-five years. Nigerian church historian Yusufu Turaki describes the indigenization principles followed by

---

2. Lambie, *Doctor without a Country*, 162.

3. Lambie, *A Doctor Carries On*, 171.

4. Lambie, *A Doctor Carries On*, 171–72.

SIM in Nigeria as consisting of self-propagation, self-support, and self-government.[5] Turaki gives credit to SIM for the establishment of the Evangelical Churches of West Africa (ECWA) in 1954. With a sense of gratefulness to God for the SIM pioneers, he writes of their role in "the founding of ECWA as an Indigenous Church and [in] its structural and leadership development."[6] The ECWA denomination in Nigeria today consists of over ten million members.

In 1941, after the Italians were defeated and SIM missionaries began re-entering Ethiopia, Laurie Davison, formerly an SIM missionary in Abyssinia and subsequently serving with the Occupied Enemy Territory Administration,[7] observed regarding southern Ethiopia: "We have found here as indigenous a church as Roland Allen ever dreamed, and it is our earnest hope that no member of our mission will do or say anything to destroy the autonomous structure."[8] Years later Donald L. Donham, a Marxist-leaning anthropologist, conducted extensive field research among the Maale of southern Ethiopia, a group to whom SIM missionaries and Ethiopian evangelists had brought the gospel. To better understand the message the missionaries and evangelists brought to the Maale, Donham undertook extensive historical research within SIM's International Archives as well. He observed of Lambie and the Ethiopia Kale Heywet Church, "In a matter of five short years, the SIM (with Lambie's reluctant permission) *would* begin baptizing, and finally (in 1956) a nationwide 'denomination,' the Kale Heywet Church *was* founded—a body that would count over three million Ethiopians as members by the mid-1990s."[9] Donham affirms Lambie's intention: "There can be little confusion that these were Lambie's intentions from the beginning. It was, in fact, this overriding commitment to evangelization and to an independent native church that set apart the SIM from virtually all other foreign missions operating in the country at that time."[10] We can say that Ras Tafari Makonnen and his officials understood that missions would play a significant role in modernizing Abyssinia. These officials were keen to have hospitals, clinics, and schools launched within their country. It appears that they did not anticipate the far-reaching impact the gospel message would have among the peasantry of southern Abyssinia.

5. Turaki, *History of SIM/ECWA in Nigeria*, 255–59.

6. Turaki, *History of SIM/ECWA in Nigeria*, 306.

7. Bahru, *History of Modern Ethiopia*, 180.

8. Laurie and Lily Davison, "The History and the Movements of Laurie and Lily Davison: 1935–1949," nd, MS, 8 pp., SIMIA, EC-1, File 4.

9. Donham, *Marxist Modern*, 93.

10. Donham, *Marxist Modern,* 93.

Lambie and his SIM colleagues adhered to the following eight basic principles of church planting.

They were committed to the power of preaching. The SIM missionaries were committed to share the message of the Bible to all those who would listen. They expected that there would be some who would accept the message, be converted, and be "born again from above" with a resulting change in their moral life and a desire to form a new spiritual community. The writings of the SIM missionaries supply numerous examples of sharing the gospel message. While Lambie and the Rhoad family were trekking to Moyale from Soddo, January 24 to March 4, 1930, he recorded in his "Jottings in My Diary" various opportunities they had to preach through interpreters.[11] Dr. Ralph Hooper, a Canadian physician, held evangelistic services in a hotel ballroom in Addis Ababa in June 1932. "The meetings were almost too much of a success," Lambie wrote, "as the Government ruled out that we could not have such meetings in a hotel again. Several hundred people heard the pure Gospel preached."[12] Dr. Percy Roberts and wife, Vi, regularly went out by mule to preach in the Wolaitta countryside.[13] When the Lambies trekked north with Rowland Bingham in 1934, they often preached, and "we always carried Bibles and Testaments, which we sold or gave away."[14] Duff confirmed the missionaries' commitment to the power of preaching, writing about "the conviction and conversion of sinners through 'the foolishness of preaching' the Word."[15] Tibebe Eshete affirms that Lambie and his SIM colleagues were firmly convinced that "the fundamental tenet of the missionary enterprise was to bring salvation through direct evangelization."[16]

In a 1929 letter to a Mr. Cooksey of London, Dr. Lambie expressed ambivalence concerning where new Abyssinian converts from the southern ethnic groups should unite—whether with the ancient Abyssinia Orthodox Church or as part of a future "non-denominational but truly Christian native church."[17] This dilemma was resolved through the implementation of the 1932 Homatcho baptism.

---

11. Lambie, *Doctor without a Country*, 187–88, 191.

12. Lambie, *Doctor without a Country*, 211.

13. Percy and Vi Roberts, letter to family in Canada, November 1, 1935, SIMIA, EE-1-104, File 6.

14. Lambie, *Doctor without a Country*, 217.

15. Duff, *Cords of Love*, 265.

16. Tibebe, *Evangelical Movement in Ethiopia*, 78–79.

17. Lambie, letter to Joseph J. Cooksey, Stuart House, London, November 29, 1929, SIMIA, EA-1-82, File 5.

Their goal was the celebration of the sacraments of baptism and the Lord's Supper. Glen Cain had been based at the new SIM station in Homatcho, Sidamo, since 1929. In 1931 he wrote two letters informing Lambie, who was in the United States on furlough, of a small group of believers in Homatcho who he felt were ready for baptism.[18] Cain expressed disappointment in the callous response offered by assistant SIM director George Rhoad. On the basis of his experience in Kenya—where "no converts were baptised during his whole first term"—Rhoad proposed delaying the Homatcho baptism.[19] On March 23, 1932, Cain, Duff, and Lewis, while in Soddo, composed a letter to both directors, Lambie and Rhoad, expressing their concern about delaying the Homatcho baptism. They wrote, "We are convinced that progress is being arrested and the working of the Holy Spirit hindered by certain restrictions upon steps needful for the advancement of the work."[20] They quoted the SIM's *Principles and Practice* which allowed that "a Missionary-in-Charge of a station in which [through] the blessing of God converts are gathered be granted permission in regard to baptizing converts and the organization of congregations."[21]

Lambie did not receive the letter from the three missionaries in a good spirit. On April 7, 1932, he wrote in rather "huffy" language, "You must realize that there are other things that must be considered and for us to hurry a formation of a native church at this juncture would seem unwise. It is a step that we should take only after the most mature deliberations and conference and prayer."[22] A month later, on May 5, Lambie shared his hesitation about baptizing converts with Bingham: "We feel that the time has hardly come. It has been so difficult to get in [Abyssinia] at all. We are in only on sufferance and we are anxious to get into a dozen other places. To begin baptizing and organizing churches now, would most certainly arouse the Abyssinian [Orthodox] Church and cause us to be bitterly opposed in new advances."[23] Another reason for Lambie's hesitation came from his initial 1928 interaction with a council of the Abyssinian Orthodox Church (Lambie's phrase was the "Abyssinian Sanhedrin"): "We sought to emphasize that we were sent to preach the word rather than to baptize and that we were in no sense seeking to duplicate any denominational organization in America or any

18. Cain, letters to Lambie, June 12 and July 3, 1931, SIMIA, EB-2-92, File 1.

19. Duff, *Cords of Love,* 268.

20. Cain, Duff, and Lewis, letter to Lambie and Rhoad, March 23, 1932, SIMIA, EB-2-92, File 1.

21. Cain, Duff, and Lewis, letter to Lambie and Rhoad, March 23, 1932, SIMIA, EB-2-92, File 1.

22. Lambie, letter to Cain, Duff, and Lewis, April 7, 1932, SIMIA, EB-2-92, File 1.

23. Lambie, letter to Bingham, May 5, 1932, SIMIA, EB-2-92, File 1.

other country."[24] Lambie assumed that the proceedings of that initial 1928 interaction with the priests would certainly have reached the ears of Regent Ras Tafari Makonnen and Foreign Minister Blattangeta Hiruy Wolde Sellassie.

Lengthy discussion took place at the SIM Abyssinian Field Council of May 16–18, 1932, about the possibility of baptizing believers at Homatcho. Lambie called upon Glen Cain to share about God's blessing in the Sidamo ministry. "Mr. Cain, in simple language, yet vividly and graphically, told of the Spirit's working there; the calling of the first believers, their choosing of elders, their clear-cut testimonies, their spiritual discernment and judgement in the problems they were called upon to deal with, expressed this to the Council."[25] Subsequent to Cain's report, Lambie made the following motion, acceding to the Homatcho baptism: "We recommend that all cases of prospective candidates for baptism be most prayerfully and carefully considered by the missionaries at the station, with the field directors."[26]

The baptism at Homatcho took place on December 25, 1932, performed together by Cain and Lambie. Subsequent to the baptism Alfred Roke reported, "Each one felt the privilege should belong to the other. It was a case of 'in honour preferring one another.'"[27] This baptism of four Sidamo believers, one older man and three young men, was witnessed by a host of Sidamo observers as well as seven SIM missionaries who were at Homatcho at that time. Looking at the baptism in retrospect, Lambie wrote, "The impression was borne in upon us that here were at least a few who understood what they were doing and were ready to be baptized."[28] Brian Fargher comments about Lambie's ill-founded fears of repercussions from either the government or Orthodox Church leaders: "The dipping of four farmers into a pond must have appeared insignificant."[29] Roke wrote a detailed account of the Homatcho baptism in his letter to Sidney Wood, who was a member of the New Zealand Council: "We were so pleased that

24. Lambie, "Christian Missionaries Appear before Church Council," report to Bingham, February 14, 1928, SIMIA, EA-1-83, File 6. See Duff, *Cords of Love*, 29, and Lambie, letter to US Embassy, February 25, 1928, affirming that he had been asked "not to build churches," SIMIA, EB-2-92, File 1.

25. SIM Abyssinian Field Council Minutes, May 16–18, 1932, SIMIA, ME-1/A-155, File 2. On this initial baptism, see further in Cotterell, *Born at Midnight*, 57–61.

26. SIM Abyssinian Field Council Minutes, May 16–18, 1932, SIMIA, ME-1/A-155, File 2.

27. Roke, *They Went Forth*, 146.

28. Lambie, report to Bingham, March 6, 1933, SIMIA, EB-2-92, File 1.

29. Fargher, *Origins of the New Churches*, 153. Ras Desta, by then governor of Sidamo, was sympathetic to SIM activities in Sidamo. He would have quelled any negative reaction to this "seemingly non-consequential" baptism.

Dr. Lambie could baptize the first ones to take the step, Mr. Cain assisting."[30] In this letter, Roke wrote a short biography of each of the four candidates for baptism. Their names were Deressa, Seda, Bareso, and Ortessa. Soon after the Homatcho baptism, the four men were offered communion of honey water and barley bread.[31]

A year later, on December 10, 1933, ten candidates were baptized at Soddo, Wolaitta, by Ohman and Lewis.[32] They celebrated the Lord's Supper two weeks later.[33] Lambie intentionally avoided being present at the Soddo baptism. He wrote to Bingham, "In another way I wish earnestly to avoid giving the impression that the Field Director is a kind of Bishop going around, so . . . perhaps it would be better for me not to be there."[34] In order not to create conflict with the Abyssinia Orthodox Church, little publicity was given to the baptisms. As Roke expressed it, "Much of the encouragement in Ethiopia must remain of a confidential character, in order that our missionaries may not be hindered in their work."[35] The April 1–4, 1936, SIM Abyssinian Field Council in Addis Ababa reported further on the increasing number of baptized believers. "On one field twenty-six have been baptized and on another twenty-five and lesser numbers on other stations. . . . We rejoice, give thanks and take these victories as the pledge and promise of greater things."[36]

The SIM missionaries assumed that converts would gather into "new churches." After the new believers were baptized and offered communion, the SIM missionaries allowed them full rights of membership in the local community of believers.[37] The new converts were not expected to be assimilated into the existing Abyssinian Orthodox Church. Rather, as Fargher has

30. Roke, letter to Sidney Wood, New Zealand SIM secretary, January 10, 1933, in Stephen Roke Special Collection of Alfred Roke materials, in New Zealand. For a detailed account of the baptism at Homatcho, see "Examination of Candidates for Baptism," in Roke, *They Went Forth*, 165–73.

31. The practice of using honey water and barley bread for communion continued among the Sidamo churches well into the 1970s, as witnessed by the author.

32. Duff, *Cords of Love*, 273.

33. Cotterell, *Born at Midnight*, 69.

34. Lambie, letter to Bingham, December 14, 1933, SIMIA, EB-2-93, File 3. See also Lambie, letter to Rhoad, December 23, 1933, SIMIA, EB-2-92, File 3: "I do not wish to pose as a Bishop going about and baptizing folks who have believed."

35. Roke, letter to Sidney Wood, January 10, 1933, in Stephen Roke Special Collection of Alfred Roke materials, in New Zealand.

36. SIM Abyssinian Field Council, Addis Ababa, April 1–4, 1936, SIMIA, ME-1/A-155, File 2.

37. Balisky, *Wolaitta Evangelists*, 110.

argued, following their baptism these new believers became leaders of local indigenous "new churches."[38] It appears that the early SIM missionaries took the teaching of Acts 15 as a biblical precedent. There the apostle Paul pled that newly converted Gentiles were not to be assimilated or proselytized into the Jewish faith. They were to be allowed to establish their own Gentile congregations. In the same way, baptisms subsequent to that of Homatcho in 1932 unleashed a new entity within Ethiopia—the "new churches movement" now evident in various evangelical denominations.

They developed a new pattern for training church leadership. The SIM Abyssinian Field Council held at Soddo, December 1–6, 1933, discussed the matter of training local church leadership. The discussion arose in response to the presence of Rev. and Mrs. Harold Street, who had been sent by SIM in the United States specifically for this ministry. The council decided, "The consensus of opinion seemed to be that a native ministry was best trained by those who had been instrumental in leading out the believers from darkness into light. This would ordinarily be by those missionaries at the station nearest the convert."[39] The council's concern was that initiating a single church leadership training school at this stage of church development would create a barrier between the scholars and their fellows in local churches. They were committed to the principle that teaching and training should be done within the local assemblies of believers, not in a specialized central seminary that might have a tendency to "exalt wisdom rather than spirituality."[40]

They established a policy regarding the construction of church buildings. The SIM missionaries arrived in Abyssinia with the conviction that the Bible teaches that anyone has the right to establish a new church. They were not extending a denomination from oversees into Abyssinia. The missionaries had no idea where new churches might spring up; they believed that was the work of the Holy Spirit. But they were committed to sowing the seed, nurturing those who believed and gave evidence of a changed life, and eventually baptizing the new followers of Jesus. For this reason Lambie was committed to establishing numerous points of outreach in southern Abyssinia, by faith confident that individuals would respond to the gospel. Once

38. Fargher, "Case Study: The Homacho Baptism," in *Origins of the New Churches*, 149–55, provides an example of this principle.

39. SIM Abyssinian Field Council, Soddo, December 1–6, 1933, SIMIA, ME-1/A-155, File 2.

40. SIM Abyssinian Field Council, Soddo, December 1–6, 1933, SIMIA, ME-1/A-155, File 2.

believers were baptized and had elected their own leadership, they became a church with full rights and responsibilities to function as a church and to begin meeting in their own building.

Discussions at Soddo during the December 1933 SIM Abyssinian Field Council included the issue of church buildings:

> The matter of having church buildings conforming to indigenous principles was discussed, the immediate cause of this discussion being the commencement of such a building at Soddo [station], using some school funds from native sources. It was felt that this was not the right method, but that churches should be built by believers themselves.[41]

Lambie wrote to Bingham soon after the Field Council's decision, stating, "Rowland Allen's books, *Expansion and the Native Church* as well as *Missionary Methods: St. Paul's or Ours*, has impacted the Abyssinian missionaries to carefully establish the native church along the principles advocated by Allen."[42] The Abyssinia missionaries gave evidence of a growing sensitivity not to transgress the principle of the "native church idea."

The SIM missionaries responded to human need. The missionaries responded to the Abyssinians' physical needs by offering medical services and opening clinics at seven of the locations where they served. The hospital at Soddo provided professional medical service to a wide population in Sidamo Province. The leprosarium at Furi on the outskirts of Addis Ababa was a haven for destitute leper patients. The work of the SIM Leprosarium was truly done in the spirit of Christ, whereas much of SIM's medical work was used as a means to open doors for evangelism. In 1935 Dr. Lambie wrote as much: "There is perhaps no country where a medical diploma acts more efficiently as an entrance *passé porte* than Ethiopia."[43] Still, the mission's response to human need was more than instrumental; one cannot disregard SIM's significant contribution of Drs. Hooper and Roberts to Unit #4 of the Ethiopian Red Cross. This was truly a ministry of love to the hundreds of wounded and disabled patriots crippled and maimed by Italian bombs and mustard poison gas.

Further, all twelve of the SIM locations outside of Addis Ababa provided limited educational services. Fargher comments, "At that time academic schools were not an integral part of the SIM policy in Ethiopia but

---

41. SIM Abyssinian Field Council, Soddo, December 1–6, 1933, SIMIA, ME-1/A-155, File 2.

42. Lambie, letter to Bingham, December 14, 1933, SIMIA, EB-2-93, File 3.

43. Lambie, "Conquest by Healing in Ethiopia," *Officers' Christian Union*, 70–72.

the missionaries did begin schools in every area," adding that "the main objective of these schools was Bible literacy."[44] The schools, even with a limited curriculum, created an appetite for learning among the believers. In the years following the Italio-Ethiopian War, SIM operated over forty elementary schools in southern Ethiopia and two secondary schools.

A contemporary scholar of the Ethiopian Kale Heywet Church, Girma Bekele, offers a critique of SIM's limited dualistic missiological framework, stating, "This type of parallelism between evangelism and social concern has its roots in the way in which SIM operated in Ethiopia."[45]

The missionaries decided not to pay indigenous evangelists. A request by SIM member Allan Smith was addressed at the Addis Ababa SIM Abyssinian Field Council meeting, March 28–April 2, 1935. He desired to serve with the Bible Churchman's Mission Society among the Boran of southern Abyssinia. The council decided that Smith would not be allowed to join together with the BCMS "as we differ from them so radically in the matter of a paid native evangelism. We are committed to indigenous church principles." This significant decision not to use mission funds to pay evangelists' salaries has steadfastly been adhered to by the mission until the present.

The SIM missionaries were committed to Bible translation. The Addis Ababa SIM Abyssinian Field Council, March 28–April 2, 1935, noted that "Dr. Lambie said he felt it to be an urgent need to get [Bible] translation work on a better basis in this area." Walter Ohman was appointed to head up a translation committee. As noted earlier, the Gospel of Mark had previously been translated by Glen Cain and the Gospel of Matthew by Clarence Duff. The Gospel of John was translated into the Wolaitta language, as was the little booklet *God Hath Spoken*, a widely used compilation of Bible texts in the Wolaitta language.[46]

In conclusion, it is evident that the SIM pioneers arrived in Abyssinia with a clear-cut goal of preaching the gospel to as many as would listen. For this reason, in the years 1928 through 1936 they established fifteen stations and centers as preaching points. They also provided limited educational and medical services. In the south, SIM missionaries were located at Homatcho, Soddo, Marako, Hosanna, Duramei, Chencha, Bulki, Jimma, Tutitti, Yerga

---

44. Fargher, *Origins of the New Churches*, 122, 176.

45. Girma, *In-Between People*, 242.

46. SIM Abyssinian Field Council, Soddo, June 3–4, 1931, SIMIA, ME-1/A-155, File 2. See also, Duff, *Cords of Love*, 265–66.

Alem. In Addis Ababa the SIM presence consisted of the SIM Bookstore, the Headquarters at Akaki, and the Leprosarium at Furi. In addition to these, Lalibela and Debra Markos were located in the north for a total of fifteen. The missionaries overcame various obstacles such as sickness, loneliness, lack of funds during the Great Depression of the 1930s, local resistance, and issues of incompatibility between personnel. But in faith they carried on, building on what they believed to be biblical principles for establishing the church in a cross-cultural situation. From very humble beginnings, a nascent church movement in southern Abyssinia has blossomed into one of the largest evangelical churches in present-day Ethiopia.

In 1927, prior to leading SIM into Abyssinia, Lambie wrote prophetically:

> [To those] who can see a big thing before the world has caught the vision and can act upon it, this opportunity comes . . . an untouched country teeming with people. Not mere savages of no intelligence but sturdy mountain folk who if won for Jesus Christ will go out all over Africa as missionaries and teachers and be far more useful than missionaries from western lands.[47]

Dr. Lambie and his cohorts did catch the vision of what God could do through the Ethiopian Kale Heywet Church. This vibrant Ethiopian evangelical church, which now comprises over nine million members, is presently sending out and financially supporting over twenty-five families as their own Ethiopian global missionaries to plant indigenous churches in more than a dozen countries around the world.[48] To God be the glory!

---

47. Lambie, "A New Mission to Abyssinia's Unknown Frontiers," ca. September 1927, 11, SIMIA, EA-1-82, File 13.

48. Jack Bryan, "Is the World's Next Missions Movement in Ethiopia?" *Christianity Today*, June 21, 2019, www.christianitytoday.com/ct/2019/july-august/ethiopia-missions.html.

Prior to the advent of Christianity in southern Abyssinia, primal or traditional religion was adhered to by the majority of the population. The peoples of Abyssinia, unlike some other people groups in Africa who no longer knew the name for their High God, knew the name of the God they worshipped. The Gedeo worshipped *Waq*; the Sidamo, the Kambatta, and the Hadiya, *Muganno*; the Wolaitta and related Omotic speakers, *Tosa*. Local traditional religious functionaries in the south included the *qalicha*, who could foretell the future by dreams, and the solitary *sharechwa*, who, under a trance, could reveal that which is hidden. These two kinds of practitioners promoted fear and anxiety among the local population.

During the 1920s in southern Abyssinia, another kind of religious functionary made an appearance. This was the prophet, defined as "a charismatic leader, free from family and social ties as well as economic interests. He creates new obligations and brings about a radical reorientation of attitudes and values."[49] A prophet was usually driven by two forces. The first was the external engine of crisis within a given society. The prophet had a message that showed the way into the future. The second was an inner spiritual force that compelled the prophet. He or she was undergirded with a strong sense of divine call to restore society to health and well-being. Unlike the *qalicha* or the *sharechewa*, who operated in a hidden manner, the prophet functioned openly and was in conversation with his society.

Abbaye became a significant prophet in Kambatta. He encouraged his neighbors to put on clean clothes on Sundays and to come to his house to hear him give advice. It was reported that Abbaye would hold up the palms of his hands and appear to be reading from the Bible. Another prophet of the south was Chelake from Gofa, located southwest of Wolaitta. He prophesied that men would fly and mountains would shake. This was interpreted as having come to pass when the Italian war machine invaded the south. Chelake also predicted that someone with a walking stick curved at the top would come by way of the river carrying a golden book. This prediction was fulfilled when a Wolaitta evangelist appeared. The most significant prophet in the south was Esa Lale (the one who releases to freedom).

Esa launched his itinerant ministry in Gamo, Qucha, Boroda, Gofa, and Wolaitta in the 1920s. He preached in these southern areas against corruption going on within society and that men and women were to live in peace with one another. Esa was arrested for predicting that eventually the tyranny of the oppressors of the southern Abyssinian peoples would be curtailed and the land would be given back to the previous owners. The ruling authorities from the north judged that Esa was inciting the local population against them and marched him off to trial and imprisonment in Addis Ababa. Evangelicals in southern Abyssinia referred to Esa as their John the Baptist. SIM missionary

---

49. Anderson and Johnson, *Revealing Prophets*, 11.

Earl Lewis trekked extensively in Wolaitta and observed the results of Prophet Esa's teaching. Unlike most of his colleagues of that time, who saw no positive aspects within primal religion, Lewis observed that Esa's teaching denounced Satan worship and encouraged the people to worship the Creator God, *Tosa*. Esa encouraged families to practice religious rituals each Sunday with the head of the household offering prayers to the high God, *Tosa*. Esa also taught some aspects of the Decalogue, such as that all people were to live at peace with one another.[50] Pre-Christian prophets such as Esa served as providential precursors of the evangelical movement in southern Abyssinia.

50. Balisky, "Esa Lale," 578–79.

9

SIM Seeks to Launch Mission Stations
in the North

*Just as truly many of us have to cross
the valley of the shadow of death.*

THOMAS A. LAMBIE, *A BRUISED REED*, 75

IN A DEPARTURE FROM its announced plan of missionary operation, in 1934 Sudan Interior Mission attempted to establish two mission stations among the Orthodox Christian population of northern Abyssinia. As related earlier, SIM in 1928 was enabled by God to overcome initial resistance on the part of Addis Ababa officialdom to its establishment of mission stations among non-Christians in southern Abyssinia. By 1932, over fifty mission personnel staffed thirteen SIM outreach centers in the south. Baptisms had been performed at Homatcho, Sidamo, and Soddo, Wolaitta. Also, official permission had been granted for the construction, at two different locations in Addis Ababa, of the SIM headquarters building and the Leprosarium Center. While the leprosarium in Addis Ababa's Furi suburb was being built, Dr. Lambie paid a visit to Ras Kassa Haylu Darge, the governor of Lasta Province situated in northern Abyssinia, who was in the capital on official business. It was known that leprosy was rampant in the province of Lasta, so Lambie, gifted as he was in public relations with Abyssinian officialdom, requested a substantial contribution from Ras Kassa toward the construction of the Addis Ababa leprosarium. The governor's response was rather curt and somewhat surprising to Lambie. "No, I will not give you anything for [the leprosarium] in Addis Ababa, but if you build a hospital in Lalibela, I will give land and three thousand thalers."[1] When Lambie remonstrated that the population in northern Abyssinia was Orthodox Christian and that the focus of SIM was on the pagans and Muslim population in the South. Ras Kassa responded, "It does not matter. They need you up there as much as the pagans; they are Christian in name only. Also there are many Mohammedans. If you like, I will put my offer in writing."[2]

Before accepting this invitation to expand the ministry of SIM to the North, Lambie felt that he should obtain the affirmation of his missionary colleagues in Abyssinia as well as agreement from the general director of SIM, Rowland Bingham. The initial goal of the mission, drafted in 1927 by the leaders of the Abyssinian Frontiers Mission, as stated in chapter 5, was to evangelize non-Christians in southern and eastern Abyssinia. Lambie commented that the request from Ras Kassa "put the whole matter of the north before us in a very definite way. There were no Protestant missions in all the north-country."[3] The response from SIM's international director was affirmative: "Doctor Bingham decided to come out again, and go with me and [to] himself see the north country."[4] By February 1934, Bingham was in Addis Ababa in attendance at the February 8–12 SIM Abyssinian Field Council meeting. Minute 38 read, "It was planned, God willing, that Dr. Bingham would first visit the North, then take a quick trip to Jimma, and then tour the stations in the South. It was expected that the North trip would take about 5 weeks."[5] Further details of the trip that reveal the character of the relationship between Bingham and Lambie appear in chapter 11.

On the question of whether SIM should open a mission station in the north, Bingham reported:

> This story [of Ras Kassa] arrested us, challenged us, fascinated us. Like Paul we "assuredly gathered" that God intended us to preach the Gospel there as well. But there were other voices that sought to dampen enthusiasm . . . [including] opposition to entering a country already occupied by the old State Church;

1. Lambie, *Doctor without a Country*, 213. At that time one thaler was equivalent to US$5.00. The offer in 1932 of 3,000 thalers would be equivalent in 2019 US dollars to a gift of approximately US$280,158 toward the construction of an expensive building (see DollarTimes, www.dollartimes.com/inflation/inflation.php?amount=1&year=1932).

2. Lambie, *Doctor without a Country*, 213.

3. Lambie, *Doctor without a Country*, 213.

4. Lambie, *Doctor without a Country*, 213.

5. SIM Abyssinia Field Council, Addis Ababa, February 8–12, 1934, Item 38, SIM-IA, ME-1/A-155, File 2.

and especially to entering Lalibella, the sacred city of the north, to which pilgrims gathered by the thousands every year at the great festivals.[6]

At the end of February, Thomas and Charlotte Lambie, together with Bingham and Dean Blanchard, an ornithologist from California, began their journey north.[7] A mission vehicle drove them over Entote Mountain, then across a long plain to where they finally reached their mule caravan. For three weeks they plodded north, traveling through deep canyons and then atop *ambas* or fortresses. (One of these fortresses called Magdala was the place where Emperor Theodorus made his last stand in 1867 against Lord Napier.) The missionaries carried Bibles and Scripture portions, written in Amharic. These were either sold or given away to those who could read. As a medical doctor, Lambie carried a good supply of medicines with him to treat sick persons who came to the missionaries' overnight camping spots. "On some plateaus it would be too cold to sleep, even with four blankets to cover one. By day we may go through some low valley and be scorched with the heat. We struggled on together."[8]

In mid-March, after three weeks of arduous trekking, the Lambie/Bingham party arrived at the historic thirteenth-century site of Lalibela, where they viewed with awe the eleven ancient churches hewn out of the red volcanic stone. A chronicler of the life of thirteenth-century Emperor Lalibela records that angels assisted Lalibela's craftsmen in constructing these churches, stating, "The greater part of the work had actually been effected not by men, but by angels."[9]

6. Bingham, "Lure of Lalibella, Ethiopia," 300.

7. Lambie, "Trip to Lalibela [daily diary]," February 23–April 11, 1934, 7pp., SIMIA, EA-1-82, File 19.

8. Lambie, *Doctor without a Country*, 213.

9. Pankhurst, *Ethiopian Royal Chronicles*, 12.

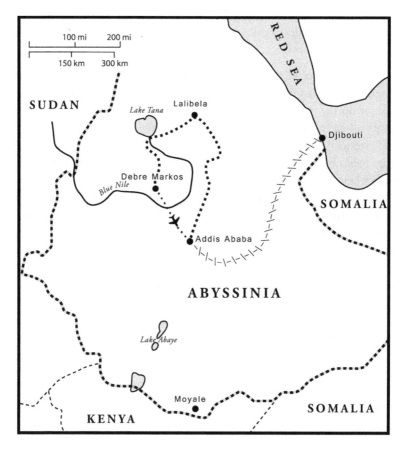

Thomas and Charlotte Lambie's route north with Rowland Bingham

Lalibela was inhabited mainly by priests and traders, but after exploring the town Lambie located a site that could serve as a mission station. A local man, appointed by Ras Kassa, was helpful in assisting the SIM party in locating the Lalibela mission site, but the local priests were less than enthusiastic about allowing foreigners to reside within the "holy domain." Lambie writes: "In vain we sought to reassure them that we came as friends and not as enemies, to build up and not to tear down. They were as adamant and proclaimed curses and maledictions upon any who bought or sold to us and who would give or sell us land."[10]

From Lalibela Lambie wrote to the mission family:

> We plan going back via Debra Tabor and Debra Markos. This
> will require more than a month. We have seen very great need

10. Lambie, "Abyssinia: Sokota and the Word of God," 213.

and will see much more and we cannot but think that our heavenly Father has guided us to take this trip, but the same blessed
Holy Spirit who led Paul to his fruitful ministry in Macedonia
showing him the beckoning man is willing to guide us as we
truly know His will for us. Let us not stagger at His promise
through unbelief but go up from Kadesh-Barnea in Victory.[11]

Accordingly, from Lalibela the Lambie/Bingham party journeyed
northwest for another week to Gondar, situated in the foothills of the towering Simien Mountains.

It appears, however, that Lambie may have struggled with the thought
of SIM's becoming involved in the North, in the heartland of the Orthodox
Church. He knew that the initial objective of the Abyssinian Frontiers Mission had been to go to "the unevangelised pagan tribes of Southern Ethiopia
rather than to the members of the Ethiopian Coptic Church."[12] Further, he
knew a move into the North would be resisted. "An adherent to the Ethiopian Orthodox Church commented, 'But why should the Church, which is
so central to the very identity of Christian Ethiopians, be destroyed? Her
children resent it.'"[13] Now, the Lambies and Rowland Bingham were making
arrangements to launch mission stations situated within the historic Orthodox Church precincts. Previously he had affirmed that "we would not speak
against the Ethiopian Coptic Church, and we believe that is right. On the
other hand we will never shade our Christian message to conform to any
opinion of men contrary to the Word of God."[14]

When Bingham and the Lambies arrived in Debra Tabor, south-south-
east of Gondar, Ras Kassa's son received them cordially and invited them
to open work. From Debra Tabor they made their way west to Lake Tsana
and arrived at Bahir Dar, where the headwaters of the Blue Nile are located.
Crossing the Blue Nile on boats made of reeds, they travelled directly south
through Gojam Province, which, as described by Lambie, "is lovely beyond
my powers of description. Forest, river, lake and plain, valley and waterfall,
unite to make some of the grandest scenery imaginable."[15] After a week,
they arrived at Debra Markos and were met by Ras Emeru, cousin of the

11. Lambie, letter to SIM fellow workers, March 18, 1934, in Duff, *Cords of Love*,
258.

12. Lambie, "A Short Statement in Regard to Mission Work among the So-called
Christian Gurages of Abyssinia," ca. 1933, SIMIA, EA-1-82, File 0.

13. Getachew Haile, "The Missionary's Dream: An Ethiopian Perspective on Western Missions in Ethiopia," in *Missionary Factor in Ethiopia*, ed. Getachew Haile et al., 7

14. Lambie, "A Short Statement in Regard to Mission Work among the So-called
Christian Gurages of Abyssinia," ca. 1933, SIMIA, EA-1-82, File 0.

15. Lambie, *Doctor without a Country*, 221.

emperor. Of the governor Lambie wrote: "He was, in my opinion, after the
Emperor himself, the very finest man in Ethiopia [Abyssinia]. Honest and
faithful to his friends, he never took a bribe or concealed a fault; he was generous and unselfish."[16] Ras Emeru invited the "Lambie Mission" to establish
work in Debra Markos. Following their nearly three months' travel, Lambie
and Bingham anticipated opening new SIM stations in Lalibela, Gondar,
Bahr Dar Giorgis, and Debra Markos. As it turned out, mission stations
were opened at Lalibela and Debra Markos, but the Italo-Ethiopian War
prevented SIM from locating in Gondar and Bahr Dar Giorgis.

In 1934 Don and Ruth Davies, together with Nick Simponis, were assigned to Debra Markos and settled into their ministry without difficulty on
land designated for them. When Dr. Harriet Skemp, Lottie Blair, RN, Ken
and Blanche Oglesby, and Jim Luckman attempted to settle on a property
in Lalibela that they had to share with several arrogant soldiers, they found
the situation impossible. Lambie wrote that he "was receiving frantic letters from Lalibela about their miserable quarters."[17] No amount of pleading
with Foreign Minister Blattangeta Hiruy in Addis Ababa served to ease the
situation. In desperation and with earnestness, Lambie spoke to the foreign
minister: "You have known me for many years, and if I have let you down
or wronged Ethiopia [Abyssinia], I will let you judge. I love Ethiopia [Abys-
sinia] and hope to spend the rest of my life serving her, and if necessary
would become an Ethiopian myself to prove the sincerity of my love."[18] The
foreign minister readily agreed to administer the oath of Abyssinian allegiance to Lambie the following day. Because forfeiting his prized American
citizenship for the sake of advancing the mission was so unusual, Lambie
asked his Excellency for a one-month deferment to think further on the
crucial step he was about to take. One month later in the presence of the foreign minister and the emperor, he took the oath of allegiance to Abyssinia.
Lambie wrote, "The whole thing made quite a stir, and I was ridiculed by
many whose good opinion I cherished; there were other thoughtful persons
who commended the action."[19] "Whether it was a misjudgement," Clarence
Duff (who had been Lambie's close associate from the entry of SIM into Abyssinia) wrote much later, "for him to give up his United States citizenship
to become an Ethiopian subject I will not attempt to judge. . . . In any case
his heart was right in the matter."[20]

16. Lambie, *Doctor without a Country*, 222.

17. Lambie, *Doctor without a Country*, 224.

18. Lambie, *Doctor without a Country*, 225.

19. Lambie, *Doctor without a Country*, 225–26.

20. Duff, *Cords of Love*, 334.

In mid-December of 1934 the Lambies found it necessary to make another trip to Lalibela to settle the land matter. Another plot of land was located for the mission station, and the Oglesbys and Luckman soon made it comfortable for habitation and conducting medical work. The Lambies began their journey homeward in mid-March, 1935, retracing their steps through Debra Tabor and beyond Lake Tsana, where they made camp. There the SIM postman finally caught up to them with a sackful of letters and papers. Lambie wrote:

> On opening the letters on that bare hillside we received the stunning news that our only son, Wallace, had met instant death in South America [Colombia] over a month before. The news got to Addis Ababa the next day, but took over a month to get to us. Weary from the exertions of two months of hard trekking and the anxieties of getting our dear missionaries really located [in Lalibela], the blow came upon us with fierce impact.[21]

The bereaved parents "stumbled back to Addis Ababa after another three weeks of hard going. When we saw the Emperor, he said no word for a space of five minutes, while the tears coursed down his cheeks in sympathy for us. It meant far more than words."[22]

Prior to returning to Abyssinia in 1927 with their daughter Betty, the Lambies had arranged for their son Wallace, then seventeen years of age, to remain with Charlotte's parents, Albert and Elizabeth Claney, at "The Meadows" in Maryland. Wallace undertook clerical training, following which William S. Lambie, a cousin to Dr. Lambie, around the year 1930 secured a position for the young man in Medellin, Colombia, at a branch of the National City Bank of New York. Upon making port in Puerto Rico while onboard ship to Medellin, Wallace wrote an endearing letter to his father. The final paragraph read:

> Dad, old man, I love you. Perhaps the end of all love is *brolie* [brotherly love?]. I mean that of child to father—but one thing has taken its place and above that is everlasting that of father to son—man to man. Brothers in Christ.
>   Write Dad soon
>   Your own son
>   Wallace
>   P.S. Pray for me more I need it.[23]

---

21. Lambie, *Doctor without a Country*, 229.

22. Lambie, *Doctor without a Country*, 229.

23. Wallace Lambie, letter to Thomas A. Lambie, n.d., MHSC.

After Wallace's tragic death at age twenty-four, four employees of the bank where he worked wrote to Dr. and Mrs. Lambie:

> February 1, 1935
> We, of the staff of the National City Bank at Medellin, partake of your sorrow which is so deep for us as companions of Mr. Lambie, whose death left us in an unexpected moment without him who was a friend, almost a brother, and a chief always dealing with mild character and gentlemanly manner. We are so deeply stricken with his absence from among us and when looking at his desk and chair [in] this bank, empty of him, we understand the unspeakable misfortune of his loss that crushes our hearts. . . .
> With deepest sympathy we remain,
> yours sincerely,
> [signed] Gonzalo Gomez Escobar, Alberto Perez, Luis E. Gil, and Jesus Mora Vasquez[24]

On February 4, 1935, the manager of National City Bank in Medellin, Mr. Carl Erickson, wrote:

> Dear Doctor Lambie,
> It is with great regret that we confirm our cable in regard to the death of your son Wallace. We wish to express to you our most sincere sympathy. Wallace was with us only a short time but he had won our affection and respect both as a conscientious employee and as an honorable, likeable young man in our midst socially. Our entire Colombian staff join us in conveying our deepest sympathy. On the night of January 28, 1935 Wallace, accompanied by Mr. Garrington of the Bank of London and South America and an elderly lady . . . went to the new theatre Alcazar, a moving picture house. . . . About an hour after the Theatre Alcazar opened the entire roof fell in without any warning. The three were killed or asphyxiated presumably instantaneously. . . . You may feel that Wallace is resting in a country where he made friends who are feeling the shock of his sudden death.
> Sincerely yours.
> Carl E. Erickson, Manager[25]

Another disappointment came to Dr. Lambie, for just over a year after the SIM missionaries were settled in the north, their ministry was cut short.

24. Four Employees of National City Bank, Medellin, Colombia, letter to Lambies, February 1, 1935, MHSC.

25. Carl E. Erickson, letter to Lambie, February 4, 1935, MHSC.

The Fascists were swooping into the north. In mid-April 1936 the Italian military invaded Debra Markos, where Glen and Winnie Cain (Cain's first wife) and Jean Cable were serving. They were evicted. Lambie wrote, "By the end of April, 1936, it was evident that the game was up. The Ethiopians were defeated on all fronts. The airplanes and poison gas had broken their morale."[26] Because the other missionaries had fled south, Mr. and Mrs. Ken Oglesby were now alone for the time being at Lalibela. So it happened that for several days the Lalibela mission station proved to be a place of refuge for the fleeing emperor.[27] Rowland Bingham records that the emperor, fleeing together with Ras Kassa from the attacking Fascists, "has never forgotten the treatment accorded him by our missionaries [at Lalibela] on that occasion."[28] Eventually, on August 5, 1938, Clarence Duff, deputy director of SIM, signed a contract—on payment of 900 pounds sterling by the Italians—turning over the Debra Markos and Lalibela buildings to the invaders.[29]

Thus ended the sad saga of Dr. Lambie's attempt to establish a bulwark for missions in the north of Abyssinia. From a historical perspective, one may ask whether SIM had undertaken adequate missiological deliberation prior to launching SIM outreach in the northern portion of the country. Viewed from today, it seems very unlikely that SIM's paradigm for establishing churches in southern Abyssinia would have been feasible as a pattern for mission work to be conducted at the heart of the Abyssinian Orthodox Church's historical bastion in northern Abyssinia. Before SIM's outreach into the north could gain a footing, the Italian war of 1935–36 disrupted the bold, yet ill-advised venture.

26. Lambie, *Doctor without a Country*, 244.

27. Cotterell, *Born at Midnight*, 91–92.

28. Bingham, *Seven Sevens of Years*, 98.

29. Duff, *Cords of Love*, 358.

Shaikh Zakaryas, 1845–1920

In 1892 Zakaryas, staunch follower of Islam, received a series of disturbing visions that culminated in his seeking out an Arabic Bible. Christian contemporaries of Zakaryas claimed that his conversion was similar to that of the Apostle Paul. His first vision presented a man from the east, sent by God to give him special wisdom and greater insight into teaching the Quran. In his second vision, three shaikhs advised him to be bold in interpreting the Quran. Two of the messengers then ascended to heaven, and one remained behind to comfort and encourage Zakaryas in his assigned task. After these two visions he set about to reform and renew Islam. From 1892 to 1895 Zakaryas preached in many places around Soqota, Wag province, in northern Abyssinia. His preaching from the Arabic Bible, which was beginning to have a Christian tone, aroused strong opposition within the local Muslim population. The Muslims launched a series of accusations against him for disturbing the local peace, but the officials, who were Amhara Christians, dismissed the case.

In 1896 Zakaryas transferred his ministry to the province of Bagemder where he began teaching conversion to Christ. With helpful Christian books in Amharic provided by the Swedish mission in Asmara, the movement to Christ among Muslims grew rapidly. Eventually, in 1907, Zakaryas was accused before Emperor Menelik by both the Muslims and the Amharic-speaking Ethiopian Orthodox Christians from the north. The Menelik/Zakaryas Council issued a "Permission and Proclamation" written on vellum that allowed Zakaryas to preach freely anywhere in northern Abyssinia. The movement continued until the leader's death in 1920, at which time his followers numbered over 7,000. Zakaryas's successor, Yesuf, continued as leader. By 1924 unabated persecution mounted against what the Orthodox Christians pejoratively called "New Christians." As Menelik was now dead, the Muslims and Orthodox in the north no longer honored the 1907 document of toleration.

Yesuf, a humble artisan from the north, was unable to get the ear of officialdom in Addis Ababa. In desperation he took his case to Dr. Lambie, who had been recommended to him by missionaries in Addis Ababa. At a special luncheon in the Lambie home in 1932, to which the emperor was invited, Lambie broke social protocol and asked Haile Sellassie to hear the issue of Yesuf. Becoming convinced that Yesuf's case was sincere, the emperor had a permission document prepared similar to that written by Menelik. Yesuf, with the document of permission in hand, was now prepared to return north to Soqota. But before leaving Addis Ababa, Yesuf begged Lambie to send missionaries to assist the new Christians in Begemder Province. Though persecution was lulled for a time after Yesuf returned with the official document, renewed violence broke out again some years later. Yesuf and many of his followers were martyred.

Unfortunately, Lambie was unable to establish a mission station among these "New Christians." Though part of history, the movement toward Christianity initiated by Shaikh Zakaryas is now only a memory.

10

Launching and Facilitating the Ethiopian Red Cross

*Disease, difficulties, and heartache did not
stop stout hearts like . . . Tom Lambie.*

V. RAYMOND EDMAN, PREFACE,
A DOCTOR'S GREAT COMMISSION, 7

AS NOTED IN CHAPTER 4, during 1915 Dr. Lambie served temporarily with
the British Red Cross Unit at a British hospital in Alexandria. He had been
appointed for five months to care for wounded British soldiers from the
Middle East warfront.[1] This experience of caring for wounded and dying
soldiers gave him unusual medical exposure. Little did he know that in
twenty years he would be directing the large and unwieldy Ethiopian Red
Cross (ERC) operation from Addis Ababa. For a missionary such as Lambie,
this task was an unusual assignment.

By April 1935, Haile Sellassie was apprehensive that war between Abyssinia and Italy had become inevitable. As early as 1934, well before the
Lambies left Addis Ababa in May 1935 for England and Scotland, Lambie
had already spoken to His Majesty about inspiring some persons in London
to organize a British ambulance service for Abyssinia. Haile Sellassie initially appeared indifferent to the proposal, but eventually he made an urgent

1. Lambie, *Doctor without a Country,* 102–5.

call to Lambie, asking him to return to Abyssinia as soon as possible.[2] When Lambie arrived in Addis Ababa on September 20, 1935, he found the country in the grip of impending war with Italy. He was soon called to the office of the foreign minister, Blattangeta Hiruy. On the basis that Lambie was now an Abyssinian citizen and that he had extensive medical experience in Abyssinia, he was informed that he was to serve as the executive director of the Ethiopian Red Cross.[3] Lambie commented,

> I was not very keen for the job; it was too late for me to make myself really useful. . . . I was to have all the liberty I needed if I consented to take on the job. . . . The first shot was fired about the time I took over which was October 3, 1935. We were given three large ground-floor rooms in a Government building on the main road, near its junction with the road connecting the two palaces. . . . Here meetings of the committee were held twice weekly to discuss the various aspects of the Red Cross work; these seldom resulted in anything practical.[4]

At the same time there were urgent SIM matters which demanded to be addressed. He convened an SIM Abyssinian Field Council meeting in Addis Ababa for November 20–28, 1935, where he presented this statement:

> In view of the catastrophe that has come upon our country in the Italian war and invasion, and because the Government has appointed me Secretary Executive of the Ethiopian Red Cross, and because it seemed to me that it is indeed God's will for me to accept this appointment; and because this takes nearly all of my time; I feel I should delegate to others most of the direction of the Mission. I, therefore, appoint Messrs. Duff and Cain to be Deputy Field Directors. . . . [I]t is understood that I do not relinquish my work as Field Director absolutely.[5]

So, on the advice of Rowland Bingham, SIM international director, Lambie delegated most of SIM Abyssinia's day-to-day operations to others. Glen Cain was to take oversight of all SIM personnel outside of Addis Ababa, and Clarence Duff was to deal with the many and varied activities and duties of SIM in Addis Ababa that previously had been performed by

2. The material in this chapter is indebted to Lambie, *Doctor without a Country*, 230–45, and Lambie, "Report and Critique of the Ethiopian Red Cross, November 5, 1935, to May 5, 1936," June 12, 1936, 5 pp., SIMIA, EA-1-83, File 17.

3. See Spencer, *Ethiopia at Bay*, 49.

4. Lambie, *Doctor without a Country*, 133.

5. SIM Abyssinian Field Council, Addis Ababa, November 20–28, 1935, SIMIA, ME-1/A-155, File 2.

Lambie.[6] The two men valiantly carried the administrative duties of SIM Abyssinia until August 1938, when they, along with other remaining SIM missionaries, sadly departed Addis Ababa by train.[7]

Foreign Minister Blattangeta Hiruy, who served as president of the ERC, communicated the will of the Abyssinia Government to the ERC Committee. On September 26, 1935, the Ethiopian Red Cross was officially recognized by the International Committee of the Red Cross (ICRC) as the organization's sixty-second member.[8] The ICRC in Geneva sent two well-qualified men to Abyssinia to assist with administrative details. Mr. Sydney Brown was a career serviceman with experience in the Far East as well as in Europe who spoke a number of European languages fluently. He was acquainted with Geneva and League of Nations methods, but unlike so many internationally-minded persons, he had a sympathetic heart for his assignment. The other Geneva representative from ICRC was Dr. Marcel Junod, an intensely practical person, who was not looking for an armchair job, but was always willing to go into the Abyssinian war zones to determine actual needs of the field ambulances and give authoritative opinion as to best practices.

Daily operation of the ERC was chaotic. Rainer Baudendistel reports that "meetings were complicated because there was no common language between the participants, resulting in time-consuming translations."[9] Lambie's ERC colleagues felt that he was not an efficient manager. Sydney Brown, the ICRC delegate, described Lambie in a rather disparaging manner: "He was the kind of person who can follow one case at a time in every detail. And who does not know at all how to make other people work. For a mule's bridle he would be quite capable of leaving his office for a whole morning, bringing with him, if possible, the quartermaster, the deputy secretary and others."[10] Lambie himself confessed that control of the finances often overwhelmed him, writing that financial control of the ERC

> was left almost entirely in my hands. I was glad that the Ethiopians trusted me. Before Count Tastitsheff came on as full treasurer, I even had to carry the money around with me, buttoned up in an inside pocket . . . for we tried to pay cash for everything. I would have anywhere from $1000 to $4000 on my person in

6. Duff, *Cords of Love*, 309.

7. Duff, *Cords of Love*, 364–65.

8. Baudendistel, *Between Bombs and Good Intentions*, 37.

9. Baudendistel, *Between Bombs and Good Intentions*, 40.

10. Baudendistel, *Between Bombs and Good Intentions*, 40.

high denominations bills, which was not very safe; but there was
no one available whom I could trust.[11]

Lambie also was disturbed by inefficiency within the ERC Committee.
On one occasion an hour was spent discussing a difference of twenty-five
cents in one of the accounts. He lamented that this type of pettiness was
occurring at the same time that men out in the war zones were dying of
untreated wounds, dysentery, and starvation.

Lambie's involvement in the Red Cross venture met with the full approval and support of SIM's international director, Rowland Bingham. In
October 1935 Bingham wrote:

> We presume that some day when war breaks out they [Abyssinian government] will take action, but, in the meantime, Dr.
> Lambie felt, with the writer, that our mission could not remain
> inactive any longer. We therefore decided to form our Mission
> Red Cross which will operate through the mission societies already on the field. There are two Swedish missions, the United
> Presbyterian Mission, and our own Sudan Interior Mission.
> Outside of these four missions we question whether there are
> more than a half-a-dozen fully qualified doctors in the whole
> country. . . . We do not forget that the first command of our Lord
> to His disciples was not only to preach the Gospel but to heal the
> sick and cleanse the leper.[12]

A succeeding issue of the *Evangelical Christian*, which Bingham edited, carried a full-page statement entitled "Our Mission: Red Cross for
Ethiopia." It stated: "Dr. T. A. Lambie, Field Director of the Sudan Interior
Mission, who is serving as Secretary of the General Red Cross in Ethiopia,
sent the following cable on November 5, 1935, from Addis Ababa. 'We are
now sending our own Red Cross unit, Sidamo South East. Dr. Hooper, A. O.
Smith, A. G. Roke. His Imperial Majesty delighted. Promises help. Further
assistance required.'"[13] Bingham's inclusion of this statement in SIM's official
magazine indicated the whole-hearted support that the international SIM
body felt for the Red Cross endeavor in Abyssinia. It gave evidence as well of
basic approval on the part of the majority of evangelical churches in North
America, Britain, and elsewhere.[14]

---

11. Lambie, *Doctor without a Country*, 237.

12. Bingham, "Ethiopia and the Mission Red Cross," 382.

13. Bingham, "Our Mission: Red Cross for Ethiopia," 507.

14. Pankhurst, *Medical History of Ethiopia*, 224, mentions that SIM "dispatch[ed]
staff to care for Ethiopian troops."

Rainer Baudendistel, a Swiss historian who specialized in the Horn of Africa and who had formerly served with the ICRC, affirmed the international support enjoyed by Red Cross operations in Abyssinia. "The [Ethiopian] Red Cross was able to mount an impressive medical relief operation. . . . Eight [hospitals] were provided for by Foreign Red Cross Societies and seven were mobilized by the Ethiopian Red Cross, or worked under its wings. These hospitals practically formed the entire modern medical service of the Ethiopian army."[15]

Sixteen ERC units from various countries served in the Abyssinian war theater. Countries represented included Egypt (headed by Prince Ismail Daoud), the Netherlands, Norway, and Finland (headed by 70-year-old Professor Faltin). Ethiopia itself provided two units, which were Unit Number Five, headed by Dr. Belau, and Unit Number Six with Dr. Mazarosh in charge. SIM contributed Unit Number Four, led by Dr. Hooper, a Canadian, who was assisted by Alan Webb, Allen Smith from Britain, and Alf Roke from New Zealand.[16] Another Canadian, Dr. Roberts, eventually joined Unit Four. This unit was assisted by dozens of Ethiopian support personnel such as ambulance drivers, over one hundred stretcher bearers, dressers, cooks, and orderlies. Unit Number Four was assigned to the southern sector and spent most of its time at Negellie, Ras Desta Damtew's advance base.

SIM Unit Number Four was only one of four Red Cross units staffed by mission agencies. Medical personnel from the Swedish Evangelical Mission supplied staff for Unit Number Two, and Unit Number Three was staffed by the Norwegian Lutheran Mission. Unit Number One, staffed by the United Presbyterian Mission and headed by Dr. Robert Hockman of Wheaton, Illinois, deserves special mention. Hockman had been called to Ethiopia from his mission base in Egypt. At Unit Number One he had a large working force, many of whom were health assistants from the Addis Ababa George Memorial Hospital. There seemed to be overstaffing, so Hockman sent half of them back to Addis Ababa, keeping the best, especially native converts, who usually stood up to arduous camp life better than the ordinary recruit enlisted in Addis Ababa. Hockman's death was the first tragedy that the ERC experienced. It occurred while Unit Number One was located at Dugahbur in the Ogaden. Ever fearless, he was unloading an unexploded bomb that had been dropped by an Italian plane, seeking to make it safe when it went off, and in ten minutes the young missionary was dead. His body

---

15. Blaudendistel, *Between Bombs and Good Intentions*, 305.

16. See Ralph Hooper, "With the Red Cross in Ethiopia," SIMIA, EA-1-82, File 18. His 31-page account covers the period November 1935–January 1936. It is a graphic story of traveling south of Addis Ababa, where there was no all-season road, to assist the Ras Desta's Patriotic Army.

was brought to Addis Ababa by air, and as Dr. Cremer, Fred Russell, and Lambie lifted the corpse out of the plane, they began to realize how awful war is. They sorely grieved for his wife and child at their mission base back in Egypt.[17]

Additional tragedies were inflicted on the ERC by the Fascist Italian military. Sydney Brown of the ICRC reported on the wanton destruction of the Swedish Red Cross Unit at Melka Dida: "I cannot say how dejected I am about the fate of our Swedish friends. Even the Great War of 1914–1918 did not witness such atrocities against the Red Cross . . . barbaric actions carried out by a Great Power [Italy] which we previously counted as one of the most civilized."[18] Dr. Marcel Junod, also from the ICRC, commented further, "It was obvious that the Swedish ambulance unit—the only source of any assistance for that whole unfortunate southern army—had been deliberately destroyed."[19]

A further agony was the loss of two SIM missionaries' lives. SIM Red Cross Unit Number Four, under the direction of SIM's Dr. Hooper, was providing medical assistance to Ras Dasta's retreating army in Sidamo. In order to replenish Dr. Hooper's medical supplies, on March 18, 1936, Dr. Lambie assigned Cliff Mitchell and Tom Devers to transport a supply of medicine by mule caravan from Addis Ababa to Yerga Alem, via Soddo. After completing their mission, Mitchell and Devers decided on May 7 to trek back to Addis Ababa. Two days later as they were returning through the Arussi desert along with a party of twenty well-armed Amharas, they were ambushed by several hundred mounted Arsi warriors, who cruelly murdered the missionaries.[20] Later Lambie was to write, "The mystery of suffering and the blessedness of the fellowship of suffering is a secret that God reveals to His people and somehow if we take it rightly . . . it seems good. Nothing is really sweeter than the fellowship of Christ's suffering if we take it rightly."[21] The deaths of Devers and Mitchell, two stalwart SIM personnel, caused deep sorrow within the entire SIM family. Further, following the May 2, 1936,

17. "Medical Missionary Heroes: Malaku Bayen, Robert Hockman, and Winifred (nee Thompson) Hockman," 4.

18. Getachew Bekele, "Origin and Development of the ERCS," in *Ethiopian Red Cross Society: 1935–1985*, 16.

19. Getachew Bekele, "Origin and Development of the ERCS," in *Ethiopian Red Cross Society: 1935–1985*, 16.

20. The demise of these two missionaries came as a heavy blow to Lambie, who felt responsible for their deaths. See Lambie, "Record of Disaster," May 15, 1936, SIMIA, EA-1-82, File 2. Also see Myrtle Mitchell (wife of Cliff Mitchell), letter to "Praying Friends," 1936, SIMIA, EA-3.

21. Lambie, letter to "Praying Friends," 1936, SIMIA, EA-3.

exit from Addis Ababa of the emperor and his official cabinet, law and order began to break down throughout the Abyssinian countryside, resulting in intertribal fighting and wholesale murder.

Not all members of the ERC committee in Addis Ababa were enthusiastic about the religious commitment of the four units staffed by missions. Dr. Hooper, for example, had gained a reputation for his evangelistic preaching while on duty with the ERC. ICRC committee member Sidney Brown wrote with tongue in cheek of Dr. Hooper's field hospital in Sidamo that Hooper "was more interested in disseminating and distributing Bibles for cash . . . than to take care of the wounded."[22] That Hooper had previously conducted evangelistic meetings in a hired hotel ballroom in Addis Ababa was no doubt known to the ICRC representatives. These meetings, where hundreds of people heard the gospel, were such a success that eventually the Ethiopian officials ruled that such religious meetings could not again be convened in an Addis Ababa hotel.[23]

The logistics of forwarding supplies and equipment from Addis Ababa to each of the sixteen ERC units were demanding. Much detailed organizing in a crisis situation was required. Unit Number Two was staffed by a German army doctor together with a young Greek doctor. Unit Number Three was headed by a skilled Austrian surgeon. Lambie, somewhat overwhelmed by their demands, commented, "These all had to have literally everything from operating tents and stretchers and motor transport down to the humble safety-pin and the amount of detail involved in outfitting them can hardly be imagined."[24]

Lambie commented that the British Ambulance Service with Dr. John Melly in charge was the finest of all sixteen Red Cross Units.[25] Melly, an Oxford graduate, who later studied medicine at Liverpool, initially came to Ethiopia in 1934 to launch a medical school in Addis Ababa. In October 1935, while he was in England to raise funds for the medical school, war broke out in Ethiopia. When a public appeal was made in England to raise funds for an Ethiopian Red Cross Unit, the appeal for the British Ambulance Service received a generous response. Upon Melly's eventual arrival in Ethiopia, the equipment was sufficient for not one, but two British Red

22. Sidney H. Brown, "Report to ICRC," 10, cited in Baudendistel, *Between Bombs and Good Intentions*, 38.

23. Lambie, *Doctor without a Country*, 210–11.

24. Lambie, "Report and Critique of the Ethiopian Red Cross," June 12, 1936, 1, SIMIA, EA-1-83, File 17.

25. See the one-page complimentary biography of Andre John Maynard Melly, 1898–1936, in Baudendistel, *Beyond Bombs and Good Intentions*, 93. His life is aptly summarized, "Even more, Melly seemed to have lived in order to die in Ethiopia."

Cross units. The units were equipped with seventeen new Bedford trucks that were provided with special tires for going through swamps, a repair car, and a car for Melly—along with the latest medical equipment. The British Red Cross units recruited dozens of hospital orderlies from Kenya and British Somaliland. The British Ambulance Service had an immense amount of stores and spared no expense in getting the best of everything. Unfortunately, British Unit One was severely bombed by the Italian Air Force north of Dessie even though large Red Cross flags were visible.[26] Melly not only served in a British Red Cross Unit in the Ogaden but also with the second British Red Cross Unit in Dessie and surrounding area, giving medical assistance to troops fighting with Emperor Haile Sellassie.[27]

Despite taking unusual risks to provide medical assistance to the wounded, Melly survived the bombing of British Unit One. He died, however, during the chaos that occurred May 2–5, 1936, in Addis Ababa. His demise was poignantly described by several of his friends. George Steer, a British war correspondent, wrote, "A drunk in khaki stuck his revolver into Melly's ribs outside Ido's ruined bar, and shot him through the lung. A fearful wound. The blood poured through his jacket as he lay back in the driver's cab and [Mr.] Gatward accelerated to the hospital. I liked Melly immensely. . . . If there had not been a Melly there would have been no British [Red Cross] unit."[28]

A medical colleague of Melly's described the fatal shooting:

> At approximately 10 a.m. [May 3] Dr. Melly had decided to take a convoy of three lorries to collect wounded. . . . The convoy consisted of Dr. Melly, Mr. Gatward and Mr. de Halpert with approximately three armed native personnel in each lorry. . . . Mr. Gatward described the incident as follows, "We saw a man on the road . . . who appeared wounded. . . . I turned round to call Dr. Melly and was just in time to see a man thrust a revolver into the cab and shoot Dr. Melly. The latter collapsed on the seat and shouted to be taken back quickly to our hospital. . . . It was at 9 p.m. on this evening [May 5] that Dr. Melly died."[29]

The entire ERC personnel, both Abyssinians and expatriates, deeply mourned the death of Dr. John Melly, one of their heroes. His interpreter, Ato Werkou, said it well: "He was a true lover of the Gospel of Jesus

26. Lambie, *Doctor without a Country*, 243.

27. Lambie, *Doctor without a Country*, 242.

28. Steer, *Caesar in Abyssinia*, 388.

29. Nelson and Sullivan, *John Melly of Ethiopia*, 260–65.

Christ. . . . He was sympathetic for the poor and mostly for the wounded and suffering."[30]

As executive secretary of the ERC, Dr. Lambie faced a number of conundrums and delicate issues related to personnel. For example, a Lieutenant Colonel Georges Argyropolous, a very well-educated medical officer in the Greek army, was supposed to be in charge of the non-existent Abyssinian army medical service. Lambie commented, "The Colonel had a magnificent uniform and for all I know was an excellent doctor, but he would not leave Addis Ababa. He said his contract forbade it. As the war was not fought in Addis Ababa, the Colonel had nothing to do. He always came to staff meetings and was always treated with deference, although he had little or no voice in anything."[31]

Difficulties in communication were a definite hindrance to efficient operation of the Ethiopian Red Cross. Had the Abyssinian government permitted it to establish its own lines of communication, it could have done much better, but permission was refused. The government would not allow the units to be equipped each with its own radio sending outfit, nor would it let the ERC establish a pony express for delivery of weekly letters. The main reason for these refusals was that the central Abyssinian officials feared that the Fascists might sabotage the ERC transmission units. Red Cross communications were so unsatisfactory that toward the end of April 1936, the ERC central command in Addis Ababa did not know the whereabouts of many of its ambulances until they returned to Addis Ababa or were captured by the Italians.[32]

Baudendistel, who had years of experience with the ICRC in various countries, carefully studied the destruction caused by Italian bombing of the Ethiopian Red Cross hospital units. The field units were bombed even though they were clearly identified with large Red Cross flags. He stated, "The party which claimed it was bringing civilization to a retrograde country was using uncivilized means to achieve the goal."[33] The ERC, under Lambie's guidance as well as that of the Addis Ababa ERC committee, did what it could to meet the overwhelming medical needs of the Ethiopian army. Still, the Abyssinian patriots were at a great disadvantage in their attempt to oppose the Italian war machine. The final report of the British Red Cross Unit summed up the situation for all of the ERC units:

30. Nelson and Sullivan, *John Melly of Ethiopia*, 277.

31. Lambie, *Doctor without a Country*, 233.

32. Lambie, *Doctor without a Country*, 238.

33. Baudendistel, *Between Bombs and Good Intentions*, 162.

Together with other ambulance units in Ethiopia some measure of relief was afforded to a suffering people. Unfortunately, the demand far exceeded the supply. Many battles were fought by the Ethiopians in sectors where on their side no [Red Cross] ambulance units of any kind were present, and thousands must have died who with adequate medical treatment might have been saved.[34]

After leading the ERC operations for eight months, Lambie divided the Red Cross workers into two categories. Classification 1: "Doctors who are old soldiers. These are accustomed to shell fire and privation and are accustomed to . . . all the dangers and privations and shocks." Classification 2: "The ones who had a real live faith in the Lord Jesus Christ as their Saviour and Lord and in whose service they were able to go through it all with a smile and come through the hardest times almost unruffled. . . . Better than any known nerve sedative is a real vital faith in our Saviour."[35]

Writing of the mix of ERC volunteers, Baudendistel summarizes:

It was, indeed, an unusual lot of people who worked for the Red Cross field hospitals in Ethiopia. It was a mix of the best and the worst humanity had to offer—not uncommon under such circumstances. Idealists worked with opportunists, the noble hearted with the vile, the generous with the self-interested, the courageous with the indecisive and the strong with the weak.[36]

Early in the war Lambie had asked the government to acquire a large supply of gas masks, but they hesitated to take any steps toward procurement. When the news that gas was being used first reached the Ethiopian military overseers, they were unprepared; by then it was too late to get masks from anywhere but Europe. Instead of doing that, however, those in authority insisted on ordering them from Japan, where they were cheaper. This meant more delay. Apparently, the masks never did arrive.

In order to assist in directing the war front against the Italians, one of the last things his majesty did before leaving for Dessie in November 1935 was to give the ERC the large Fokker airplane that was in his personal possession, purchased several years earlier. With the Swedish Ambulance Unit was a young aviator, Count Karl Gustav von Rosen, who had flown a small

34. Cited from Baudendistel, *Between Bombs and Good Intentions*, 97.

35. Lambie, "Report and Critique of the Ethiopian Red Cross," June 12, 1936, SIMIA, EA-1-83, File 17. War correspondent George Steer, no evangelical, commented, "The most indefatigable people I met in Ethiopia were the missionaries" (*Caesar in Abyssinia*, 366).

36. Baudendistel, *Between Bombs and Good Intentions*, 82.

plane from Europe to Ethiopia for ERC use. Unfortunately, the small plane had proved unable to cope in the high altitudes of Abyssinia, but the Fokker was a great success. Lambie comments, "Young von Rosen, a Swede, was a real airman, courageous and resourceful; on the several occasions when I flew with him, he seemed to me all a pilot should be. . . . The wings on [the pilots'] uniforms usually cover hearts that are not only true but that are simple and kind."[37]

Buying medical supplies in Addis Ababa proved to be a challenge, and Lambie was frustrated in his attempts to procure medicine in amounts large enough to meet the needs. For example, to provide an adequate supply of quinine for an army of 200,000 men in the low-lying Boran and Ogaden districts would have cost more than US$1,000 per day. The Red Cross budget did not have sufficient funds. Also, each patriot soldier needed vermifuge once a month, the commonest remedy being oleoresin of male fern, a dose of which cost five or ten cents—another $10,000 a month for getting free of tapeworm. Emetin for amoebic dysentery was equally expensive. Lambie wrote: "We never got within miles of supplying their needs."[38]

Tumultuous Days in Addis Ababa, April–May, 1936

During Lambie's final days in Abyssinia, he wrote, "By the end of April, 1936, it was evident that the game was up. The Ethiopians were defeated on all fronts. The airplanes and poison gas had broken their morale."[39] Charlotte Lambie wrote to her daughter Betty Rees in Britain, "Many wounded and weary soldiers are coming back from the North these days. The [Ethiopian] Red Cross has asked all the missions—American, Swedish, SIM, BCMS, to cooperate in giving food, medicines, etc. Bread is being bought up all over town."[40] Locations within Addis Ababa were designated as feeding centers, and tents were erected for the soldiers who straggled into the city. Adequate food was provided, and doctors and nurses were assigned to the feeding centers. In a single day as many as six thousand returnees were fed. First aid was also administered and, when possible, those in need were hospitalized. After giving the soldiers something to eat, missionaries took advantage of the big crowds to hold gospel meetings.[41]

---

37. Lambie, *Doctor without a Country*, 238.

38. Lambie, *Doctor without a Country*, 241.

39. Lambie, *Doctor without a Country*, 244.

40. Charlotte Lambie, letter to Betty Rees, April 27, 1936, MHSC. See also Duff, *Cords of Love*, 312.

41. Charlotte Lambie, letter to Betty Rees, April 27, 1936, MHSC.

But, as usual, some persons took exception to using a feeding center or a Red Cross field hospital for missionary activity. Lucie Odier of the ERC Commission responded to the antireligious bias: "In our opinion, the Red Cross does not need to show that it has no religion. Quite on the contrary. In almost every country it works in close cooperation with all religious agencies pursuing humanitarian goals. It thereby affirms that it respects all religions, and it is tolerant, to the exclusion of no denomination."[42]

Charlotte Lambie commented to her daughter, "I wish this unrighteous war would cease. . . . Addis Ababa is full of wounded and retreating soldiers, who jammed the roads and whose condition was pitiable in the extreme."[43]

During the final days of chaos in the city at the end of April 1936, Dr. and Mrs. Lambie had to deal with the question of providing medical assistance to a small staff of Ethiopian government officials assigned to Gorei. The emperor and his military were in the north attempting to hold back the Fascist advance. Abyssinian officials based in the capital felt that an authentic government presence should be retained somewhere in the country. They decided to move the seat of government to Gorei, some 250 miles west of Addis Ababa. Whether or not this relocation of the government was implemented is debatable.[44] Lambie wrote:

> The Ethiopian [Abyssinian] Government discussed moving the capital to Gorei, where a British Consulate was based, and asked me to go along as physician. If the Italians entered [Addis Ababa] it was evident that not much Red Cross work could go on. Foreigners were fleeing Addis Ababa by every train. . . . There was no other physician available, so we decided it was our duty to go with the Government to Gorei and Charlotte and I immediately commenced to make preparations and to get six-months' supply of stores together. We did not go to Gorei. . . . The last day of April [1936] His Majesty suddenly appeared at Shola, the other side of Entoto, five miles from Addis Ababa. He refused to go to Gorei. He was discouraged, tired and hopeless."[45]

Haile Sellassie was now back in Addis Ababa, but not for long. Pandemonium broke out in the city after the emperor and his official entourage

42. Lucie Odier, member of the International Committee Red Cross, cited in Baudendistel, *Between Bombs and Good Intentions*, 40.

43. Charlotte Lambie, letter to Betty Rees, April 27, 1936, MHSC.

44. According to Haile Sellassie (*My Life and Ethiopia's Progress*, 291), official plans had already been made: "Hence, as previously planned, let the government move to Gorei and let Bitwadid Walde Tsadeq stay there acting as Regent."

45. Lambie, *Doctor without a Country*, 245.

secretly departed from the capital by train on May 2, 1936.[46] Historians have asserted that with Haile Sellassie's departure, "the Ethiopian [Abyssinian] Government ceased to exist."[47] Regardless, the deposed emperor made his way to Geneva, where he delivered a speech to the League of Nations, pleading the cause of Abyssinia.[48] Was there indeed a legitimate Ethiopian Government in Gorei after the emperor departed? This is a confusing aspect of Ethiopian history that remains unresolved. According to John Spencer, an American legal advisor to the emperor, "The Ethiopian delegation [to the League of Nations] demonstrated that there was indeed a government operating in Gorei under the ex-president of the Senate, Wolde Tsadik."[49]

When the Fascists finally drove their tanks into Addis Ababa on May 5, 1936—with their soldiers marching behind—order was somewhat restored. Lambie writes, "That night the Italian army came in. We could hear the thousands of trucks and caterpillars [tanks] long before they came. The night throbbed with the sound of them. The shooting that night was if anything more intense, but the next day it quieted down and we were able to go to town and see what dreadful carnage had taken place."[50]

Around May 8, Lambie was called to appear before the Italian officials to report on the whereabouts of the existing ERC field units. The Italian High Command and other officials were well aware of Dr. Lambie's prominent role in the ERC. Because all the records and medicines worth thousands of dollars contained in the ERC bureau had been destroyed by looting or fire, all that Lambie could show the Italian officials was his daily diary that he kept on his person. War correspondent Steer reported, "When Bentinck arrived at the Red Cross Headquarters to see if the records could be saved, he found that the place had been housebroken already."[51] All ERC

---

46. Lambie wrote, "The ministers left in Addis Ababa wanted to move the Government out to Western Abyssinia [Gorei] but to this the King objected and as everyone knows, stole away first to Palestine then to England and Geneva." See Lambie, "Record of Disaster," May 15, 1936, SIMIA, EA-1-82, File 2.

47. Baudendistel, *Between Bombs and Good Intentions*, 291.

48. Mockler, *Haile Selassie's War*, 151. The emperor concluded his speech with the question, "What reply shall I have to take back to my people?"

49. Spencer, *Ethiopia at Bay*, 79. While still in Addis Ababa, Spencer recorded, "As to the move to Gorei, no attempt was made to implement the procedure, presumably because the government was now awaiting the return [from the north of the country] of the Emperor," 59. Mockler, *Haile Selassie's War*, 163–65, states that the presence of a British Consulate in Gorei, with international communications, would have made the site a legitimate location for a Provisional Ethiopian Government. On September 29, 1936, the British Consulate in Gorei was officially closed.

50. Lambie, *Doctor without a Country*, 247–48.

51. Steer, *Caesar in Abyssinia*, 393.

office files and equipment were littered on the floor. Although the Italians were aware that Lambie had previously written strong letters to the London *Times* and other journals accusing the Italians of bombing ERC units in the war zones as well as of having sprayed poison gas (yperite) on innocent Ethiopian victims, the Fascist military treated him cordially.[52] The Lambies remained in Addis Ababa until August 21, 1936, albeit under stress from Italian henchmen who treated them as spies.

Thus ended Dr. Lambie's somewhat inglorious episode (September 20, 1935 to May 5, 1936) as executive secretary of the ERC. During these eight months he experienced disappointment, misunderstanding, and, no doubt, feelings of defeat in war-devastated Abyssinia. To the best of his ability he sought to serve wounded soldiers and suffering patriots by means of the sixteen Red Cross units. Without doubt, he and the ERC were able to provide some measure of relief to some of the injured. But Lambie was aware that thousands died on the war front without adequate medical treatment. For all his sacrificial service to the ERC, Lambie received no official thanks from his beleaguered chief commander, Emperor Haile Sellassie, who arrived in Addis Ababa at the end of April, exhausted and forlorn, from the northern battlefront. Steer wrote, "Horror and alarm struck the people when the Emperor alighted. The face always sensitive, was haunted now. . . . The eyes seemed to have lost their quiet resolution. . . . The steps and carriage were no longer resilient."[53] It was a defeated monarch who boarded the train for exile on May 2, 1936. Lambie was left in turbulent Addis Ababa, no doubt questioning whether his contribution through the Ethiopian Red Cross had indeed furthered "the welfare of the Kingdom of God."[54] Dr. and Mrs. Lambie finally left Addis Ababa by train and reached Djibouti on August 21, 1936. They then made their way by ship to England to visit their daughter Betty and her children before continuing on to the United States.[55]

52. Lambie, *Doctor without a Country*, 249. In a letter to the London *Times*, Lambie "reminded Londoners that Charing Cross might one day be gassed as easily," March 24, 1935, cited in Steer, *Caesar in Abyssinia*, 282.

53. Steer, *Caesar in Abyssinia*, 356.

54. Lambie, "Record of Disaster," 1, May 15, 1936, SIMIA, EA-1-82, File 2.

55. Charlotte Lambie, letter to Betty Rees, August 28, 1936: "Djibouti is full of spies and other Italians," MHSC.

11

Thomas Lambie and Rowland Bingham: Trekking Together in Africa

*And Jonathan made a covenant with David
because he loved him as himself.*

1 SAMUEL 18:3 (NIV)

THOMAS LAMBIE AND ROWLAND Bingham traversed hundreds of miles together—in 1930, 1934, and 1937—by mule and horse in Abyssinia and by vehicle in Sudan, as well as sharing trans-Atlantic flights and traveling together by train and ship. Their journeys were for the purpose of furthering the work of God's kingdom in Africa, and in this chapter large sections of that story will be given in their own words. Months of shared experience of the tropical sun by day, cold nights, thirst, hunger, and malaria served to deepen the bond between the two mission leaders.

Around 1929 Lambie invited Rowland Bingham to visit Abyssinia. Earlier in that year Bingham was anticipating crossing Africa from Nigeria to Kenya by car. Afterward Bingham wrote regarding plans for the trip:

> We knew motor roads were being extended [across Africa] in many directions under British, French and Belgian rule, and that what was impossible only five years before was fast becoming feasible. It was hard to get any information that would be satisfactory, but we [Guy Playfair and Rowland Bingham] finally decided to attempt it. We wrote Nigeria of our coming in the

Fall and to Ethiopia we sent word that if we succeeded in crossing the continent they might look for us at the southern border
of Ethiopia in early March [1930].[1]

Lambie opens his account:

For months we had been expecting our leader [Bingham], who
was visiting Nigeria. . . . He was planning to drive across Africa
in a Ford station wagon from Lagos to Nairobi, and from there
to go by government transport to Moyale, on the southern border of Abyssinia. Mr. and Mrs. Rhoad and I were to meet him
in Moyale and bring him back to Addis Ababa, visiting mission
stations on the way.[2]

In March 1930 the Lambie/Rhoad party waited three weeks in hot and
inhospitable Moyale on the border between Kenya and Abyssinia for Bingham to arrive. Finally on March 25 he arrived aboard a Kenyan supply truck
from Nairobi. Early rains had turned the heavy clay soil into a quagmire,
and at times twelve strong bullock teams were required to pull the truck out
of the mire. Bingham's clothes were streaked with mud but he was in good
spirits. Lambie wrote:

Mr. Rhoad, George [Rhoad's son], and I went over at once to
welcome our beloved friend and General Director. He indeed
gave traces of having a long and hard journey, as he was much
travel stained, but very cheerful. We were so glad to see him that
I think if it had not been for the presence of the English officials
we would have fallen on his neck and wept.[3]

He continued:

It is so good to have Rev. Bingham with us. He is so helpful,
and his counsel is always so sagacious, and his experience so
worldwide that one feels proud to be associated with such a man
in service for God. . . .
    We are praying that his visit will be the thing used of God
to open doors for us into all these southern areas to which no
missionary has as yet come. . . .

1. Bingham, "Across Africa by Mule and Motor," 260.

2. Lambie, *Boot and Saddle*, 123. Playfair, *Our Trip across Africa*, 1–19, gives a short
account of crossing the continent with Bingham.

3. Lambie, "How We Met Mr. Bingham, and Accompanied Him to Addis Ababa," 1,
SIMIA, EA-1-82, File 19. This 31-page typescript covers Lambie's 1930 mule trek from
Soddo, Wolaitta, (January 25, 1930) to Moyale (March 4) and then on to Addis Ababa
(May 25).

The three Rhoads slept inside the one tent, and Mr. Bingham and I were out under the veranda. It seems that Mr. Bingham and I snored so that the dogs must have imagined the camp was being attacked by some strange animals. . . .

Mr. Bingham is proving an exceptionally good traveller and is so entertaining with his anecdotes of Christian work and Christian leaders all over the world. . . .

We had such a good day in camp at Arboar [Borana] last Sabbath [April 5, 1930]. Mr. Bingham gave us missionaries [Dr. Lambie and the Rhoads] a Bible reading from Matthew, proving to us conclusively that Matthew is not, as some people would almost place it, an appendix to the Old Testament or a Gospel especially written for the Jews, but that it is indeed a real living Gospel to Jew and Gentile.

Writing from Dilla on April 15, Lambie added:

Had a long journey to this place in the Darassa country. It is indeed a beautiful country. . . . There are immense groves of a wild plant or *ensette* as it is called, and large coffee orchards. Coffee does wonderfully well in this region, and the hillsides are simply studded with little hamlets and villages where lives a large population. We reached here just as a large market was gathering. Mr. Bingham took some moving pictures of it. We were a great source of amusement to the large market crowd, who acted as if they had never seen white people before.[4]

The party of Bingham, Rhoads, and Lambie arrived in Soddo on April 19, 1930. On the following day, Bingham conducted a three-day spiritual life conference for thirteen SIM workers at Soddo. Lambie summarized Bingham's impact on the SIM mission family, "At every station, Dr. Bingham gave us most helpful messages from God's Word and his own experiences— messages that some of us at least will never forget. He had an autoharp with him, and with his musical, if somewhat husky voice, he would teach us songs and choruses."[5]

---

4. Lambie, "How We Met Mr. Bingham, and Accompanied Him to Addis Ababa," 7, SIMIA, EA-1-82, File 19.

5. Lambie, *Boot and Saddle in Africa*, 135.

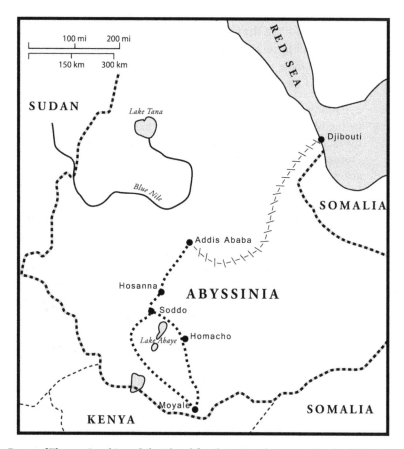

Route of Thomas Lambie and the Rhoad family to Moyale to meet Rowland Bingham

On May 25 Lambie accompanied Bingham by train to Djibouti. Together they traveled by ship up the Red Sea, through the Suez Canal, and finally on to Marseilles. At Marseilles Bingham decided they should fly, first to Paris and then to London, where he had important meetings. En route to Paris, while flying aboard a small aircraft through some rather violent thunderstorms, Lambie became quite airsick and began retching. From across the aisle, Bingham read a scripture verse to Lambie: "Asa encouraged his heart in the Lord." Lambie responded by writing on a scrap of paper, "Dr. Bingham, it's not my heart, it's my tummy that needs encouraging."[6]

As related in chapter 9 (see map there), the year 1934 saw the two men traveling together again. In 1932 Lambie had informed Bingham of an invitation from Ras Kassa for SIM to launch mission work in the north

6. Lambie, *Boot and Saddle in Africa*, 138.

of Ethiopia. Lambie's report caught the attention of SIM's entrepreneurial leader, who reasoned that the invitation might be a "Macedonian call." But as he realized, other factors also needed to be considered before attempting to plant churches there within the sacred territory of the established Abyssinian Orthodox Church. For example, they could expect to encounter

> opposition to entering a country [province] already occupied by the old State Church; and especially to entering Lalibella, the sacred city of the north, to which pilgrims gathered by the thousands every year at the great festivals. And so we postponed action till such a time as we might join our veteran leader [Dr. Lambie] in a tour of investigation.[7]

It was anticipated that the northward leg of an exploratory journey would require at least a month. The young California ornithologist Dean Blanchard, who accompanied the experienced missionary party, offered to cover the costs of the mule trek north.[8] The addition of the ornithologist placed an added burden on Charlotte Lambie, the chief provider of nourishing food three times a day. Lambie praised his wife for her thorough planning and provisions.

> We never started off without our bowl of hot oatmeal porridge, coffee, jam and toast; bacon and eggs too, if we had them. This would be before daybreak. We would ride on until about eleven o'clock; then sit under some trees and have a lunch of bread and cold meat, hard boiled eggs, hot tea and cake, or a tin of fruit. While we had this our caravan passed us and would go on to the camping site and get the mules unloaded, by which time we would arrive and help in putting up tents and getting camp in order, cots made up, and mule lines staked off. Then came an hour's sleep, which would bring us up to half past three, when we usually had hot baths in our canvas bathtub and a cup of tea and bread and butter, with a warm supper just after nightfall.[9]

Along the journey north, Bingham expressed some misgivings about the northern venture. Would the mission have the necessary finances for this new venture? Would skilled medical personnel volunteer for the

---

7. Bingham, "Lure of Lalibella, Ethiopia," 300.

8. Dean Blanchard's report of his research on bird life in northern Ethiopia is located in the Huntington Library, San Marino, California. See Lambie, *Doctor without a Country*, 221.

9. Lambie, *Doctor without a Country*, 217.

envisioned leprosy medical work in Lalibela? He asked for the prayers of the home constituency, "that we might be rightly guided."[10]

Back in 1930 in the lower altitude of southern Ethiopia, Bingham had experienced trekking with some ease. But traveling north of Addis Ababa presented special challenges.

> February days were desperately trying, when we had first to climb down the rocky zigzag trail, four thousand feet, then rise up two thousand; then drop two thousand to the water level, and the same day scale the heights another 4,000 feet to bring us back to our nine thousand altitude. . . . Sometimes we climbed down paths where we could not trust our nimble-footed mules, and in the ascent for long stretches we hadn't the heart to sit in the saddle, even if they were able to rise with us on their backs over the rocks. . . . As I sit in my tent door and write, the glories of a beautiful sunrise are before my eyes, reminding one of the day when for this old world's woes "the Son of Righteousness shall arise with healing in His wings."[11]

After three weeks of strenuous trekking, the SIM pilgrims and Blanchard arrived at Lalibela with its eleven famous rock-hewn churches. Lambie wrote:

> They are not as famous as they deserve to be, due to their isolation and difficulty in approach, so when we saw them they had been visited by scarcely a score of Europeans. The first record of them was sent to Europe by Alvarez, a Portuguese monk, who visited them at a very early date [ca. 1520–30], and who, after briefly describing their wonders, says that if he continued he would only be disbelieved.[12]

Soon after the mission entrepreneurs arrived at Lalibela, they began seeking out possible locations for a mission station. They soon found what they thought would make an excellent mission station site, a setting that also met with approval from the man whom Ras Kassa had appointed to assist them in their search. Bingham enthusiastically reported:

> The [site] selected just a little way out of town, was beautiful beyond description. Situated on a terraced slope behind which the mountains rose up for a thousand feet, it dropped off at the

---

10. Bingham, "From Aden to Addis Ababa and Beyond," 193.

11. Bingham, "From Aden to Addis Ababa and Beyond," 194. See also Lambie's account of the journey to Lalibela, "Abyssinia: The Road of the King's Son," 290.

12. Lambie, *Doctor without a Country*, 218–19.

foot to a beautiful valley a thousand feet or more below. On either side of this site were two beautiful streams of water running strong at the close of the dry season. . . . Each was skirted by trees of all sizes right up to the majesty of an immense wild fig tree. . . . Here we knelt on the Sunday afternoon and dedicated the site to the Lord.[13]

Lambie commented more cautiously, "The priests . . . did not seem very enthusiastic about our coming. This was to be expected."[14]

Taking leave of Lalibela, the missionaries journeyed to Debra Tabor and Lake Tana, which they found to be equally beautiful. Lambie expands on the site:

The cold, wind-swept, treeless plateau of Wollo [Province] gave place to rolling country with frequent bits of forest and stream which were really charming. At Debra Tabor was Ras Kassa's oldest son, Wanda Wossan, who received us most cordially and invited us to open work in his country as well. Gondar, the old capital [of Abyssinia], was spoken of as a desirable Mission location. Debra Tabor itself is a large town of ten or twelve thousand people, with Greek and Indian shopkeepers, and a very productive surrounding country.[15]

The explorers then made their way through beautiful forest, river, lake, and plain in the province of Gojjam, where they finally reached Debra Markos. As mentioned in chapter 9, SIM was invited to open work at both Debra Tabor and Debra Markos.

The journey through the north had taken the Lambie/Bingham party some three months. Because Charlotte was not feeling well after such demanding mule travel, in April Lambie sent a message via Ras Emeru's radio to ask if the emperor could send his plane to fly Charlotte and Rowland Bingham from Debra Markos back to Addis Ababa. Because the plane had room for three passengers, all three of the Lambie/Bingham party arrived back in Addis Ababa following a mere one-hour and twenty-minute flight. "As we gazed down on the mighty [Blue] Nile in its mile-deep gorge, we congratulated ourselves on being able to fly over it instead of painfully climbing down and then even more painfully climbing up its precipitous sides."[16]

Prior to returning to Canada, Bingham once again toured the southern SIM stations. It is worth noting that on this tour he heard some

13. Bingham, "Lure of Lalibella, Ethiopia," 302.

14. Lambie, *Doctor without a Country*, 219.

15. Lambie, *Doctor without a Country*, 219–20.

16. Lambie, *Doctor without a Country*, 222.

missionaries criticize Lambie for locating missionaries on properties without having obtained definite contracts or title deeds. Apparently around 1916 Abyssinia enacted a law forbidding foreigners to buy land from Abyssinians. The reason for the new regulation was that previously enterprising Greeks and Armenians had acquired large holdings for their personal gain. But the implications of the law made it stressful for missionaries outside of Addis Ababa, residing on rented land, to carry on stable mission work. Minute 28 of the February 1934 SIM Abyssinian Field Council addressed obtaining legal papers for SIM stations. "It was agreed that Dr. Lambie had done everything possible in the endeavour to obtain papers to protect our station[s], but that with the present governmental attitude, it was most difficult, if not prejudicial to the work, to press for written documents."[17] A week later, Lambie took Bingham to visit the American minister, His Excellency Addison Southard. When Bingham inquired about getting land contracts finalized by the Abyssinian officials, the American minister responded, "It is impossible to get the Ethiopian to commit himself on paper. . . . We have tried to get a paper for the property we Americans rent from them here in Addis Ababa, but we cannot get it. I do not think Dr. Lambie should be criticized for his failure when we legations fail to do what we attempt."[18] After the meeting with the US official, Bingham's concern about indefinite contract deeds was somewhat allayed.

Before taking leave, Bingham summarized their trek to northern Abyssinia.

> We have had the joy of seeing the beginning of the harvest of souls in Ethiopia [Abyssinia], and in participating with our beloved field director Dr. Lambie (and Mrs. Lambie), in prospecting our lines of advance into the great north, and in knowing that ere we reach home [in Canada] our first party is already posted at that first station [Lalibela] in that hitherto unoccupied territory.[19]

Soon after their return from the north, however, Lambie seemed to sense some ambivalence on Bingham's part. When he questioned him about the advisability of launching mission stations in the north, Bingham responded that he had had difficulty sleeping the previous night due to concern about that very issue. The verse that kept coming to him was Proverbs 11:24, "One man gives freely, yet gains even more; another withholds

17. SIM Abyssinia Field Council, February 8–12, 1934, Item 28, SIMIA, ME-1/A-155, File 2.

18. Lambie, *Doctor without a Country*, 222–24.

19. Bingham, "The Editor Safely Home," 304.

unduly, but comes to poverty." Bingham was committed to act on the first part of the verse—about giving freely because God will give the increase, in spite of commitments in Nigeria, French West Africa, and southern Ethiopia. Lambie affirmed: "Dr. Bingham's faith was always like that. Present faith built upon past faith in a faithful God, whose promises are faithful—Yea and Amen."[20] During 1934 SIM missionaries were based in Lalibela and Debra Markos.

Bingham and Lambie's final expedition together took place in the Anglo-Egyptian Sudan, March 14–25, 1937.[21] By this time the Italian Fascists had made the SIM missionaries feel no longer welcome in Abyssinia. The purpose of the two-week survey trip, launched from Khartoum, was to determine the feasibility of relocating former SIM missionaries from Abyssinia to work among unreached Sudanese ethnic groups residing near the Abyssinian highlands. Previously Bingham and Lambie had visited the British Foreign Office at 10 Downing Street in London to propose that SIM launch mission activity in Sudan. Official approval of their request had been graciously granted; now both were convinced of God's call for SIM to launch into the Anglo-Egyptian Sudan. Lambie wrote, "I believe we have that call. For six months now some of us have been praying about it, and the call seems to come clearer and clearer with an insistence that brooks no denial."[22]

His report of the trip stated:

> A week ago today (March 16), we started from here (Khartoum), in a Ford V8 [rented with driver] to do some exploring. We went first to a place called Wisko, which is not far from Karmuk. We went that night to Wad Medani. Dr. Bingham was very tired when we got there as he was having a go at malaria, so we did not feel we could go on the next day, but rested at a Greek hotel. Our room was pretty fair, but the sanitary conditions were terrible.[23]

The travelers continued in a northwesterly direction to Rosaires, near the Blue Nile. They then traveled in a southerly direction with the Blue Nile to their west until they came into the Inghesana Hills, which were about

20. Lambie, *Boot and Saddle in Africa*, 152.

21. The opening of chapter 13 of this volume gives further details concerning the Bingham/Lambie exploratory trip through the eastern portion of the Anglo-Egyptian Sudan. They arrived in Khartoum on March 14, 1937.

22. Lambie, "A New Challenge to the Sudan Interior Mission," 133.

23. Lambie, "Report of the Anglo-Egyptian Sudan Exploratory Trip with Dr. Bingham," March 16–25, 1937, SIMIA, KB-1-122, File 21.

2,000 feet in elevation. They found these hills a delightful place that had potential for a mission rest home. They observed streams of pure water flowing down the Inghesana Hills escarpment, a welcome sight that cheered the weary and thirsty travelers.

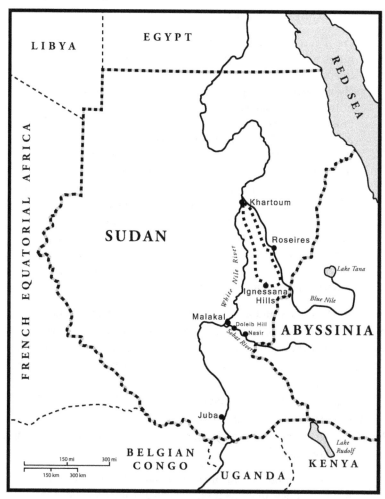

Lambie and Bingham survey eastern Sudan, 1937

Lambie continues:

> We got to Wisko about 1:00 p.m. and went into the Govern-ment Rest House which is very clean and nice and we had a good rest. The people look something like the Anuaks only bet-ter looking and finely built. It seems easy to make friends with them. They are very black and very primitive. . . . It is on the

direct Kurmuk–Khartoum Road, which is opening up to trade famously. Dozens of motor trucks are on the road day and night. I think the mission would be well received here.[24]

Soon after returning from the Anglo-Egyptian Sudan to the United States, Lambie wrote enthusiastically:

> We [Drs. Lambie and Bingham] made a trip of nine hundred miles, much of it over rough, dry-season roads, and saw some interesting sites. The new irrigation system in the Gezira is an absolute marvel of engineering skill and resourcefulness. South of this area one comes into the districts where rain crops are possible and large Arab villages line the banks of the Blue Nile. At Roseires we left the river and struck off southward towards the Inghesana Hills. . . . These hills rise up majestically from the flat plains and are only separated from the Abyssinia high lands by a comparatively narrow belt of flat country. . . . On the sides of the hills are clustered the Inghesana, from whom the hills take their names. . . . It is our plan to start in this area amongst the Inghesana in October [1937]. We wish to send some experienced missionaries [relocated from Abyssinia] at first to study the area and locate, with the cooperation with the Sudan British officials, the mission at the most strategic points.[25]

If the Fascists would no longer allow the Abyssinian SIM missionaries to remain in Abyssinia, it is evident that both Bingham and Lambie were convinced that they should be redeployed to the Anglo-Egyptian Sudan. Further, the British Foreign Office had also opened the door for SIM to venture into this new country.

Bingham and Lambie's exploratory journey of 1937 into the Anglo-Egyptian Sudan brought an end to their extended travels together. Following the trip, Bingham published a strong affirmation of Dr. Lambie's character and leadership abilities.

> Coming into our Sudan Interior Mission, the director [Lambie] of that new movement [in Abyssinia] has led in one of the strongest missionary advances of the past decade in Ethiopia, a movement that gave promise of reaching the whole country in ten years more. Now Dr. Lambie, the best known and most loved white man in the whole of Ethiopia, finds himself and his missionary co-workers being forced out of the land by the

24. Lambie, "Report of the Anglo-Egyptian Sudan Exploratory Trip with Dr. Bingham," March 16–25, 1937, SIMIA, KB-1-122, File 21.

25. Lambie, "Our New Task," 292.

combined action of both State and Church under an intolerance [the Fascists] unknown in territory ruled by any other power in Africa. Every other nation but Italy has recognized the altruistic labors of the missionary of all nationalities and permitted them to continue their work of mercy and enlightenment.[26]

The two men had a sincere and deep respect for one another based on their mutual obedience and love for their Master, Jesus Christ. When Bingham died suddenly at the end of 1942, Lambie lost a trusted and loyal colleague in Christian mission. Rowland Bingham's demise may well have been one of the factors that led Dr. Lambie to seek another mission agency through which to serve in Palestine from 1946 to 1954. That story will be told in a later chapter, but first—as related in the following four chapters—Lambie was to experience considerable stress and misunderstanding as SIM leader in both Abyssinia and Sudan.

26. Bingham, "On Ethiopia's Frontiers," 308.

12

Estrangement from Haile Sellassie

*Thus comes a sad ending to what had been a great
enterprise. It seems to have gone down to defeat
through circumstances over which we had no control.*

THOMAS A. LAMBIE, *A DOCTOR WITHOUT A COUNTRY*, 251

DR. LAMBIE INITIALLY MET Ras Tafari Makonnen in his Addis Ababa palace in 1922. The meeting took place soon after the Lambie family arrived
in the capital after trekking from Sayo, Wellega, in western Abyssinia (see
chapter 4). Their meeting began a cordial fourteen-year relationship; they
were initially bound together by the building and staffing of a new hospital
in Addis Ababa. The facility served the medical needs mainly of the Addis
Ababa population. A previous Russian medical facility was in disrepair and
was not adequately staffed. Lambie successfully built and staffed the Tafari
Makonnen Hospital/George Memorial Building under the aegis of the
United Presbyterian Mission. Up through 1926, development and construction of the hospital bonded the regent with Lambie in a unique manner.[1]
When Lambie returned to Abyssinia in 1927, he was the leader of a new
organization, the Sudan Interior Mission. That each of the two leaders now
had his own agenda in time led to tensions between them.

---

1. See Lambie, *Doctor without a Country*, 150–61, for a full account of the funding
and building of the Ras Tafari Makonnen/George Memorial Hospital in Addis Ababa.

During the political machinations of the following years, Ras Tafari was crowned as Emperor Haile Sellassie I in 1930. At times Lambie felt that he was being controlled and manipulated by the emperor, especially when permission for establishing schools and medical clinics was withheld. Their tenuous relationship was somewhat ameliorated, however, when Lambie was appointed as executive secretary of the Ethiopian Red Cross during the Italo-Ethiopian war, 1935–36.[2] At this point Lambie was in league with Emperor Haile Sellassie, who was fighting for his own life and for the entire nation against the Fascists (see chapter 10).

It appears that cracks in the relationship between Lambie and the emperor deepened on May 2, 1936. The Italian war machine was at the doorsteps of Addis Ababa, and the emperor departed from the city without notice to Lambie, fleeing in secrecy by train to Djibouti. Lambie no doubt had expected some word of appreciation from the emperor for his eight months of sacrificial and dedicated service as executive secretary of the Ethiopian Red Cross. Another incident might also hint at cleavage between the two men. Dr. and Mrs. Lambie were initially invited to join a core group of Ethiopian officials in Gorei. These officials had been sent to Gorei, in western Abyssinia, to establish a new seat for the Ethiopian government when it became clear that Addis Ababa would fall.[3] At that time the emperor was in the north with his troops doing battle with the Italian invaders. In preparation for the possible move of government, Charlotte Lambie had packed provisions for six months, but Lambie tersely records, "We did not go to Gorei."[4] One may ask whether Haile Sellassie on his return from the north had blocked the Lambies from joining the Abyssinian officials in Gorei.

Lambie wrote, "His Majesty Haile Sellassie is a broken-hearted and disillusioned man. He has taken temporary refuge in England, where he has a place at Bath. . . . The old Ethiopian [Abyssinian] nobility is broken, destroyed, save only a few that left with His Majesty."[5] His comment about Haile Sellassie and the Abyssinia leadership may well reflect his own

2. Baudendistel, *Between Bombs and Good Intentions*, 38.

3. An article in the London *Times*, May 8, 1936, substantiates this step. See Mikre-Sellassie, *Church and Missions in Ethiopia*, 64fn59. See also Richard Pankhurst, "Hakim Warkineh: Propagandist for Ethiopia at the Time of the Fascist Invasion," in *Ethiopian Studies at the End of the Second Millennium*, ed. Baye, 435–49. Hakim Warkineh comments that Ras Emeru was captured on December 16, 1936, as he was attempting "to organize an Ethiopian Government in the west of the country," 443.

4. Lambie, *Doctor without a Country*, 245.

5. Lambie, *Doctor without a Country*, 251.

thinking subsequent to the Italian army's victorious entry into Addis Ababa on May 5, 1936.

Unprecedented chaos and looting took place in Addis Ababa from May 2 through May 5 following the departure of the emperor with many of the nobility. The arrival of the Italian military brought about a measure of stability. Lambie had telegraphed the London *Times* on March 25, 1936, regarding the Fascists' use of mustard gas which contravened stipulations of the Geneva Conventions.[6] His previous condemnation of the Italians' aggression was well known, but his position after May 6 is not clear. Did he begin to vacillate? He later wrote: "The day after the Italians entered I called on the High Command and told them what we had been doing and of the Red Cross activities. I told them that although I had been against them I was not going to oppose them, but took Paul's word in Romans 13:1 as my guide, 'Resist not the powers.' They were very polite."[7]

It appears that Rowland Bingham, SIM's international director, approved of Lambie's appeasement in regard to the Fascist conquerors: "As soon as the Italians were in charge in the capital Dr. Lambie offered his services to the new rulers in any way that he could aid in the Red Cross sphere, assuring the Italian leader of the Mission's non-political principle."[8] It is not clear why Lambie capitulated to the Italian regime. Was it that he feared for his life?[9] Or was it that he hoped that SIM might continue its work in Ethiopia under the Italian regime? The latter hope, if it was such, seems to contravene what he had written to the Lambie prayer and financial supporters a year earlier: "If Italy should succeed in her desires to take the country [Ethiopia], what would result? It would result I fear as it has in Eritrea, in the expulsion of all Protestant missions and the gracious work would cease."[10] A month later, in June 1935, he had made a similar statement to a New York newspaper reporter, Josephine Rickard. About that interview, Rickard wrote: "The work which the Americans and British have

6. See also Bingham, "Italy and Ethiopia," 220, where he quotes Lambie's protest "against bombing and gassing country villages and cities of no military significance. . . . Ruthless destruction."

7. Lambie, *Doctor without a Country*, 249.

8. Bingham, "The Situation in Ethiopia," 258.

9. Charlotte Lambie, letter to daughter Betty Rees, late 1935, "They say the Italians have a 'White nigger list' whom they plan to shoot as soon as they arrive, Dr. Hamer and dad and one of the journalists is on the list," MHSC.

10. Lambie, "Letter to Prayer and Financial Supporters," May 25, 1935, sent from Buxton, England, SIMIA, EA-1-82, File 3.

been doing in Ethiopia in education, medicine and Christian ministry, Dr. Lambie fears will be barred in the event of Italian domination."[11]

SIM missionary Malcolm Forsberg expressed the views of most of his SIM colleagues concerning Lambie's unusual ambivalence, stating, "Dr. Lambie thought that by ingratiating himself with the Italians he could arrange for the continuance of the work in Ethiopia, but I deny that the Lord has to depend on disloyalty and inconsistency to maintain His work."[12] John Spencer, a young American legal advisor within the Ethiopian Ministry of Foreign Affairs, considered Lambie's "giving his hand" as a defection to the Italians.[13] Sidney Barton, the British minister in Addis Ababa, also condemned Lambie's statement to the Italians as "a pusillanimous attempt to curry favour with the Italians."[14] Regardless of what Lambie expressed to the Italian officials, he later acknowledged that it was a false hope.[15]

At the time, the Italian authorities asked Lambie to put into writing his statement about the Italian bombing of Ethiopian Red Cross trucks and mini-hospitals. This he consented to do.

> I wrote nothing but what was true, but I should not have written as I did. The Italians, I heard, made quite a lot of this letter, and gave it wide publicity. Mr. Duff, our Deputy Field Director, came to me and frankly told me that he thought I was wrong in writing as I had done, and he wanted to resign as Deputy Field Director. . . . I at once wrote a second letter to the Italians, in which I said that they made too much of my first letter.[16]

What Lambie wrote the Italians in his second letter found support among some of Lambie's SIM colleagues based in Addis Ababa. But Clarence Duff, his deputy in Addis Ababa, stated, "Sometimes his judgement or his actions proved to be unwise," and some felt that he had overstepped his authority as the mission leader.[17] Not only that, but the Fascists were keen to discredit Lambie and to drive a wedge between him and Ethiopian officialdom, especially Emperor Haile Sellassie. It was assumed that the emperor would have been informed about Lambie's letter to the Fascists.

11. Josephine G. Rickard, interview with Thomas Lambie, June 1935, 10 pp., quotation from p. 4, SIMIA, EA-1-82, File 20.

12. Forsberg, letter to Bingham, January 16, 1942, in Roke, *They Went Forth*, 203.

13. Spencer, *Ethiopia at Bay*, 84.

14. Baudendistel, *Between Bombs and Good Intentions*, 43.

15. Lambie, *Doctor without a Country*, 250.

16. Lambie, letter to Bingham, March 16, 1942, in Roke, *They Went Forth*, 211.

17. Duff, *Cords of Love*, 334.

Lambie attempted unsuccessfully to reconcile with the emperor while Haile Sellassie was in Bath, England, from 1936 to 1939. In 1940, Haile Sellassie was in Khartoum, en route with the British military to return to his throne in Addis Ababa. Lambie was also in Khartoum in 1940 and made a second attempt at reconciliation. Forsberg, who accompanied Lambie to the Anglican Cathedral, described the event:

> One day there was an ecumenical gathering at the All Saints Cathedral (Anglican) in Khartoum. Dr. Lambie sat by the aisle down which all the Khartoum church leaders and bishops would march. HIM [His Imperial Majesty] was to come down that same aisle. He did come down the aisle but paid no attention to Dr. Lambie going or coming.[18]

Lambie was thoroughly perplexed by the emperor's complete rejection.[19] He surmised that the emperor may have seen his first letter to the Italians which would have provoked the breach, but not the second letter.[20] Lambie wrote to Bingham, "It was said that I said that the Italians had not used poison gas. I never said any such thing. I said the opposite. It was [also] said I wrote to Geneva against him. I never did. Someone has lied but I could not find out who."[21]

During the subsequent months there was growing criticism against Lambie from his Sudan SIM colleagues. In 1942 Lambie attempted to clear himself for the rather compromising letter he had sent to the Italians soon after May 5, 1936. On March 16, 1942, he sent a "Statement" to Rowland Bingham, SIM's international director, stating, "You will remember that I was counted as an Ethiopian at that time and had undergone great mental and physical strain. At that time I was also vitally concerned over the very lives of some of our missionaries who were in danger of death, and at the

---

18. Forsberg, letter to Brian Fargher, October 9, 1980, Paul Balisky Special Collection (hereinafter PBSC). See also Forsberg, *Land Beyond the Nile*, 182.

19. Matilda Jean Prenter, "Oglesbys—Tea with Emperor" (diary entry), October 28, 1940. The Oglesbys had shown special hospitality to Haile Sellassie in their Lalibela home during his April 1936 flight from the Italians, something that he never forgot. The Prenter diary was sent to me by Matilda's daughter Gwen Stavely, November 28, 2017, copy in PBSC.

20. See Lambie, *Doctor's Great Commission*, 261, where he states, "Something I said earlier in this book had greatly offended him. I never quite knew what it was, and would have done anything possible to be reconciled to him, but it was not to be."

21. Lambie, letter to Bingham, March 16, 1942, in Roke, *They Went Forth*, 212.

same time I was most anxious to get permission for the mission work to go on."[22]

Lambie appreciated the opportunity to inform Bingham of his reasons for having written the appeasement letter to the Italians. He continued, "The appeasement policy will never work with the Germans or Italians, and I should have known better and acted differently. I hope I will never do so again." He concludes his "Statement" with the following confession:

> For the pain and injury done to my benefactor and onetime friend, His Imperial Majesty Haile Sellassie, I can only say that I am very sorry and, if he sees this statement, [I hope] that he will accept my humble and sincere confession of wrong done in writing that letter. As far as I know, this is the only thing that I have ever written or spoken that would give aid or comfort to his enemies. That I ever said [anytime] that the Italians did not use poison gas or anything like that, as has been reported, is not so. I have reportedly said that it was the cowardly use of poison gas that alone enabled Italy to win the war.[23]

Lambie was unaware of the Italian propaganda machine which had drafted two letters in his name (following considerable investigation I consider these two letters to be spurious). A four-page letter, dated May 21, 1936, was signed "Dr. Lambie" and sent to the International Red Cross Committee in Geneva. The second letter, two pages in length, was sent to the London *Times* (unpublished with no date) and signed "T. A. Lambie." Lambie's comments in his two letters just cited to Rowland Bingham contravene the basic substance contained in the two spurious letters.

The two letters that I consider to be spurious state categorically that the Italians did not use mustard gas and that they did not bomb Ethiopian Red Cross trucks or their temporary field hospital units.[24] Ethiopian scholar Mikre-Sellassie G/Ammanuel accepts both as bona fide letters written by Lambie. He concludes,

> Thus, Lambie's declaration confirmed the Italian excuses for bombarding the Red Cross ambulance units. The declaration

22. Lambie, letter to Bingham, March 18, 1942, SIMIA, Forsberg, Malcolm and Enid, Box 09, File 4.

23. Lambie, "Statement" to Bingham, March 16, 1942, SIMIA, Forsberg, Malcolm and Enid, Box 09, File 4. I am grateful to Mrs. Evie Bowers, SIM IntArchivist in Charlotte, NC, for her painstaking work in differentiating between Lambie's March 15, 1941, letter to Bingham and Lambie's "Statement" written one year later, on March 16, 1942, also addressed to Bingham.

24. Mikre-Sellassie, *Church and Mission in Ethiopia*, Appendices 1 and 2, 378–83.

was immediately published by the Italian press and broadcast from Rome with the premeditated plan to divert the public opinion of the world against Italy for its violation of the laws of war by attacking the Red Cross camps.[25]

It would appear that by writing his first letter Lambie made himself vulnerable to the devious clutches of the Italian war machine. The Italians manipulated his initial letter, superimposed their own idea that no war crimes had been committed by the so-called "civilizing" Italians, and submitted their version of Lambie's letter to the IRCC under his signature as "Dr. Lambie." The documents were intended by the Italians as well to enhance public opinion in Italy, that even an American of the stature of Dr. Thomas Lambie would affirm the justice of the Italo-Ethiopian war.

When Peter Cotterell wrote in 1972 that "Lambie was too small a pawn in the complex game of international politics to be employed" by the Italians, he was unlikely to have been aware of these forged documents.[26] But Cotterell may also have underestimated the significance that Lambie had in the eyes of the Italians. In Ethiopia and abroad Lambie was recognized as a reputable observer and writer about the war situation in Ethiopia. The Fascists' spurious letters, however, had the effect of undermining the long-standing relationship of trust that had existed between Lambie and Haile Sellassie. Dr. and Mrs. Lambie departed from Addis Ababa by train on August 21, 1936, never again to set foot in Ethiopia.[27]

Even though he was shunned by the emperor, Lambie was keen to assist the emperor to get back to his throne in Addis Ababa. When the British military approached the Lambies, who were at that point residing in Khartoum, to accept a two-month assignment in Malakal, the Lambies acquiesced. They were to be based in Malakal, with him serving as a "propaganda agent," beginning in February 1941. From that base they were to send leaflets and other messages to the Abyssinian patriots to revolt from their Italian masters and to assist their *negus* (monarch), Haile Sellassie, get back to his throne. The Lambies lived in the Malakal British Government House and recruited Abyssinians who had deserted from the Fascist forces and were now living in Sudan. Of his tactics, Lambie wrote,

---

25. Mikre-Sellassie, *Church and Mission in Ethiopia*, 63. Following considerable investigation, my judgment is that the two "Lambie letters" found in Appendices 1 and 2 of *Church and Mission in Ethiopia* are indeed spurious.

26. Cotterell, "Dr. T. A. Lambie: Some Biographical Notes," 52

27. Charlotte Lambie, letter to daughter Betty Rees, August 28, 1936, MHSC. Charlotte mentions that the Lambies left Addis Ababa on August 21.

What we wanted was to have them [Abyssinian patriots] just as ragged and dirty as possible. They were to have a few score leaflets carefully written in Amharic and Galla concealed under their rags. These were to be given to influential Abyssinians across the border. . . . They were to travel by night and lie up [sleep] at day. Each man was to go to his own particular district. . . . The propaganda leaflets usually bore reproduced photographs . . . of surrendering Italian prisoners . . . and one picture of their Negusa Nagast [Haile Sellassie].[28]

Bahru Zewde observes that "a prominent role was played in the field of intelligence by *ya west arbanyotch* [Ethiopian soldiers involved in espionage]. From their vantage point inside the enemy's organizational network they passed on crucial information about enemy strength. . . . In general terms, therefore, the Resistance forms a glorious chapter in the history of modern Ethiopia."[29] One may surmise that Lambie's service at Malakal contributed significantly to this effort. We have no indication that Emperor Haile Sellassie was cognizant of Lambie's successful service as a propaganda agent or of Lambie's desire to get the negus back on his Addis Ababa throne. But letters written to Lambie by patriot fighters who were former acquaintances from western Abyssinia indicated progress was being made on the battlefield.[30]

Be that as it may, the Lambies never returned to Ethiopia, and the rift between Dr. Lambie and His Imperial Majesty Haile Sellassie was never healed. Lambie, however, was able to outlive his 1936 Ethiopian mistake. His next venture, into another fruitful ministry with SIM in Sudan, spanned from 1939 to 1942. This venture, recorded in his book *A Doctor Carries On*, is the subject of the following chapter.

28. Lambie, *A Doctor Carries On*, 103–4. For Lambie's Malakal propaganda mission, see chap. 8, "With the Forces," 98–110.

29. Bahru, *History of Modern Ethiopia*, 172–73.

30. Lambie, *A Doctor Carries On*, 105–6, mentions correspondence between a local Wellega headman and Lambie.

13

Tensions with British Administrators

Empire was about individualism; it was about character
and personality, about the rule of the strongman,
who, through a mixture of personality, intellect and leadership,
could dominate his peers and the world around him.

KWASI KWARTENG, *GHOSTS OF EMPIRE*, 233

AFTER SPENDING A YEAR (1936–37) in the United States, Thomas and Charlotte Lambie felt that they should return to Africa and assist in establishing the Sudan Interior Mission in the Anglo-Egyptian Sudan. Inwardly they believed they had the "necessary equipment" for this task because of their previous experience there (1907–18) with the United Presbyterian Mission. In a letter to SIM supporters Lambie wrote, "Few have the equipment we have for the Sudan—viz. (1) A knowledge of the country, and (2) A knowledge of the language [Arabic], which though somewhat rusty from disuse can be brushed up, and (3) A knowledge (though somewhat out of date from disuse) of tropical medicine."[1]

In early 1937 Lambie made a two-week survey trip in the Anglo-Egyptian Sudan with Rowland Bingham, SIM's international director. The purpose of their trip was to place Abyssinia-based SIM missionaries, who had been evicted by the Italian Fascists, among unreached people groups of southern Sudan.

1. Lambie, Prayer Circular to Supporters, December 1939, SIMIA, EA-1-82, File 6.

Lambie wrote:

> This was my first visit [to southern Sudan] after eighteen years
> absence in Abyssinia where my early missionary years were
> spent. We [Bingham and Lambie] were both quite thrilled at the
> thought of getting to Khartoum, and filled with a great sense of
> responsibility that was ours in meeting government officials and
> in spying out the land that might become the scene for future
> labours of the Sudan Interior Mission.[2]

Lambie had served in Sudan for a decade under the aegis of the Foreign Missions Board of the United Presbyterian Church, so he knew the
country well. During his absence, many changes had taken place in the
country. Roads had been built in all directions and the city of Khartoum had
grown into a modern metropolis. What had not changed was the religious
situation. The north of the country remained fanatically Muslim but was
less strict in observing religious tenets. Lambie observed that the traditional
religionists of the south, except those near mission stations, were almost
exactly as they had been thirty years before. With British security and freedom from slavery, the population of the southern ethnic groups had greatly
increased. But Lambie noted that sadly the United Presbyterian Mission had
reduced its missionary force somewhat and that the remaining missionaries
were somewhat discouraged. But he was heartened by the positive gains
the Anglican Church Missionary Society had made among the Dinkas. The
Sudan United Mission, also, had opened stations among the Dinkas and
other people groups residing in the Nuba Mountains.

The purpose of the Lambie/Bingham expedition was to survey the
large Sudanese population along the Sudan-Abyssinia border, which extended for more than a thousand miles. The one mission station near that
border was Nasir, under the direction of the United Presbyterians and located on the Sobat River. The station had been previously pioneered by the
Lambies (1915–19). Lambie and Bingham hired a vehicle and in February
1937 made a nine-hundred-mile tour over southern Sudan's rough roads.
At the end of their tour they visited Sir Stewart Symnes, governor-general of
the Anglo-Egyptian Sudan, in his Khartoum office. He commented, "You do
not need to convince me of the value of Foreign Missions. I am sure they are
a good thing."[3] Lambie later summarized the interview with the governor
general: First, any mission advance in the "Boma Area" must be withheld for
political reasons. The Italians based near Kurmuk would misconstrue such
activity as "English incursion" near Italian-occupied Abyssinia. Second,

2. Lambie, "I Have Begun to Give . . .," 387.
3. Lambie, "Our New Task," 292.

the proposal of establishing a work in the southern "Fung Area" would meet with approval if carefully-thought-out plans were made. But General Symnes did not agree with the argument that former SIM New Zealand and Australian missionaries evacuated from Abyssinia "needed a place" to serve. Such "dumping" (General Symnes's word) did not appeal to him. Third, establishing a station among the Inghessana people group was encouraged as the Inghessana Hills were "an attractive place." Lambie understood General Symnes to say, "As to work in distinctly Moslem areas, the Government had to be very careful as to the attitude in permitting the introduction of Christian Missions as Government permission for such work would result in attacks on Government policies by the watchful Moslem Press and embarrass Governmental relations with Mohammedan People."[4]

Throughout most of his career, Lambie had a respectful opinion of British officials. He writes, "They were, as a rule, from very good British families and schools of England; some had gained honour in sports. The large power delegated to them frequently enlarged their heads. The whole system of government was conducive to this; yet they were, by and large, a wonderful set of administrators. The British officials in the Sudan were above any suspicion of bribery or dishonest dealings."[5]

In response to the British policy against Christian missionary involvement among Muslims, Lambie wrote,

> By wishing to avoid a rumpus in admitting Christian missionaries, a temporary wrong and injustice is perpetrated as well as a permanent one. This policy encourages intolerance and fanaticism which may prove to be a boomerang, may prove to be the

---

4. Lambie, "Report of the Interview between Governor General of the Anglo-Egyptian Sudan, Sir S. Symnes, and Drs. R. V. Bingham and T. A. Lambie at Khartoum, Anglo-Egyptian Sudan, on March 14, 1937," SIMIA, Box KB-121, File 1. In his "Note for S.I.M. File," January 22, 1940, Juba Archives, South Sudan National Archives (hereinafter SSNA), Upper Nile Province (hereinafter UNP) 46 B 3, Douglas Newbold stated: "Bishop Gwynne has seen Dr. Lambie recently—he has known him for 30 years and can handle him—and has told him not to resist the Government policy about non-proselytisation in Moslem areas and that his (the Bishop's) view is that Christianising influences in these areas can best come (in the fullness of time) from the example of adjoining indigenous churches (e.g. Nuba)." (These SSNA materials were sent to me as email attachments, June 2, 2015, through the kindness of Douglas H. Johnson, a specialist on the history of South Sudan, whom I met at the International Conference of SIM History in Africa, Addis Ababa, July 9–13, 2013.)

5. Lambie, Doctor without a Country, 25.

seedbed for the cultivation of a Mahdi or Mohammed Grany to plague us at some future date.[6]

By July 1937, SIM, under Glen Cain's supervision as acting director, had placed eleven missionaries at the following five locations: among the Dinka at Abayath; among the Uduk at Chali; among the Mabaan at Doro; among the Dinka at Banjang (north of Melut on the White Nile); and among the Dinka at Melut, formerly a Sudan United Mission station, south on the White Nile, that was subsequently transferred to SIM.

After two and a half years in the United States, the Lambies arrived in Khartoum in November 1939 for him to assume the role of director for SIM Sudan, replacing Glen Cain. They decided to tour the five SIM stations, departing in December.[7] Cain served as driver of the Ford V8, which was christened "Dorcas" because it was "full of good works." The passengers were Thomas and Charlotte Lambie; Caroline Cain, Lambie's secretary (but not a relative of Glen Cain); and Mohammed, the guide and interpreter. With Khartoum as the starting point, the first SIM station they visited was Banjang, located among the nomadic Dinka tribe, one of the larger people groups of Sudan. The Alf and Tina Roke family and Norman Dunn were located there. The next SIM station, Melut, lay further south in the Upper Nile Province (UNP). It served as the base for Earl and Pauline Lewis, Lois Briggs, and Daisy McMillan. Because of its location along the White Nile, the Melut station proved to be a strategic center for the mission's other four stations. The station at Abaiyat, some forty miles east of Melut, was also among the Dinka people group. John and Peggy Phillips and Phyliss Hawkins were based there. The SIM station at Doro lay fifty-five miles southwest of Kurmuk, an Abyssinia/Sudan border center that was staffed by a British officer. The Doro station was located on the banks of the Khor Yabus River, which drains the western slopes of the Abyssinian mountains. Dr. Robert and Mrs. Claire Grieve, Ken and Blanche Oglesby, and Zilla Walsh were involved in teaching Mabaan children in the recently established school at Doro. The fifth SIM station was at Chali, among the Uduk, located south some thirty miles south-southwest from Kurmuk. The Malcolm and Enid Forsberg

6. Lambie, "Closed Minds and Open Doors," ca. 1938, 10, SIMIA, EA-1-82, File 0. This 14-page pamphlet was initially distributed by the Fellowship of Faith for the Muslims, 106 Highbury, New Park, London.

7. Lambie, *A Doctor Carries On*, 24–44. Lambie, report to August Holm, November 23, 1939, SIMIA, KB-1-121, Box 3, states that the Lambies arrived in Khartoum that day. Lambie continues, "Mr. Cain is expected around the first of December and I think we will be making a tour of the stations soon after our arrival."

family together with Nick Simponis were based at this well-forested site, with the Ethiopian mountains in clear view.[8]

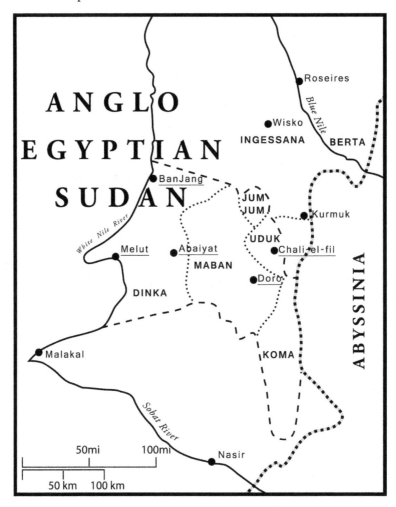

Five SIM stations (underlined) in Sudan

After this extended tour, Lambie, as director of SIM operations in southern Sudan, was keen to expand the mission's sphere of influence further south among the large Dinka population. He was optimistic that the colonial officials in Khartoum would be obliging. In a November 1939 letter to August B. "Gus" Holm, SIM secretary in New York, Lambie confided:

8. Forsberg, *Land beyond the Nile*; see pp. 118–72 for Forsberg's account of missionary life among the Uduk at the Chali station.

There is a new Civil Secretary [in Khartoum] since a few months [ago] and our missionaries speak so highly of him. He is the official that has most to do with our Government contacts. He is said to be a real Christian and he has kindly asked [Norman and Flossie] Couser and us to meet him at his home for dinner and after this meeting I am in hopes that I can write to you of future prospects.[9]

With this encouraging prospect, Lambie submitted a proposal to launch two additional SIM stations among the Dinka in the Upper Nile region. Douglas Newbold, the civil secretary in Khartoum, responded:

I refer to your letter of December 19th, 1939, conveying an application to open two new mission Stations among the Dinka south of the Sobat. I informed you in January that it might be some time before I could obtain a definite decision owing to the war preoccupations and the necessity for consulting the Director of Education and Governor [of] Upper Nile [Province]. I have now submitted your application to His Excellency the Governor-General, who regrets that a permit cannot be given for any more stations until (a) the existing stations are developed and established, (b) some educational results are apparent, and (c) the responsible authorities of the American Mission [that is, the FMBUPC] have been consulted. Apart from these considerations, it is obviously difficult for the Sudan Government to encourage new and uncertain commitments in time of war.[10]

From correspondence available it appears that the British officials in Sudan did not have a wholly favorable opinion of Lambie. On January 18, 1940, Newbold wrote an internal four-page memo titled "Note on Dr. Lambie, Field Director, Sudan Interior Mission" and marked "Strictly Confidential." Lambie had previously given Newbold a copy of his autobiography, *A Doctor without a Country*. Apparently, Newbold gained several telling insights about Lambie's character from the book as well as from some conversations. To his Foreign Service colleagues, Newbold confided:

He appears to be a likeable, humorous, forceful and slightly mischievous personality. He is a missionary of some thirty years, an "old timer" in character as well as in age, whose strong individualism has had defects as well as advantages. He has a good knowledge of native mentality, interested in politics, keen, by his

9. Lambie, letter to August Holm, November 23, 1939, SIMIA, KB-1-121, Box 3.

10. Newbold, civil secretary, memorandum to Lambie, March 23, 1940, SSNA UNP SCR 46, B.3, December 1939–January 1940.

own account, to cooperate with Government and obey Government regulations, strongly opposed privately but loyal (he says officially) to the ban on proselytisation in Muslim areas, a fully qualified doctor with good leper experience, very pro Haile Sellassie (naturally), anti-Italian, and rather contemptuous of the American Mission, which he describes as 'stagnant'. Lambie was warned about 'gate-crashing' into American Mission area.[11]

Newbold and his Foreign Fervice colleagues had by now sized up Lambie as, from their point of view, a forceful hustler who was keen to expand his mission.

On January 27, 1940, Lambie wrote to R. V. H. Roseveare, director of education in Khartoum,

> In the Sudan Interior Mission we are from many denominations and we desire to present a pure Gospel message in the hope that the church which will one day eventuate will be along indigenous lines conforming to the best principles of Christianity. . . . Missionaries do not come to Sudan for pleasure or for personal gain. We are not misguided fanatics."[12]

On March 23 that year Newbold wrote to Lambie informing him that permission for SIM to open two additional stations among the Dinka south of the Sobat River had been denied. The following forceful letter was rather discouraging to Lambie.

> I am fully aware from your conversations with me and the Governor of the Upper Nile [Armstrong], that this decision, though perhaps not unexpected, will be a disappointment to you. I know that expansion is always more attractive, and more lucrative, to a mission than is consolidation, but "digging in" has a great strategic value, and the Government's view is that there is plenty of scope for years ahead for your staff and your funds,

---

11. Newbold, "Note on Dr. Lambie, Field Director of Sudan Interior Mission" (Strictly Confidential memorandum), January 18, 1940, SSNA UNP SCR 46, B.3. Denys Heseltine Hibbert, director of education, wrote to Newbold on January 20, 1940, "The Sudan Interior Mission has money, recruits, and drive behind them. Dr. Lambie is excitable and regards the Government with its spheres and policies as a bogey thwarting his legitimate work," SSNA UNP SCR 46, B.3, December 1939–January 1940.

12. Lambie, letter to R. V. H. Roseveare, director of education, Khartoum, January 27, 1940. See also Lambie to C. L. Armstrong, governor of UNP, February 20, 1940, SIMIA, KB-1-121, Box 3: "The tendency for me is to return to Khartoum profoundly discouraged over the failure of our trip to Malakal."

in the areas already allotted to you, and in which I wish you the best of luck.[13]

That same day, Newbold wrote to Governor Armstrong in Khartoum, "I hope that Dr. Lambie will build his efforts inwards and not outwards."[14]

Immediately after receiving Newbold's letter, Lambie wrote dejectedly to Bingham:

> It is indeed disappointing. If this is carried out it means that we give all our time and efforts to making these five stations what the Sudan Government thinks adequate and that if our educational efforts please them . . . then they may give us more. Doubtless the war does have something to do with the decision and also pressure brought to bear from Egypt opposed to increase of Christian Missions. . . . We praise God for the Sanatorium in Equatoria and please God it may lead to more.[15]

Four months later, on July 23, Lambie wrote more positively to Bingham:

> For the moment I think we will gain nothing by pressing the government about new work and would I believe to be the losers. They are great and good men working in a good cause, often overworking and suffering from the heat and strain and lack of accustomed vacations and separations from their loved ones. I have a lot of sympathy for them and would certainly like to help them. . . . I believe that we will accomplish far more in the end by showing our appreciation of present difficulties.[16]

In his letter of March 24 to Bingham, Lambie confirmed that permission was granted for the Mission Rest Home designated as the "Sanatorium in Equatoria" to be built at a higher elevation in a forested area of the Issorie mountain range, some 150 miles west of Juba. The government authorities made it clear that this was not to be used as a base for "outreach" to the sparse local population but as a "Mission Rest Home." Glen and Winnie Cain and Norman and Flossie Couser were assigned to build the Sanatorium.

---

13. Newbold, letter to Lambie, March 23, 1940, SSNA UNP SCR 46, B.3.

14. Newbold, letter to Armstrong, March 23, 1940, SSNA UNP SCR 46, B.3. Kwarteng observes, "He [Douglas Newbold] was a cerebral man who was a popular workaholic. He was a pragmatist and yet was conservative and somewhat reactionary in his administration"; see *Ghosts of Empire*, 254.

15. Lambie, report to Bingham, March 24, 1940, 4 pp., SIMIA, KB-1-121, Box 3.

16. Lambie, letter to Bingham, July 23, 1940, SIMIA, KB-1-121, Box 3.

Kwasi Kwarteng's critical analysis of British imperialism, *Ghosts of Empire: Britain's Legacies in the Modern World*, offers insight into the struggles that Lambie experienced in Sudan with the rather "hard-nosed" officers of the British colonial service. A Foreign Office veteran called the colonial officers the "finest body of men in the world."[17] The men in the Sudan Political Service were said to be a "cut above average," for the Foreign Service was keen to recruit "sound, competent men."[18] All had attended public schools and were athletes, and the majority were graduates of either Oxford or Cambridge Universities. Individualism was a sought-after quality among the recruits. Notably, over one-third of the recruits to the Sudan political service were sons of the clergy.

Lambie may well have attempted to negotiate with the young British colonial officers in a manner similar to the way in which he successfully dealt with the Abyssinian governors. In Abyssinia Lambie was thought of as an American, with no colonial aspirations and with a willingness to provide medical assistance as well as education to the local population. Also, Lambie represented the epitome of "American individualism." It was at this very point that he clashed with the British colonial officers, for they too were strong individualists. Kwarteng acknowledges that "everything about the British pointed to individualism."[19] "Individualism and character … was prised above all else."[20] Doubtless it was the shortcomings of the British colonial officers' individualism and the individualism of Lambie that blocked SIM from its desired expansion in the Sudan. Douglas Newbolt, the British civil secretary, assessed Lambie to be a "likeable but mischievous old man. To be frank, I do not believe that S.I.M. can deliver the goods that we want. They are not interested in education like the CMS or the Catholics. Dr. Lambie is an expansionist, and his history of cooperation with the Government and fellow Missions is *not* encouraging; his technique is 'itinerant' rather than 'consolidatory.'"[21]

Lambie explained the Sudan situation to SIM colleague Guy Playfair, who was based in Kano, Nigeria:

17. Kwarteng, *Ghosts of Empire*, 236.

18. Kwarteng, *Ghosts of Empire*, 238. Sharkey, *Living with Colonialism*, 68, states that the district commissioners were from the "'upper-middle' classes."

19. Kwarteng, *Ghosts of Empire*, 232.

20. Kwarteng, *Ghosts of Empire*, 239.

21. Newbold, note in file, December 19, 1939, SSNA UNP SCR 46, B.3. Forsberg, *Last Days on the Nile*, 84–85, confirms the hard-nosed attitude and policy of the British officials in Sudan: education first, then evangelism.

We had hoped to get into new areas and open more stations, but there were, humanly speaking, two reasons which did not permit this:

1. The unwillingness of the Government to make new commitments while [the Italo-Ethiopia] war was in progress.

2. The Government's desire to see us engaged in school work which they could approve of before granting us new mission stations.

The Government in A.E. Sudan has tied up schools and missions so that unless we prove ourselves successfully in the scholastic sphere we are not to be given opportunity of doing [new] missionary work.[22]

The response of the British administrators to SIM's attempt to expand its sphere of influence by opening additional stations within southern Sudan was discouraging to Lambie. He sincerely believed that SIM had the resources to expand with two additional stations among the unevangelized Dinka. But he was blocked by the colonial officials, from whom he felt rather estranged.

We conclude this chapter with an objective statement by Douglas H. Johnson, a person who has carefully studied the correspondence in the years 1937–54 between the British colonial officials and SIM leadership in Sudan.

The real problem lay not so much in the nationality of the missionaries, their class, or their "Low Church" outlook; it was the sheer impracticality of the SIM missionaries that struck most officials who came in contact with them. Their seemingly underhanded and duplicitous attempts to expand their operations into areas where they had been forbidden earned them the distrust not only of the government but of rival missions. All mission organizations chafed against the sphere system and tried to circumvent it where they could, but the SIM was seen as taking evasion to the extreme. Ironically, it is probably their language work among the Uduk and the Mabaan, dismissed by the government as ineffectual and inadequate, that has been the SIM's most lasting contribution to the region and its peoples . . . Christian and non-Christian alike.[23]

22. Lambie, report to Playfair, December 31, 1940, SIMIA, KB-1-121, Box 3.

23. Douglas H. Johnson, "Tacking to the Winds of Change: The SIM and Education Policy in South Sudan, 1937–1954," in *Transforming Africa's Religious Landscapes*, ed. Cooper et al., 147–69; quotation from 165–66.

14

Death of Dr. Robert and Mrs. Claire Grieve at Doro Station

Face to face with Christ, my Savior,
Face to face—what will it be,
When with rapture I behold Him,
Jesus Christ who died for me?

HYMN BY CARRIE E. BROCK, 1898 (PUBLIC DOMAIN)

THIS CHAPTER BEGINS WITH a short biographical sketch of Dr. Robert and Mrs. Claire Grieve, who were stationed in the Sudan at SIM's Doro station. Located some fifty miles southwest of Kurmuk, it was on the border with Abyssinia.[1] Robert and Claire met at Wheaton College, Wheaton, Illinois, in the 1930s. Following college, Robert enrolled in medical school while Claire served for a period in Alaska under the Presbyterians, teaching at a mission school. They were challenged by Malcolm Forsberg to serve in Africa with SIM. After Robert graduated from medical school, World War II prevented him from attending the University of London's tropical medicine program; as an alternative, the Grieves served temporarily with the American Mission Hospital in Assiut, Egypt. At the hospital Robert was

1. Though in much pain prior to her death at Doro, Claire Grieve sang the hymn "Face to Face with Christ my Savior," saying, "I want to see my Savior face to face"; see Lambie, *A Doctor Carries On*, 67. The hymn's first stanza serves as the epigraph for this chapter.

able to work with experienced staff and to acquire valuable knowledge related to tropical diseases. Early in 1940 they arrived in Khartoum and by February were comfortably settled at Doro in a residence constructed with local materials. Robert soon began serving the Mabaan population from a small but well-equipped clinic. The couple applied themselves to adapting to the language and culture; Lambie affirms that they "made great strides with the language."[2]

The situation along the border between southern Sudan and Abyssinia was tense. In midyear Lambie reported in a two-page letter to Rowland Bingham that the Italian military was making forays into Sudan.

> I would like to write to you about a lot of things but probably they would not pass the censors but just remember that this country is at war too with all that it means in dislocation of not only these mails mentioned but all mails. We have had no letters from America for almost two months. . . . We are all pretty poor as allowance received last week was only two pounds ten shillings per worker. . . . Weather here has been exceptionally trying, such awful heat and dust storms, prickly heat and biting insects. . . . I am going to write to all our missionaries to do as little moving about as possible while conditions are as they are.[3]

On August 6, 1940, Lambie sent a telegram to Bingham indicating that "Italian border activities render future mission work in Chali and Doro somewhat perilous."[4] On August 20 he wrote to August Holm, the SIM secretary in New York, stating that he had not received any reply from Bingham.[5] In the same letter, he mentioned to Holm that he had engaged in discussion on the topic with Douglas Newbold, the British colonial administration's civil secretary who was based in Khartoum. Newbold's response was: "I do not think the Italians will infiltrate as far as your missions."[6]

On August 23, however, the Italians attacked Kurmuk and took possession of that British outpost. Kurmuk had played a key role for SIM's communications. The Doro and Chali stations would send occasional runners to the British border outpost in Kurmuk to meet the fortnightly mailbag from Khartoum and carry out financial transactions with a friendly Greek

---

2. Lambie, *A Doctor Carries On*, 66.

3. Lambie, letter (from Khartoum) to Bingham, July 23, 1940, SIMIA, KB-1-121, File 3.

4. Lambie, telegram to Bingham, August 6, 1940, SIMIA, KB-1-121, File 3.

5. Lambie, letter to August Holm, August 20, 1940, SIMIA, KB-1-121, File 3.

6. Lambie, communication of Douglas Newbold's response to August Holm, August 20, 1940, SIMIA, KB-1-121, File 3.

merchant as well as to socialize with the British assistant commissioner, who also was friendly. Following the Italian takeover of Kurmuk, the SIM personnel at Doro and Chali lost contact with the outside world. Though both the Doro and Chali stations were staffed by Americans, missionaries from a neutral nation, Malcolm Forsberg felt uneasy about the close proximity of the Italian army. To make it clear that SIM personnel were not involved in any kind of political or espionage activity, he wrote tactfully to the Italian commander.

> Sudan Interior Mission
>
> July 27, 1940
>
> The Commander,
>
> Italian Army at Dul,
>
> Ethiopia
>
> Sir:
>
> This is to inform you that there are two men, one woman and a child at Chali, all of whom are Americans.
>
> There are two men and three women at Doro, one young lady of whom is Australian. The rest are Americans.
>
> We are engaged solely in missionary work among the Uduk and Mabaan tribes. We have placed an American flag on one of the houses at Chali.
>
> Sincerely yours,
>
> M. I. Forsberg,
>
> Sudan Interior Mission[7]

The Italians were now figuratively at the doorstep of the two mission stations.[8] With Doro only fifty miles from Kurmuk, the missionaries felt vulnerable. Except for Robert and Claire Grieve, the SIM missionaries at Doro and Chali (Ken and Blanche Oglesby, Zillah Walsh, Malcolm and Enid Forsberg, and Nick Simponis) had all experienced the trauma of the Italian invasion of Abyssinia several years before. Now they feared for their lives. After several days, a response arrived from the Italian military commander in Kurmuk. Exactly as written, it read:

---

7. Forsberg, letter to the Italian commander in Kurmuk, July 27, 1940, cited in Lambie, *A Doctor Carries On*, 60.

8. See Lambie, *Doctor's Great Commission*, 255–56, gives a brief account of the Italian bombing at Doro Mission Station.

Governo Dei Galla E. Sidama

Karmuk 2nd August 1940 XVIII

Mr. M. I. Forsberg

Sudan Interior Mission

Chali.

I have received your letter of which I understand the presence of your Mission in my territory. I shall be glad you all men and women [come] here at Kurmuk everyone with his own passport.

I hope that the travel by Chali and Doro to Kurmuk it would like to you.

Please my best wishes to ladies and my salutations to gentlemen.

Commander Italian Army, Kurmuk.

(Signed) [name illegible][9]

When the Chali and Doro missionaries notified Lambie as field superintendent of the situation, he was caught between a rock and a hard place. On one side was the short memo he had received from Douglas Newbolt, the British civil secretary in Khartoum, "I do not think the Italians will infiltrate as far as your missions."[10] On the other side, evacuating the missionaries from the Doro and Chali stations was a physical impossibility. The rainy season made the roads impassable and no vehicles could get through. Also, neither station had riding animals available. Further, Claire Grieve was pregnant as well as recovering from a bout of malaria. Relying on the advice from the British civil secretary, Lambie did nothing about evacuating the mission personnel, but sought advice by telegram from Bingham.[11]

On August 23, 1940, the Italians bombed SIM's Doro station. Ken Oglesby wrote the following account at 2:00 pm that same day. His account is somewhat incoherent because of shell shock and his recent recovery from malaria.

This must be brief. Great sorrow here. God never led us to flee—we had to stay at our post by wish of all here. Planes came from

9. Cited in Lambie, *A Doctor Carries On*, 62.

10. Newbold, memo to Lambie, August 9, 1940, SIMIA, KB-1-121, File 4.

11. Lambie, telegram to Bingham, August 6, 1940: "ITALIAN BORDER ACTIVITIES RENDER FUTURE MISSION WORK CHALI AND DORO SOMEWHAT PERILOUS BUT FAVOURABLE POSSIBILITIES EXIST. COMMUNICATIONS QUITE SPORADIC. HAVE ADVISED ALL REMAIN STATIONS. PLEASE CONFIRM." Two weeks went by with no response from Bingham; see Lambie, letter to August Holm, August 20, 1940, SIMIA, KB-1-121, File 3.

East at 9:00 A.M. Today (2 planes) and dropped over 30 bombs here and around. None any other place.

The first bomb did the damage—no houses hit, but Dr. Grieve is dead—shrapnel in forehead, died one hour later. Mrs. Grieve badly wounded in back just above hips, but not in abdomen we think. She is [in] great pain—we don't know if [she] will live, can't tell. Blanche [Oglesby] was wounded in legs and hip but no bones broken—4 places, and many little ones on left arm. She can walk as yet. I got it in back at right shoulder but no bones broken, 2 places. Zillah [Walsh] O.K. She was at her house. She ran to us after first bombs and she [Blanche] and I ran to big trees when planes returned, so no more hit us but they fell many places. Some incendiary bombs and burned my chicken house and chickens (16). No one else hurt at all. My arm hurts so I can't write much. Don't worry, praise God for His mercy. I am in a daze and can't cry or think. Don't know about Chali.

Police soldiers here (from Boin) to help bury Dr. and they are bringing this letter to you. . . . Dr. [Grieve] felt if he held up his U.S.A. flag they would not bomb us and I ran to help him hold up the flag.

I got 16 Mabaans to dig the grave for Doctor. The police helped so faithfully. 5 were here. Blanche [Oglesby] was carried to the grave in a chair as her legs pain her so to walk, she can walk altho. Zillah stayed with Mrs. Grieve who was conscious as yet. We had a most blessed service for Mabaans (a lot) and preached the blood to them. The police left after funeral and also helped carry Mrs. Grieve to house from clinic. They had been gone only a few moments when the Lord took "Claire" [Grieve] to himself and to be with Bob [Grieve]. My, oh, my![12]

Lambie wrote later:

It was a whole week after the bombing of Doro before news reached us in Khartoum. The first information we had of it was a visit paid to us by a high official of the Government, the Deputy Civil Secretary, Mr. G.R.F. Bredin, who broke the sad news as tenderly as possible. It was broadcast to the world from London

12. Ken Oglesby, letter sent by runner to SIM stations at Abiyat and Melut, August 24, 1940. See also Blanche Oglesby, letter to August Holm, September 27, 1940, 3 pp., in which she gives details of the Doro atrocity, and Douglas Newbold, "Report from Upper Nile Province," August 29, 1940, which covers the August 23 attack on the SIM station at Doro and the deaths of Dr. and Mrs. Robert Grieve. These two letters and the report are located in SIMIA, KB-1-121, File 4.

either the same day or the next. It was frequently mentioned in the press of Britain and England.[13]

In a six-page letter to Newbold, the British civil secretary in Khartoum, Lambie carefully detailed the events leading up to the tragic bombing at Doro.

1. That the missionaries were known by name to the Italians who asked them to come to Kurmuk to report.

2. The missionaries informed the Italians of the difficulty and practical impossibility of going to Kurmuk at that time.

3. The Italians were displeased at the message and said they would look in on the places by airplane.

4. They did so with dire results.[14]

Newbold subsequently sent the following report to his superiors.

On August 23rd at 10:30 a.m. the Sudan Interior Mission Station at DORO (alias Boing) on YABUS River 55 miles S.W. of Kurmuk was attacked by 2 Italian aircraft. The Italian commandant at Kurmuk had earlier in August sent a message that they and their missionaries at CHALI station (30 miles S.S.W. of Kurmuk) were to report to him with their passports. A reply was under consideration when the attack at DORO occurred. The station is quite isolated and unprotected and near no military objective of any sort. Dr. and Mrs. GRIEVE were killed by machine gun fire as they ran out waving an American flag. Rev. and Mrs. OGLESBY were wounded in the back and leg respectively. Miss WALSH was unhurt. All four victims were American citizens. At least 30 bombs were dropped. One girl and two boys of the Mabaan tribe were wounded. The location of the Mission was known to the Italians and the attack must have been deliberate.

(Initialed) D.N.

29.8.40.[15]

Lambie wrote to Bingham: "I must say the death of our dear workers has greatly touched the Government who are very sympathetic indeed. I have had a letter from the Governor-General and telegrams and letters

13. Lambie, *A Doctor Carries On*, 70.

14. Lambie, letter to Newbold, September 2, 1940, SIMIA, KB-1-121, File 4.

15. Newbold, Civil Secretary's Office, Khartoum, "Report from Upper Nile Province," September 29, 1940, SIMIA, KB-1-121, File 3.

from many."[16] Lambie concluded his letter by asking Bingham to pray that
wisdom would be given as hard decisions needed to be made.

After conducting a thorough investigation of the fatal bombing, the
Foreign Service of the United States of America in Cairo on November 1,
1940, made a formal protest to the Italian government in Rome. A section
of the protest was forwarded to Dr. Lambie; it read:

> My Government is confident that the Royal Italian Government
> will promptly condemn the acts of those responsible for the bru-
> tal unprovoked attack against four American citizens concerned
> and that prompt steps will be taken to punish those guilty of
> an outrage shocking to all those who continue to preserve any
> respect for the principles of civilized behaviour. My Govern-
> ment must of course make full reservations concerning the sub-
> sequent entering of claims for compensation for the killing of
> Dr. and Mrs. Grieve, wounding the Reverend and Mrs. Oglesby,
> and for any property damage suffered by American interests.[17]

The Italian government responded to the American Embassy in Rome
on January 31, 1941, completely denying any responsibility for the August
23, 1940, bombing of the Doro station.

> The said authorities after careful investigation state that it is to
> be excluded that the air action in question was carried out by
> Italian planes and emphasize the point that the government of
> the province concerned had in fact given orders that the two
> stations whose presence at Doro and Chali was perfectly well
> known should be left undisturbed where they were.[18]

The historian Rainer Baudendistel, who initially served with the International Committee of the Red Cross, focused his research and writing
on the Horn of Africa. By dint of careful research in Italy's war archives in
Rome, he discovered a statement made by a high ranking Italian military
officer: "With immediate effect all restrictions on targets in Juba sector
must be lifted, including those on civilian populations, urban centres and
cattle."[19] It is clear that what counted for the Italian leadership in Rome, and

16. Lambie, letter to Bingham (Confidential), September 2, 1940, SIMIA, KB-1-
121, File 4.

17. Raymond A. Hare, Charge d'Affairs, Foreign Affairs, United States of America,
Cairo, to Lambie, Khartoum, February 28, 1941, SIMIA, KB-1-121, File 4.

18. Raymond A. Hare, Charge d'Affairs, Foreign Affairs, United States of America,
Cairo, Italian letter forwarded to Lambie, Khartoum, February 28, 1941, SIMIA, KB-
1-121, File 4.

19. Baudendistel, *Between Bombs and Good Intentions*, 163fn16.

particularly for the military based in East Africa, was the achievement of their goal—the conquest of East Africa. It could well be surmised that the bombing at Doro was rooted in the spirit of the Italian Air Force, in the Italian high command, and in the entire Fascist system—the conquest of East Africa. Unfortunately, Dr. and Mrs. Robert Grieve, the innocent medical couple residing at Doro, were the victims of Fascist bombs.

The Doro tragedy made much additional work for Lambie and his secretary, Miss Caroline Cain. Besides correspondence with the British officials in the Anglo-Egyptian Sudan, in behalf of the American Embassy in Cairo they had to prepare valid affidavits, obtained from those who had witnessed the deaths of the Grieves. Lambie commented to the American Minister Plenipotentiary Judge Bert Fish: "The preparation of these affidavits has consumed a great deal of time and thought, and I hope you will agree with me that they are very well done."[20] They also sent letters of sympathy to various members of Dr. Robert and Claire Grieves' next of kin in the state of Washington in the United States.[21]

In writing to Mr. and Mrs. James McClenny in Edmonds, WA, Lambie indicated that most of the personal effects of the Grieves had been sold to various members of the SIM family in Khartoum. The letter indicated that Dr. Grieves' medical instruments were in safe keeping in Khartoum, stating, "We hope that God will raise up a successor soon to use them."[22]

Lambie wrote to August Holm, "I may say that things continue to look up in the Sudan and everyone is very confident. There have been no Italian bombers over for a long time and we think that the danger is about passed."[23] A month later Lambie wrote to Holm even more optimistically, "We are in high hopes that our missionaries will get back to Doro and Chali soon. The Government has authorized the Oglesbys to go back for a four-day visit which will, we trust, be the precursor of their permanent return."[24]

Thus ended another stressful period, 1939–42, for Lambie in Sudan. He had not anticipated the sudden death of Robert and Claire Grieve, these two keen and gifted volunteers who were just starting out on their missionary careers. The tragedy was a heavy load for Lambie, together with his wife, Charlotte, and the SIM personnel in South Sudan, to shoulder. Despite

20. Lambie, letter enclosed with affidavit to Judge Bert Fish, September 29, 1940, SIMIA, KB-1-121, File 4.

21. By my estimate more than fifty documents in the Lambie correspondence held by SIMIA relate to the death of Dr. and Mrs. Grieves.

22. Lambie, letter to James McClenny, brother of Claire Grieve, December 26, 1940, SIMIA, KB-1-121, File 4.

23. Lambie, letter to August Holm, December 3, 1940, SIMIA, KB-1-121, File 4.

24. Lambie, letter to August Holm, January 28, 1941, SIMIA, KB-1-121, File 4.

the deep sorrow it brought to the entire SIM Sudan family, Dr. Lambie was not deterred from carrying on his missionary mandate within the Anglo-Egyptian Sudan.

Postscript: After the tragic deaths of the Grieves and the evacuation in 1940 of the remaining SIM personnel based at Doro (among the Mabaan) and Chali (among the Uduk), it appeared that ministry among the Mabaan and Uduk people groups might be permanently curtailed. But that was not the case. Wendy James, in a perceptive chapter, follows the story of the Christianizing of the Uduk of Chali from 1941 to the present.[25] In 1941 SIM assigned Mary Beam and Elizabeth Cridland to Chali. Known to the Uduk as "Miss Beam" and "Miss Betty," the two missionaries supervised and taught in the Chali elementary school, mastered the Uduk language, and did Bible translation. Their ministry produced encouraging results. A baptism conducted at Chali in 1949 resulted in the establishment of the first church among the Uduk.

Over a period of years, the number of conversions among the Udak grew, and the mid-1960s saw a mass baptism of over 600 converts. Unfortunately, in 1964 all SIM personnel were expelled from Sudan. One of the cardinal teachings the Beam and Betty team, who were like mothers to the young church, had emphasized among the Uduk Christians was "Stand on your own two feet." In the years that followed without SIM personnel among them, the Uduk attempted to internalize cardinal Christian truths. Certainly during this process, the Uduk Christians as a community struggled with competing loyalties to their former primal religion. But by 1972 the Uduk had established eight new chapels in and around Chali. They showed that they had truly imbibed their mentors' watchword to "Stand on your own two feet."

The eruption in 1983 of civil war in Sudan eventually forced large-scale Uduk dislocation. By 1987 the majority had fled Sudan to the safety of refugee camps in Ethiopia. Located near Assosa (east/southeast of Chali) and Bonga in the south (east of Gambeila), the camps were temporary "holding" places for thousands of Uduk. While in the two camps, the refugees retained their Christian beliefs and practices. In writing their reports, Ethiopian UNHCR officials have regarded the Uduk community at Bonga, numbering some 14,000, as "model refugees" with strong cohesion and inner structure, no doubt due to their Christian heritage.

25. See Wendy James, "Remembering Chali: The SIM in the Sudan–Ethiopian Borderlands (1938–1964) and its Social Legacy," in *Transforming Africa's Religious Landscapes,* ed. Cooper et al., 171–97.

In spite of unusual and grave setbacks for Lambie and his SIM colleagues in Sudan, their 1940 vision for evangelizing among the Uduk and the Mabaan continues to be realized.

15

Misunderstandings with SIM Colleagues

A beloved elderly missionary who realized
something of my inner conflict said,
"Take up the cross into your bosom."

THOMAS A. LAMBIE, *A BRUISED REED*, 43

FROM 1939 THROUGH 1942 friction developed between Dr. Lambie and
mission personnel serving at SIM's five stations in Sudan. Of the SIM missionaries who had earlier served in Abyssinia, only eighteen transferred to
Sudan, and they became increasingly estranged from him.

When the Lambies returned from the United States to Sudan on November 19, 1939, Rowland Bingham, SIM's international director, appointed Lambie as SIM's director for the Sudan. Unfortunately, Bingham did not
officially notify the person then in charge that he was being replaced. Since
mid-1937 Glen Cain had been serving as acting director for SIM in Sudan,
a position he held until July 1939, when he left for furlough in Australia.[1]
On Glen and Winnie Cain's return to Khartoum in December 1939, Lambie
had already been installed as the new SIM director, and Cain came to realize that SIM had no administrative position for him. So, as mentioned in
chapter 13, the Cains (together with Norman and Flossie Couser) oversaw

---

1. Roke, *They Went Forth*, 231.

the construction of SIM's new rest home in a mountain range near Issorie in Equatoria Province, some 150 miles west of Juba.[2]

These changes and reassignments to the SIM Sudan administrative structure were not handled well. Alfred Roke writes, "To the embarrassment of all concerned, an estrangement built up between the two leaders [Lambie and Cain] and the Cains went to live at Issorie in the Upper Nile Province."[3] The discord continued to fester until 1941. At that point Bingham mentioned in a letter to Alfred Roke and Walter Ohman that Glen Cain had accepted a position with the British military, supplying language assistance to the British troops as they began combat missions from Sudan into Abyssinia. It appeared to Bingham that Cain had taken on this assignment without consulting Lambie. He commented, "I judge from this that there was lack of fellowship somewhere."[4] But it may well be that Bingham himself had unintentionally planted the seeds of "lack of fellowship" between the two leaders.

Apparently, Glen Cain did notify Lambie that he would begin working with the British armed forces, but only after he had already made the decision. On February 2, 1941, he wrote:

> Dear Dr. Lambie,
>   This letter may bring you a real surprise. I have offered my services, especially in language help to the army, which offer has been accepted. It appears that I may be taking up my various duties the beginning of March. You may be wondering why I did not get in touch with you first. The responsibility of this decision rests on Winnie and me and I did not want you in any way to be involved or the mission.
>   Signed, G.H. Cain.[5]

Soon after Cain's move into the British army, Lambie himself was not entirely open and forthright with his Sudan SIM colleagues about his own plans. Early in 1941 he offered to serve the British forces as a "Propaganda Agent," based in Malakal. His two-month assignment involved sending

2. Lambie, *A Doctor Carries On*, 52–53.

3. Roke, *They Went Forth*, 197.

4. Bingham, letter to Roke and Ohman, April 24, 1941, in Roke, *They Went Forth*, 198.

5. Cain, letter to Lambie, February 2, 1941, SIMIA, KB-1-22, File 3. See also Forsberg, letter to Bingham, January 16, 1942, SIMIA, Forsberg, Malcolm and Enid, Box 09, File 4.

coded messages through informers to Abyssinian resistance fighters.[6] Further, while serving as SIM director of Sudan, Lambie observed that British soldiers and airmen were arriving in Khartoum in growing numbers. Ever the entrepreneur, he felt that he and his wife should launch a new ministry to British military personnel. As they struggled with knowing God's will in the matter, Lambie decided, "The inner conviction should be strengthened by providential circumstances. When He leads, the work is undertaken for His glory and one can be sure that He will guide and bless."[7] The Lambies decided to "throw open our house and try to do all we could to restrain [the soldiers] from going to dens of infamy and drink shops and to point them to the Saviour."[8] So the Lambies proceeded to open the new ministry, placing a large sign on their gate: "SOLDIERS AND AIRMEN WELCOME." They purchased a number of games which were set up on their spacious veranda with its matted roof. They provided tables for writing letters home. "What gallons of tea and what mountains of cakes disappeared. My wife had to spend a good deal of every day in the kitchen baking homemade cakes, which miraculously vanished each evening. Finally she got a servant trained to do it."[9]

The Lambies recruited other SIM personnel to assist in this service to the soldiers and airmen. When hundreds of Greeks from Cyprus, which the British controlled, were transferred for a time to Khartoum, Nicholas Simponis, a Greek-American, was of special assistance. He was able to distribute hundreds of Greek New Testaments, which the Greek soldiers appreciated receiving. SIM missionaries who assisted this ministry for a time included Zillah Walsh, Carolyn Cain (Lambie's secretary), Alfred Roke, Norman Nunn, and Ken and Blanche Oglesby.[10] Letters received by the Lambies leave little doubt that the Khartoum ministry to servicemen was much appreciated.

> One officer wrote to his wife in India about us. She wrote to some friends in England, who in turn, wrote to two splendid English women residing in California. The women in California

6. This "Propaganda Agent" assignment is fully written up in Lambie, *A Doctor Carries On*, 98–110. See also Lambie, letter to Bingham, February 11, 1941, SIMIA, KB-1-22, File 3.

7. Lambie, *A Doctor Carries On*, 86.

8. Lambie, letter to August Holm, January 15, 1941, SIMIA, KB-1-22, File 3.

9. Lambie, *A Doctor Carries On*, 88.

10. Lambie, *A Doctor Carries On*, 93–94.

knew us and were [so] pleased to get news about us by this long route that they immediately sent us a generous gift.[11]

Another project, making bamboo crates for the long-distance transport of vegetables, also caught Lambie's interest about this time. Seen as another diversion of their director's attention, this project would not only have caused raised eyebrows, but also grumbling and voices of protest among SIM missionaries in Sudan. Through his creative genius, Lambie was able to construct three-quarter-bushel-size bamboo crates, complete with lids. The split bamboo was wired to slats of local mahogany. He reported that over 14,000 of these vegetable crates were eventually manufactured in the Khartoum military shop and put to good use. Soon after, the British military presented Lambie with an additional challenge: "Would he be able to devise a sturdy bamboo fuel carrier that would hold two four-gallon containers [called "debbies"] of either petrol or kerosene. These would be used to transport fuel loaded on trucks traveling on rough non-existent roads."[12] The fuel was destined for the war effort to liberate Abyssinia.

Whenever he was faced with a material, personnel, or spiritual challenge, Lambie would ask God for wisdom. As he prayed about the need for a means to transport the debbies of fuel, an idea evolved. Lambie recounts:

> They wanted a crate or a box that could be used over and over again and this added to the difficulty. At last however the problem was solved, a few strips of mahogany, some [split] bamboo stalks, a bit of wire and a few nails, and there it was. Two tins of gasoline held tightly, and one could use them over and over again. . . . Thus it came about, that more than twenty thousand were made and the army got its gasoline with a minimum of loss in time for the big push, and the war was won with the aid of the crates.[13]

During those three years in the Sudan, Lambie was much troubled with poor health. The intense heat put an added strain on his weakened heart, which meant that he had occasional dizzy spells. At times these symptoms would obligate him to take complete rest for a day or two. After partially recovering, he would return to work.[14]

---

11. Lambie, *A Doctor Carries On*, 96–97.

12. Lambie, *Doctor's Great Commission*, 259.

13. Lambie, *Doctor's Great Commission*, 259–60. Lambie, letter to "Friends," January 26, 1941, mentions the "special crates," SIMIA, KB-1-22, File 29.

14. Lambie, *Doctor's Great Commission*, 259–60. See also Lambie, *A Doctor Carries On*, 134–57.

Because of Lambie's ill health, the British doctors serving in the non-military hospital in Khartoum strongly urged him to get away to a cooler climate for at least two months. The Lambies then traveled to the Holy Land from the end of August to mid-October, 1941, where they were entertained by Alfred P. S. Clark, director of the Barclays Bank branches in Palestine, and his wife, who were sympathetic to the cause of missions.[15]

When the Lambies returned to Sudan following his brief medical leave, Lambie's role as director for SIM Sudan began to unravel. In mid-January 1942, Malcolm Forsberg wrote a three-page letter to Bingham, SIM's international director. Salient points are:

> Opposition to Dr. Lambie's leadership is nothing new. I think you could discover that in Ethiopia there was considerable lack of confidence in him. . . . When Dr. Lambie left to take up Government [British] duties in Malakal he did not consult anybody about the wisdom of his going. . . . Last November a number of our missionaries were gathered together at Melut on their way to their stations after an educational conference at Malakal, convened by the government. We were unanimous in feeling we could no longer continue working under Dr. Lambie's leadership. . . . I suggest that Dr. Lambie's recall be effected at once. . . . The workers are unanimous in asking for Dr. Lambie's recall. . . . The situation is tense. We are sorry that you must be burdened with such things at such a time. But since the matter has been opened up, we feel that a speedy disposal of the problem will do much to alleviate your anxiety and ours. Signed, M. Forsberg.[16]

During wartime the sending and receiving of mail was slow; therefore, Bingham was intent on flying to Sudan to hear both sides of the situation. But because the United States suddenly decided to enter the war, no planes were available, and trans-Atlantic Ocean travel was precarious. Bingham then decided to respond to Forsberg in writing. On February 18 he sent a two-page letter addressed to Forsberg and Roke.

> Now, let me say that I believe in our Practice and Principles, and I feel that the work, in both the Anglo-Egyptian Sudan and in Ethiopia, calls for leadership, but it is not my intention to appoint anyone who cannot command the confidence of his fellow missionaries. I cannot appoint a perfect man, because I know of none. . . . I can assure you therefore, if I succeed in coming

15. Lambie, *Doctor's Great Commission*, 261–62.

16. Forsberg, letter to Bingham, January 16, 1942, 3 pp., SIMIA, Forsberg, Malcolm and Enid, Box 09, File 4.

to the field, I shall want to have your fullest expression in these spheres, and trust we may be brought to a real unanimity in the appointments made. He would be a foolish man who would consent to accept a leadership place, who would not have the confidence of those with whom he has to labour.[17]

By July 8, 1942, because of Lambie's recurring ill health, Thomas and Charlotte were prepared to leave Sudan. Alfred Roke drove them out to the Omdurman airport, where they spent the night and prepared for an early flight on July 9. Roke writes:

I wished we had been able to have a formal and public farewell meeting for them which the circumstances forbade. We owed Dr. Lambie much for the years of loving and invaluable service in that very difficult war period. Very early in the morning we were called to the [airport] assembly area, and there I expressed the prayer for God's blessing and protection, and waved them goodbye. It was Thursday, July 9, 1942, that the Lambies flew out from Omdurman.[18]

Dr. Lambie experienced alienation on various sides while in Sudan. Initially the British civil servants in Sudan curtailed his attempts to expand the number of SIM's mission outposts. Then, the sudden deaths of Dr. and Mrs. Grieve at Doro completed his alienation from the Italians. His alienation from Emperor Haile Sellassie was an enigma to Lambie, who felt its cause was not entirely his own doing. The Italians had falsified letters and attributed them to Dr. Lambie, an action that was carried out by persons whom Lambie had thought he might trust and through whom he believed he could gain permission for SIM to continue missionary activity in Abyssinia.[19] But that proved to have been a false hope. His final alienation came at the hands of his own SIM Sudan colleagues who judged him inept as their leader.

Regardless of the tensions and stresses that he experienced, Dr. Lambie's missionary career of some thirty-five years in Africa is a remarkable story. He was a close friend to all: the local people as well as those in high office. He mastered several Sudanese languages as well as both Arabic and Amharic. His mission commitment to all ethnic people groups in Abyssinia and Sudan caused him to make unusual sacrifices: neglect of his own

17. Bingham, letter to Forsberg and Roke, February 18, 1942, SIMIA, Forsberg, Malcolm and Enid, Box 09, File 4.

18. Roke, *They Went Forth*, 239–40.

19. I deem two letters supposedly written by Lambie to be spurious because of their content and irregularities in Lambie's signature. See details in chapter 12.

health, loss of friendship with Emperor Haile Sellassie, and loss of confidence among his colleagues in mission. Lambie's love for and loyalty to his SIM colleagues is evident from his hand-written letter to Alf and Tina Roke at the death of Gordon, their two-year-old son. "Charlotte and I know what it is like to lose a son. No one but parents can really understand. There is not much we can say, only to assure you that we weep with you. Jesus knows and cares."[20]

Years later Clarence Duff, Lambie's deputy in Addis Ababa, wrote, "I regard Dr. Lambie one of the best and greatest [missionaries] it has been my privilege to know. If sometimes his judgment or his actions proved to be unwise, he rose above his faults, outlived them and the criticism incurred, and went on to fresh achievement."[21]

20. Lambie, handwritten letter to Alf and Tina Roke, June 27, 1942, in Roke, Gordon of Bajang, 30.

21. Duff, Cords of Love, 334.

Dr. Thomas A. Lambie, passport photograph, 1907
(Courtesy of Margaret Hall Special Collection)

By boat from Khartoum to Doleib Hill, first on the White Nile, then on the Sobat
River, a tributary (From Francesco Pierli, et al., *Gateway to the Heart of Africa*, 133)

Thomas and Charlotte Lambie, initially stationed in South Sudan
(Courtesy of SIM International Archives)

Thomas and Charlotte Lambie's first home, Doleib Hill, South Sudan, on the Sobat
River (From Francesco Pierli, et al., *Gateway to the Heart of Africa*, 93)

The Lambie family: Charlotte, Thomas, and children Wallace and Betty, ca. 1922
(Courtesy of Margaret Hall Special Collection)

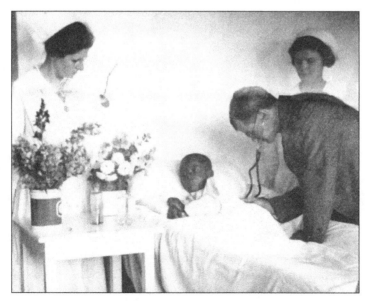

Dr. Lambie treating a patient with nurses Viola Bayne
and Hazel Ewing assisting, Ras Tafari Makonnen and George Memorial Hospital,
Guleile, Addis Ababa, ca. 1925
(Courtesy of SIM International Archives)

Abyssinian Frontiers Mission

in fellowship with

Worldwide Evangelization Crusade

Headquarters: 113 Fulton Street, New York

You and your friends are cordially invited to the

INAUGURAL MEETING of the ABYSSINIAN FRONTIERS MISSION

MONDAY, APRIL 4, 1927 at 8 P. M.

at 113 FULTON STREET, NEW YORK CITY

SPEAKERS:

MR. and MRS. A. B. BUXTON, REV. GEORGE RHOAD (Africa)
DR. T. A. LAMBIE (Abyssinia)

Soloists — Mrs. G. W. Cleveland, Mr. H. Sweet, Mr. H. I. Meredith
Chairman — Rev. C. S. Kidd (Brooklyn)

Song Service 7:45
Leader H. I. Meredith

Constance J. Brandon, Gen. Sec.
113 Fulton Street, New York City

Launching of the Abyssinia Frontiers Mission, New York City, April 4, 1927
(Courtesy of SIM International Archives)

The pioneer AFM/SIM party arriving in Addis Ababa, December 1927.
From left: Thomas A. Lambie, Walter A. Ohman, Betty Lambie, Carl H. Rasmussen,
George Rhoad (son), Clarence W. Duff, George W. Rhoad.
Seated: Mrs. Charlotte Lambie, Mrs. C. H. Rasmussen, Mrs. George Rhoad.
Missing: Mr. Glen H. Cain.
(Courtesy of SIM International Archives)

AFM/SIM missionaries preparing to trek to South Abyssinia for gospel outreach, ca. 1929. *From left*: Walter Ohman, Thomas Lambie, Glen Cain, George Rhoad, and Clarence Duff.
(Courtesy of SIM International Archives)

Grand opening of Leprosarium with royal family, dignitaries, and AFM/SIM members, in Furi, Addis Ababa, 1932.
(Courtesy of SIM International Archives)

Headquarters of AFM/SIM, Guleile, Addis Ababa, erected 1932.
The site is presently occupied by the Dutch Embassy.
(Courtesy of SIM International Archives)

From left: George Rhoad, Rowland Bingham, and Thomas Lambie
visiting AFM/SIM stations in southern Abyssinia.
(Courtesy of SIM International Archives)

Dr. Thomas Lambie and Irma (his second wife), serving tuberculosis patients
at the Ain Arruob Sanatorium, ca. 1953.
(Photo by Rev. Keith Coleman, IBPFM)

Gravestone of Dr. Thomas Alexander Lambie,
Berachah Presbyterian Church, Bethlehem, Jordan.
(Courtesy of Mr. Lloyd Long, 2016, son-in-law of Rev. LaVerne Donaldson
who officiated at Dr. Lambie's funeral)

The legacy of Dr. Thomas Lambie lives on at the Lambie Cafe located in Guleile.
(Courtesy of Mr. Zenebe Gebrehana, 2018, manager of SIM Publications, Addis Ababa)

16

Dr. Lambie's Letters to His Wife Charlotte and Daughter Betty

And everyone who has left houses or brothers
or sisters or father or mother or children or fields
for my sake will receive a hundred times as much
and will inherit eternal life.

MATTHEW 19:29 (NIV)

DR. LAMBIE WAS OFTEN absent from home for extended periods of time. When he was separated from his wife and daughter, he wrote tenderly to them. This chapter presents select quotations from his letters to two who were near and dear to him. They reveal a side of his person not seen in his official correspondence. The first letters, from 1929, were to his wife, Charlotte, who was in the United States for medical treatment. The second group of letters were addressed to his married daughter, Betty Rees; they date from 1946 to 1952. At that time Betty was residing in England. Lambie's style of writing to his wife and daughter was very personal and intimate. Little did he realize that a future generation of researchers would have access to these personal musings, many of them handwritten.

Alone in Abyssinia in 1929, Lambie poured out his heart to Charlotte. He revealed in an endearing manner the personal burdens and struggles he was experiencing while alone.[1] In a manner of communication very different from his public writing, Lambie expressed vital themes such as lament, suffering, and costly discipleship. The letters read like laments from the Psalms.

Lambie's June 17, 1929, letter to Charlotte from Hosanna, Abyssinia, reflects the emptiness he felt with both Charlotte and Betty gone. The two had recently arrived in the United States. "Dearest Wife, It's three weeks tomorrow since I left you on the station platform at Djibouti and it seems like an age. My, when I got back to the house in Addis Ababa, I just thought I couldn't stand it. I felt so bad." He later elaborated in *A Doctor without a Country*.

> My own fortunes were at a low ebb at this time, my wife's sickness and trip to America and all these extra journeys, the expense of only part of which was borne by the Mission, had exhausted the slender missionary allowance. My shoes were literally worn out, and I had no money to replace them. Still, what matters a pair of burst shoes in the rainy season when the Gospel was triumphant and Sidamo was open?[2]

In a six-page handwritten letter to Charlotte, written on August 4, 1929, Lambie was apparently concerned about his future son-in-law, Herbert Rees, who had Anglican ties to the Church of England. This young and well-educated English suitor was seriously courting the Lambies' daughter, Betty, who was eighteen years of age and at that point was in the United States completing her secondary education. Herbert's theological leaning was toward the "High Anglican Church," a position not entirely compatible with Lambie's own Presbyterian theological stance. He writes, as he often did, using an endearing variant of the name "Charlotte":

> Dearest Charliot,
>   I think Herbert ought to go into the ministry or priest-hood as he calls it. I would give anything I've got to see him an Evangelical rather than an Anglo Catholic. But maybe you and your daughter [Betty] may be the means of getting him to see the light on this. . . . Of course I want him to be honest in what he does believe. I like the Church of England, all but its exclu-siveness and its Anglo Catholic or High Church party in their flirting with Rome with her fatal Christ-dishonoring mistakes. I cannot see how there can be any mediator but our Lord Jesus

---

1. Unless noted otherwise, the letters in this chapter from Lambie to his wife, Charlotte, all from the year 1929, are located in MHSC.

2. Lambie, *Doctor without a Country*, 184.

Christ or any confessional or exalting the communion into a pretended eating of Christ's very body and flesh. . . . Of course as I said before that I do not wish Herbert to do anything that he does not believe in his heart but it certainly will be a great sorrow to me if he takes the high church position in these things.

Both Charlotte and Betty, however, believed that Herbert would make a wonderful husband for Betty. Probably for this reason Lambie wrote three weeks later, August 26, in a more conciliatory manner: "I am glad you find Herbert more loveable and true all the time. He does seem like a fine young man."

In his letter of August 4 to Charlotte, Lambie had also expressed concern about their personal finances. At that time, SIM used a "pooling system" in handling financial support for its missionaries. All funds donated for the personal finances of SIM members were pooled, and each SIM member in West Africa and Abyssinia received an equal share of the pool each month. Lambie wrote:

I hardly know what to write about finances. I do not at all want to blame you, dear, but I certainly got a shock when I heard that you had to cash the emergency check. I, of course, will have to pay this back, and just when I thought I had saved about enough to pay our Ghanotalsis bill [Greek grocer/entrepreneur in Addis Ababa] and Mohamedally bill [Addis Ababa Indian entrepreneur who rented rooms to SIM], it does hit me pretty hard. I think that by being very careful I may be able in a month or so to get straight again, but it will take all I can scrape up. I have a good many stores [groceries] left, and I am trying to be very careful of them, so I think that they will last me three months or more. I am really very comfortable and the boys look after me fine. [Lambie was living "off the land" in Soddo, where local produce was much cheaper than in Addis Ababa.] Milk is plentiful here, also potatoes and tomatoes and some other vegetables. God has provided every need and will provide. I had hoped to be able to save so as to send to you, but He will do the things for you that I cannot if you believe in Him. I do not mind one bit having to do without things if only you are happy and do not have to pinch yourself too much. . . . Do not let this worry you now, but I do think that God wants us both to be more careful.

That Lambie found his relationship with his SIM colleague George Rhoad, who was also the SIM assistant director, to be a struggle is perhaps an understatement. Rather wisely, no hint of the Lambie/Rhoad interpersonal difficulties appears in the books Lambie published. But in the same August 4 letter, Lambie confided to Charlotte,

> He [Rhoads] has his failures like all the rest of us and the Holy Spirit has sometimes a tremendous struggle in his life to get the better of George Rhoad but in the end He does triumph over George. George will not always (I sometimes think never) admit to others that it is so and is prone to blame others and all that kind of thing instead of being just broken hearted before the Lord. . . . He is selfish, at times very selfish. I guess I can't say anything, for I am, too. . . . The real thing in the man is his real faith in God and an intense longing to do God's will. For this I love him and D.V. [God willing] will work with him as long as God desires.

On another matter, Ras Tafari, the regent of Abyssinia, approached Lambie in 1928 about the need for a leprosy center that could supply medical treatment to the hundreds of lepers. These desperate people from the countryside were crowding into the center of Addis Ababa, begging for medical help, food, and shelter. In his August 4 letter, Lambie mentioned this possible project.

> I am not saying anything about the leper work at Addis Ababa, but I have a deepening conviction that it must be done and am praying and want you to pray with me that all may be convinced of its necessity and advantage if indeed it be God's will. Otherwise I do not want to do it. I had a nice letter from Mr. Danner of the Leper Mission [in the US]. Maybe he will ask you to go to New York to see him.

Later, in *A Doctor without a Country*, Lambie confirmed that Charlotte had made an excellent presentation at the American Mission to Lepers in New York and had received a positive response.

> In my wife's year alone in America [1929] she did one piece of work that was destined to bear much fruit. She gave an address at the annual meeting of the American Mission to Lepers in which she presented the needs of the lepers in Abyssinia. God used her message to interest them in Abyssinia, with the result that they agreed to give five thousand dollars a year for five years to build a leprosarium there. Other sums of money were given as well, and the leprosarium was assured.[3]

---

3. Lambie, *Doctor without a Country*, 209.

The property known as The Meadows, where Charlotte's parents, Albert and Elizabeth Claney, resided in Owing Mills, Maryland, was a financial concern to Lambie. Charlotte's parents were advancing in years, and the property needed constant maintenance. In his letter of August 26, Lambie wrote,

> Dearest Charliot,
>   It is better to sell the place than to let them [the Claneys] suffer want. As for going into debt, I refuse. It is too much of a burden for us to both carry. I cannot and will not do it, and I will not be a burden to our friends. Debt is not right for us who have, as we believe, fully yielded ourselves to God for His service. . . . Of course it comes down to us at last! Are we in this work heart and soul and spirit, to bring Christ to Abyssinia, [and] is it the dearest thing in the world to me, and are we willing to give it all that we have? If we are thus willing, then I have no fear that any of us will starve or be discredited before God. We may have to sell the place [The Meadows]. All right. God to me is a million times dearer than The Meadows. For Wallace and Betty? Yes, that [is] all right but God is looking after them and will look after them too. If you have faith to believe God and to really trust Him and to get things thus from Him . . . do not let it get on your nerves. It is going to be all right if we trust God. . . . If any of this seems harsh or hard, forgive me, as it is all meant in utter love for you. Dear, how I miss you, but this work is very important and if I know you are strong and capable and not self-contained but contained in Christ and resting in Him and not on me, then I feel the great strain out here much less. God is showing forth His arm. . . . Be anxious in nothing, but in everything let your wants be made known to God with thanksgiving.
>   Your lovingest,
>   Tommie

On Sunday, September 1, Lambie wrote to Charlotte from near Alatta Wondo. He was on his way by mule caravan to Ager Selaam, the provincial government center of Dejazmatch Birru.

> Dearest One,
>   We had such a good day of prayer Friday, and I was so much in prayer for you, dear, and for our dear folks. It does seem to me that we ought for their sakes, if not for our own, to sell the place [The Meadows] and get into town somewhere near Baltimore or I think near Pittsburgh. We can get a little place for them [Charlotte's parents] a mile or so from town on a

main road where electric light and bus line goes past the door, have an acre or two of ground for chickens and garden. . . . I feel with Daddy's eyesight going, and even if it were not going that it is too much for them to be way out in the country with no neighbors or nothing. It is up to you and me to get them out of this and not get ourselves into debt. . . . What would you think of going to Ohio, getting on the National Rd. to Muskingum? It seems to me that this would be a good solution. It would give the folks lectures to attend and be in a United Presbyterian community. . . . I do feel that God has called us to Abyssinia. He is blessing us in this work. The missionaries are such a wonderful group of people, practically everyone fully yielded to God. Mr. Rhoad is so much better than before, more humble, confesses his own sins and seems to want to work with me in everything. . . . I have had so much to learn, and actually if I let myself go I could just get so lonesome and so out of sorts with none of my family near that I just want to cry, and it's not just the family so much as just missing you. . . . It is just like a big ache all over. I just have to remind myself that we are doing it for His sake, and then it gets better and I get a joy out of life again. . . .

Your loving,

Tom.

Lambie and Rhoad reached Ager Selaam the first week of September. The official letter signed by Regent Ras Tafari, which they carried from Addis Ababa, was handed to Dejazmatch Birru, governor of Sidama Province. This letter, written in Amharic with the stamp of the regent's official seal, did not appear to give a clear directive to grant "Dr. Lambie's Mission" official permission to launch mission work in Sidamo. But it served its purpose. On September 7, Lambie wrote:

Darling,

Well, Birru was simply great. He got up and bowed, read the letter standing, bowed very low, said in turn . . . this is all I need. I did not want to send you all away last year but I had orders from Addis Ababa. He showed us the orders. . . . We all were absolutely on our faces before God and He has heard and given a marvelous deliverance. How good he is. . . . [Birru] has just been too kind for words. I told him plainly that we are here because we believe that God has sent us and we will proclaim Jesus Christ and will preach Him to the Sidamo natives. "Yes I know that," was his reply, and, "That's all right." So our position is clear and right. How grateful we are to Him who has alone given us this land. . . . No post this week and no word from

my dear Charlotte, only I seem to have the assurance that all is
well with you too. . . . God is, I feel, sure and will bring you and
me closer through this separation and sacrifice for Him. He will
never fail.

Your loving,
Tom.

On September 15, Lambie was again writing from Ager Selaam.
Together with George Rhoad he had scoured the area southeast of Ager
Selaam for several days, attempting to assist Dejazmatch Birru in finding
a better official government location at a lower altitude. In his tent on that
Sunday afternoon, he wrote a four-page letter.

Dearest Darlingest,

Last week the A/A post had not come in and this week we
were off 20 miles from here looking up possible sites for *De-*
jazmatch Birru and the mission, the postman tried to follow
us and never caught up, this is another story, and he has not
gotten to us yet. We arrived back at Ager Salaam yesterday after
going many weary miles to the south and east, wet, cold, and
mud. . . . We made camp about 5:30 in the rain, no firewood,
all very tired, cold, wet, hungry, and all the rest of it. A more
disgruntled bunch of men you never saw than our servants
were, and the missionaries were not much better. . . . I just lie
awake at nights thinking about you all and praying for you and
loving you. Sometimes I get so lonesome to see some of you and
especially you that I just think I will burst, but then I just take
it to the Lord and it is all right and His grace is sufficient, and
His blessing I sometimes think in proportion as we are willing
to sacrifice for Him. The missionaries have all been very lovely
to me and sympathize with me and pray for you all. I was so
concerned for Wallace and was praying for him and I seemed
to see him surrounded by rings of shining metal and it seemed
to me that God said, "This is how I am protecting Wally" and I
have not worried at all about him since, though not of course
ceasing to pray for him.

Your loving,
Tom.

P.S. I do hope you did not borrow money. It is so much
better to sell the place [The Meadows]. Pay what we owe and get
a smaller place for the folks.

A later letter from Lambie to Charlotte again addresses matters between their daughter Betty and her suitor, Herbert Rees. On September 22

on his return from Ager Selaam, he wrote a seven-page letter from Alatta Wondo, Sidama.

> Dearest Charliot,
>
> As for Herbert [Rees] I love him immensely and all that, but I do think he ought to stop mooning around Betty and get a job. Now, here is the situation. #1. He does not feel called to be a preacher. All right there, that's off unless God definitely puts His hand upon him. #2. He does not want to be a teacher. All right there, that's off but seems a pity, for it is the only thing he seems really qualified to do and I think he would make a good one. #3. He has the idea of Y.M.C.A. work or social service of some kind. Well, let us think of that and what is open to him—say, Y.M.C.A. work itself. As a rule, American Y.M.C.A. has found that American workers are the best both in America and in foreign lands. The English do not take so well. Herbert . . . would seem to be a charming person but flighty. . . . He has no athletic ability of any kind. I certainly do not think it right for him to think of marrying Betty until he is more definite and has some prospects, and I feel that you and I must insist on this. The very fact of his being willing to live on you for weeks in Owing Mills [at The Meadows] and on us in Addis Ababa and put us so far in debt that it has taken me until now to dig out . . . seems to me to indicate a lack of appreciation or something. . . . I meant to write to Betty and Herbert today but am not up to it. You can read them parts [of this letter].
>
> Your lovingest,
> Tom.

On September 29, Lambie wrote again from Ager Selaam. He continued to be concerned about Betty's suitor, Herbert Rees, and gave rather forceful advice prior to their intended marriage in 1930:

> Dearest Wife,
>
> I wrote you last week that long letter about Herbert which I do hope that he and you will see the sense of and be led to do the right thing. Then I wrote to Herbert himself asking him to let you and Betty read it. God surely has something more for Herbert than to be a Y.M.C.A. secretary. In saying this I do not mean to decry the Y.M.C.A. secretaries either. It seems to me in brief that Herbert needs: 1st A definite surrender of his will to God. 2nd Definite orders from God through an enlightened spirit, quickened heart and mind to do some definite work. 3rd Undertaking that work. Marriage afterwards. Please think and

pray this through and I feel sure you will conclude that this is the right course for him to take. I do not approve of his staying longer at Owing Mills in idleness. It's not good for Betty or for himself or for any of you. . . . I must close this. I wish I could hear from you oftener. It seems 400 years since you left.

Your loving,

Tom.

By mid-October two months had passed since Lambie had received a letter from Charlotte. After four months of trekking by mule, he was finally in his own house in Soddo, Wolaitta, and slept in a proper bed, which was much more comfortable. On October 13 he wrote:

Dearest wife,

I am sorry Herbert is having trouble getting a job although sort of glad that he did not go into the Y.M.C.A. as I do not think it is the thing for him. I would be very pleased if he came into our mission for language work but only if he felt a real call to do so and only if he came in as everyone else does, as a regular missionary I mean. I fear he has not felt a real call, a real surrender of all to Christ, although I do not think he is far from it, and I think we ought to pray very earnestly for him that he might be led to surrender himself.

The letter goes on to discuss at length the sale of The Meadows and how best to handle money through its sale. Lambie continues:

I have omitted to tell you of the trip over [back to Soddo]. It was not easy. In fact, the past months have been about the hardest I have ever had. Not having you with me has been so hard. Every place that we saw together before makes me want to cry or something. I just feel so kind of burdened that it hurts. Still I am glad we did it [the long trekking], as you never could have stood the physical strain and stress. Spending an entire rainy season in a tent and travelling about in the rain and mud has been far from pleasant. The incidental things, too, but I will not go into them for God has abundantly compensated for it in the victory He has accomplished through us for which we are humbly and exceedingly grateful.

It appears that Charlotte had shared in her letters to her husband what she had experienced herself, enduring heartaches and difficulties while separated. Lambie attempts to encourage her to bear all these as a good soldier of Jesus Christ. He ends his October 13 letter:

Think a little, too, of what a time I have been having these four and a half months of which I have tried to say nothing, but God knows they have not been easy months, out in the rain and mud and cold, poor food and all the rest of it not alone—the tremendous mental and spiritual strain and uncertainty and all. I think when you think of this you will not write as you did.

Your loving,

Tom.

In mid-December 1929, the SIM staff from the Soddo station traveled a six-hour journey south to Lake Abaye for a relaxing day excursion. Lambie's special dog, Bill, took a fancy to another member of the party and together, man and dog, went off to explore the shoreline of the lake. Unfortunately, the dog did not return to camp. Several of the missionaries joined in Lambie's search for Bill, but to no avail. Lambie's letter of December 22 ends on a rather sorrowful note.

Dearest Charlotte,

Whether it was a crocodile or a leopard, I do not know. . . . I feel like I have lost a brother almost. One of the best friends I ever had. I could hardly sleep the first night thinking of how he used always to lie beside my bed and if I spoke to him in the night, as I was so tired and thirsty to sleep much, his old tail would thump the ground. . . .

All my heart and greatest love,

Tom.

On December 25 Lambie wrote his final letter to Charlotte prior to his trek with the Rhoads family to meet Rowland Bingham at the Kenya/Abyssinia border town of Moyale. Charlotte had been advised by their family physician in Philadelphia, Dr. Howard Kelly, that she should undergo an operation. The medical examination had been thorough, but she was apprehensive. Her caring and loving husband attempted to allay her fears, writing, "Don't you worry the least bit. There is practically no danger in an operation like this in the hands . . . of Dr. Kelly and his assistants."

In the same December 25 letter, he mentioned having received a conciliatory letter from Herbert Rees.

I had such a nice letter from Herbert which I propose to answer today. Isn't it fine he could get his M.A. and B.A. both at the same time. I am sure I must have seemed a little harsh but I think it will work good in the end. The young man will surely realize that he was never angled for or encouraged, and I believe it will make for future happiness.

> All my best and greatest love,
> Tom.

Lambie wrote that letter eleven months before Betty and Herbert were to be married on November 20, 1930. He arrived in the United States at the end of May 1930.

The foregoing excerpts come from personal letters Lambie wrote to his wife. They recount concerns he had regarding a variety of issues, not least of which was his loneliness for Charlotte. Now we come to a series of letters, from 1946 to 1952, that he wrote from Palestine to Betty, who was residing with her four children in England.[4] By this time Betty and Herbert had been separated. The following correspondence began soon after Charlotte's death on January 25, 1946, in Port Said, Egypt, and continued until 1952 (Lambie's own death came in 1954). The letters portray deep loneliness at the death of Charlotte and the sincere loving care of a father for his own special daughter and his four grandchildren residing far away in trying times.

His letter of July 14, 1946, to Betty was addressed: Mrs. A. H. Rees, Chiswick Vicarage, 'The Mall,' London, W. 4, England.

> My darling,
>   Yes, we certainly do understand one another, and I feel deeply touched and unworthy that you should regard my prayers. I feel sure that some of these days the blessed Holy Spirit will take hold of you and cause you to make a clean sweep of everything. . . . You came pretty close to doing so when Charlotte fell asleep [January 1946] and it may take my departure to complete it in your heart. You have so much against you. . . . I realize it will be very hard for you to come to Palestine with your family hanging on your every motion. . . . I will not selfishly urge you to do this. . . . Getting away from them [the children] for a time would be very good for you and would certainly make them appreciate you more. . . . Now I must close with tons of love, sympathy and understanding,
>   Dad.

On March 19, 1946, Lambie had written to Betty following the sudden death of his wife, Charlotte.

> My Darling,
>   I get ever so many letters of sympathy and condolence and some of them are simply beautiful. Shall I send them to you or would they harrow up your feelings needlessly? I will do

4. Lambie's letters to his daughter Betty, 1946–52, are in the MHSC, located at 25 Park Avenue, Kerry, nr. Newton, Powys SY 16 4AD, UK.

whatever you say. I have been sleeping much better recently and
I am glad for that.
    Much love,
    Dad.

A year later Lambie wrote from Jerusalem on Easter Sunday, April 6,
1947:

My darling Betty,
    It's a lovely day, almost too beautiful, and all the field flow-
ers are in bloom and the city looks so clean and nice as long as
you don't look too closely. I am rather tired as we have had a
series of Jerusalem Easter Keswick meetings, and as I was one
of the leaders I found it rather strenuous. Then this morning
they asked me to be the annual speaker at the Garden Tomb
Easter sunrise meeting, and although I was greatly honoured
and greatly humbled I did find that it took a great deal out of
me. I spoke about Mary Magdalene as in Luke 7. . . . Now I am
getting busy at Ain Arrub [just south of Bethlehem] getting the
house plastered. . . . I do get pretty tired sometimes. I do not
have your mother to tell me to stop working. . . . I spoke to you
some months ago about [my] ever re-marrying, but I am glad
to say that there is nothing of that on the schedule for me as I
have no plans whatever that way. . . . Today is our wedding day
[anniversary] April 6, 1909, and how happy we were. I do hope
everything is well with you my darling and with the dear family.
    Affectionately,
    Dad.

On April 27 Lambie wrote in the midst of busy renovations on his
future house near Bethlehem:

My darling Betty,
    No letter from you this two weeks and no cablegram. I hope
everything is well. I sent you a check for $100 which I hope ar-
rived safely. I have been so busy at Ain Arrub trying to get the
house in order. It seems to take a good while but it is shaping
up rapidly now. . . . I wish you were here to advise me about the
house and tell me what to do as I feel kind of hopeless about
furniture and things. . . . The country out here is so lovely. . . . I
have planted a lot of trees around the hospital site. Will have to
water them some this year. . . . Do write to me my darling. I get
such a lonesome feeling when I do not hear from you.
    Dad.

> P.S. Yesterday was Wally's birthday. I am sure you
> remembered.[5]

Betty and Herbert were married in 1930. Lambie's letter of May 3, 1947, indicates that all was not well with the marriage even before the two separated. He wrote:

> My darling,
>   Your letter came yesterday and evidently Herbert has not been forwarding my letters to you as I have written once a week. . . . I have written the Bishop of London. I hope it does some good. You must have gone through some terrible times with Herbert and I am so sorry. The thing is to try to endure for the children's sake. . . . The Bishop should know and should help. Go to him as a daughter and ask for help. . . . You are such a dear and such a sweet doting little mother and wife and do not think I am criticising you, for I would not want you to feel that. You are so unselfish and helpful. . . . I will send all letters care of Monica until I hear from you. . . . I will look after you all I can my darling, so let me know your needs. I sent you a parcel from Denmark—butter, bacon, etc. I do hope you got it and also the $100. Herbert must support you. Do you want me to write to him? Would it do any good? Now write me often and tell me all about everything.
>   Oceans of love,
>   Dad.

From a May 12, 1947, letter, it appears that Betty and Herbert's marriage continued to unravel. That month Betty and the four children moved into a rented facility at Street Farm Cottage, Great Hallingbury, living there until February 1949. Lambie wrote:

> My darling Betty,
>   Your sweet letter arrived Saturday. . . . Since Herbert is not confidential with you I want you to feel you can be confidential with me and tell me everything. . . . If you really got up on your hind legs and told him what was what, would it not help? Tell him it is no way for a priest, a supposed man of God, to act. . . . What you are going through is Satanic, and only the Lord can help. He can and He will. . . . It is terrific, I am sure, what you are going through. May the Lord bless you my daughter. . . .
>   Goodbye my darling,
>   Dad.

5. For details of the sudden death of Thomas and Charlotte Lambie's son Wallace in Medellin, Colombia, see chapter 9.

On October 6, 1947, after his marriage to Miss Irma Schneck, who was a former missionary with SIM, Lambie wrote to Betty. Irma had first served in Jimma, Abyssinia (1931–37), then during the Fascist invasion was assigned to Nigeria. Some months after Charlotte's death, Lambie invited Miss Schneck to assist him in Palestine. He wrote later that he might have been "guilty of duplicity and guile, for I needed help for more things than the sanatorium."[6] The two were on their honeymoon near the Sea of Galilee, when he wrote to Betty.

> My Darling,
> The wedding was a great success. Irma went over early to the Clarks [manager of Barclays Bank, Palestine] to get dressed in her wedding dress which was of light blue nylon and lace with a white hat. . . . We are very happy together as we have so much in common and she is so kind and good. I think I told you she is of Swiss descent, and this I think makes her very practical although very spiritual. . . . She will be like a big sister to you I hope. She will be 49 this month while we are at sea.
> With very much love,
> Dad.
>
> P.S. Irma says to tell you that she knows she can never take your mother's place but does so much want to be as a helpful loving big sister [Irma was only thirteen years older than Betty].

Two years later, August 1, 1949, while Lambie and Irma were returning aboard ship from New York to Palestine via Beirut, he concluded a letter,

> Someone else wrote me that they were sending you a care parcel. Be very meticulous in answering at once to these parcels, as Americans are like that. Otherwise they think you do not appreciate them or never got them or something. So be sure you answer every one at once. It pays off.
> Love to you my darling and a kiss for each of the children.
> Love,
> Dad.

Earlier that year, in February, Betty and the four children had already moved from London to their new residence called "Gilmans," Great Canfield, Essex, England. This dwelling was a historic cottage built in 1485 with no piped water and outside lavatory facilities. It was surrounded by

---

6. Lambie, *A Doctor's Great Commission*, 274.

adequate pasture land where Betty tended sheep, had several milk cows, and kept pigs and chickens to sustain herself and her family.[7]

His letter of October 2, 1950, bearing the return address of Box 1, Bethlehem, Hashemite Kingdom of the Jordan, begins,

> My darling,
> A glorious October day here. . . . Your eagerly expected letters usually arrive on Saturday but none for the past two or three. Tears! Convulsive sobs!! Sackcloth and ashes!!! God bless you and keep you my darling. Much love from Irma.
> Dad.
>
> P.S. You will be answering all my questions, won't you?

Lambie's December 3, 1950, letter to Betty sounds "grandfatherly":

> My darling,
> Cheers for a letter from yesterday. It told all about the pigs. I think you ought to give them up. It's too much. Especially in the winter. . . . Had a very charming letter from Margaret Mary [Betty's oldest daughter, b. 1932]. Made me want to send her another birthday gift as soon as possible. . . . You are a brave good girl and I am proud of you.
> Yours,
> Dad.

Lambie's September 9, 1951, letter begins:

> My darling,
> Your birthday is Wednesday [Betty will be 40]. I wish I might be there to celebrate it. Not this year. . . . Now please dear, answer some of my past questions and also write for me the addresses of the children and their birthdays . . . and just state how long Julie [b. 1936] and David [b. 1934] are to be at their respective schools [Betty's fourth child, Tommie, was born in 1947].
> Much love,
> Dad.

Lambie begins a March 2, 1952, letter to Betty by describing the Palestinian weather.

> My darling,
> What an awful day. Blowing a perfect gale and rain in gusts and fog and most anything. Still we are warm and comfortable in our little house. We surely have lots of guests. We had two

7. Margaret Hall, email to Paul Balisky, November 27, 2018, PBSC.

R.A.F. men for most of the week. . . . I was interested in your new chicks. That's the right idea. Get them early and they will lay in the autumn when egg prices are high. My, what a time you had with those big pigs. Our little Betty armed with a lead pipe on the front line. I don't know what to think about your going into the pig business yourself again. Too heavy work I think. . . .

Now, with very much love to my sweet child,
Dad.

On January 13, 1952, Lambie wrote the last letter we have from him to Betty. He was concerned that she had not been responding to his many questions.

My sweetie,

At long last came a letter from you and the dear letters from the grandchildren. . . . Betty, would you please answer if you got all the dishes or not? I have asked you six times. What do I have to do to get an answer? If only myself was concerned I would simply let it go, but other people [continue writing and] bother Irma. . . . It's been so cold, and the refugees' clothes are thinner and get worse all the time. It's depressing to see them and be able to do so little about it. So glad for that wonderful stove. If it were equally suited for wood fuel I might get one. It is a miracle from what you say.

Much much love,
Dad.

This very personal correspondence from Lambie, first to his wife Charlotte, during the latter part of 1929, and then to his daughter, Betty, from 1946 to 1952, is honest, open, and endearing. In perusing the letters, the reader almost feels like an intruder into the private domain of the Lambie family. They show the tender, caring heart of a husband and father as well as a grandfather. The next chapter records "dark days" in Abyssinia. There Lambie's tender heart was bleeding for the devastation that was facing the people of Abyssinia, under the tyranny of the Fascists

17

Lambie and the Dark Days of War in Abyssinia

God had something good still in store for Ethiopia:
but the last word was still with God;
and this brought a feeling of peace to us.

THOMAS A. LAMBIE, *A BRUISED REED*, 99

WHEN THE CLOUDS OF war began to gather over Abyssinia in October 1934, Dr. Lambie bore responsibility for nearly eighty SIM workers who were based at sixteen stations spread across the varied geography of the country. He was also responsible for the well-being of personnel attached to the sixteen Ethiopian Red Cross units serving the Abyssinian troops (see chapter 10). What account did those leave behind who experienced firsthand the devastation caused by the Italo-Ethiopian war and the intertribal attacks? Expatriates would have echoed the sentiments of Charlotte Lambie: "The Italians say they want to civilize Ethiopia. They certainly are not acting as if they were civilized themselves, let alone Christian."[1]

By May 1936 the Fascists were pursuing the war with bombs and poison gas, and the future for expatriates residing in Ethiopia looked foreboding. The British and US governments ordered all nonessential expatriate personnel (women and children) serving in Abyssinia to return to their

---

1. Charlotte Lambie, letter to daughter Betty Rees, January 7, 1936, MHSC.

home countries. Rowland Bingham telegraphed to SIM Ethiopia: "You are under higher orders than those of the King of England or the President of the United States. Get your instructions from Him and we are right with you. We approve the sending home of mothers with children who cannot help."[2]

John Spencer, from the United States and a specialist in international law who served the Abyssinia government, 1935–36, reported:

> The morning of May 2 was a lovely, bright spring-like day with, as usual, not a breath of wind stirring under a startlingly blue sky. One glance down the broad Station Road, however, caused me for an instant to think it had snowed. The entire asphalted pavement down to the station itself was an unbroken stretch of white. I soon discovered that the incredible appearance of the avenue was caused by the feathers of hundreds of pillows and mattresses that had been disemboweled onto the street by looters who had gone methodically from house to house; what they could not carry away, they scattered onto the road. How my house had been spared, or how I had not paid closer attention to the tumult, I do not know. Entering the many shops, the looters delighted in mixing paints with marmalade and canned goods. Marshal Badoglio had delayed the entry of the Fascist forces in order to give time to these shiftas [local militias, whether brig-ands or lawful in intent], the Azebu Galla, to loot and ravage the countryside and towns. In that fashion, the Italian troops would have the way cleared for them and would be welcomed as liberators. Badoglio had supplied the shiftas with Maria Theresa thalers minted in Venice.[3]

George Steer, a war correspondent sympathetic to the Abyssinian cause, offered the following description of the May 2–5 devastation in Ad-dis Ababa:

> It was reported that the Emperor had ordered to open both offi-cial palaces, and . . . that all his possessions should be distributed among his people. It was between nine and ten [on May 2] that hell broke loose in the capital: a general sort of hell to begin with. . . . The police had got out of hand. Apart from the few behind Abebe [chief of police] none had yet been allowed to go and loot their share in the palaces.[4]

2. Bingham, *Seven Sevens of Years*, 96.

3. Spencer, *Ethiopia at Bay*, 65.

4. Steer, *Caesar in Abyssinia*, 371–72.

While on his way to exile in England, Emperor Haile Sellassie became aware of false reports that he had ordered his own citizens to loot and burn Addis Ababa. He remonstrated:

> We learned from the newspapers, after passing through Jibuti [Djibouti], that the Italians had spread the exceedingly shameful and despicable falsehood that it was the departing Emperor who had given instructions that the city be set on fire and property be looted. While We were thinking only of the preventing of death at the hands of the enemy of those who were our own people, how could We contemplate that by Our own advice they should exterminate and plunder each other.[5]

Clarence Duff was at the Akaki SIM headquarters on the outskirts of Addis Ababa during May 2–5. He gives the following account of the chaos in the city.

> The news of the departure of the government [on May 2] soon spread. Early in the morning we heard the sound of much shooting in the city. I drove into the centre of town to get Miss [Leona] Kibby whose [SIM] school for the blind was right in the path of the armies from the north. The streets were ominously deserted except for a few people wildly running in different directions, mostly towards the palace or the stores, where the looting soon began. Sporadic shooting made the way hazardous. As I passed the Bible House, Mrs. [Anne Marie] Bevan called from an upstairs window to warn me to get out of town quickly. She said the palace treasury had already been looted. I drove on and got Miss [Leona] Kibby with a few of her belongings without much trouble, although plenty of rifle-fire and an occasional burst from a machine-gun were heard in the vicinity. When we got back to the centre of town the goods from the quality store of Ghanatakos [Greek shopkeeper] were strewn all over the street outside, while the men and women, with their arms and outer wraps full of loot, including bottles of wine and liquor, were scattered in every direction. Other shops were broken into. By the time Dr. Lambie, delayed by a flat tire, tried to get to the Red Cross Bureau, too much of the liquor had begun to create an ugly mood in the crowd.... The road past the back gate of the [SIM] Headquarters [at Akaki] was soon crowded with people hurrying out of the city with their loot, anxious to get into the open country to the west.... All day Sunday, Monday, and Tuesday the shooting and looting continued. Threats were made, but

5. Haile Sellassie, *My Life and Ethiopia's Progress*, 292.

there were no attacks at our place [Akaki] or the Leprosarium
[Furi]. . . .

A bright spot in the midst of all the lawlessness was the
complete loyalty of our Ethiopian staff. So far as I could observe
there was never any thought on their part of deserting in time of
danger. . . . The missionaries at Headquarters numbered only five
men and eleven women. There was also the little Mitchell baby
[Cliff Mitchell and Tom Devers had been sent with Red Cross
medical supplies to Sidamo]. The arms among us all amounted
to only a couple of shotguns and two twenty-two calibre rifles.
[At night] we did not lie in terror, for we had committed ourselves into God's hands for whatever might be His purpose for
us. He was pleased to spare our lives and we, Ethiopians and foreigners, unitedly thanked Him. Tuesday, May fifth, Marshall Ba-
doglio's troop trucks and tanks rolled into town from the north,
meeting no resistance. . . . As Italian troops spread throughout
the city all was soon quiet.[6]

Rowland Bingham, SIM's international director, applauded the missionaries who remained at their post: "They were not offered nor would
they have accepted the offer to depart with the fleeing officials by train; they
neither appealed to nor took refuge in either of the defended Consulates,
British or American, but the fourteen ladies, two children, and four men
elected to stay on their mission station."[7]

Lambie commented on the bedlam in Addis Ababa:

Some weeks before, we had called a special meeting of our missionaries, to discuss what we should do if things got in a bad
way in Addis Ababa. The British Legation had an armed camp,
manned with Sikh soldiers and British officers, where they expected to look after all British subjects. At the beginning of the
war both the British and American Legations had advised us
to leave the country; but we felt it our duty to disregard this.
With no dissenting vote we decided that we would stay at the
Mission station [and also at the Leprosarium at Furi] and trust
God to carry us through. Now [May 2] hour by hour, the rifle
fire became more intense. Most of the shooting was simply into
the air; there was an apparently endless amount of guns and ammunition [looted from the two palaces], and as they went along
the streets people would shoot up into the air in exuberance of

6. Duff, *Cords of Love*, 313–15.
7. Bingham, "The Situation in Ethiopia," 258.

spirits, or perhaps to warn others that they had a gun as well as other loot and were not to be trifled with.[8]

Elsewhere Lambie wrote:

> The sound of rifle fire increased all that night. It seemed that before leaving, His Majesty had thrown open his treasures and household goods and munitions stores and bade his soldiers to take what they wanted. The soldiers and servants had not been paid for many months, needed no invitation, and fought and killed each other for the richest loot.[9]

For reasons of security the Lambies decided to vacate their small residence at the lower end of the Akaki compound and to join the eighteen SIM men, women, and children in SIM's main headquarters building at Akaki. His account continues:

> The following day, Sunday, was probably the most trying day we had. God brought to our attention the wonderful forty-sixth Psalm, beginning "God is our refuge and strength . . . therefore we will not fear, though the earth be removed." The earth seemed to be coming down over our heads that day; we were surrounded by tens of thousands of murderers and looters; you could hardly hear yourself speaking for the rifle fire. . . . The Mission servants were all about to leave us, which put us in a very serious position. After prayer, God seemed to bring to my mind the shipwreck scene from Acts. Paul said the sailors must stay on the ship, and by doing this they would all be saved. Calling the servants together, I made them a little speech, and gave them practically the same words, saying I confidently believed this was God's word to them. They all agreed to this, and consented to remain. Wonderfully enough, not one of them suffered the slightest harm.[10]

Lambie did admit to personal fear and anxiety during this May 2–5 time of chaos: "We did not say that we did not fear, for I, at least, must confess that something like a weight of lead seemed to press down on my diaphragm whenever stronger than usual bursts of firing broke out. All I could do was confess it to the Lord and then He would give rest and peace."[11]

---

8. Lambie, *Doctor without a Country*, 246.

9. Lambie, "God's Guidance in War's Alarm," 332–33, 347–48.

10. Lambie, *Doctor without a Country*, 247.

11. Lambie, "Record of Disaster," May 15, 1936, SIMIA, EA-1-82, File 2. See also Lambie, "When Addis Ababa Fell. . .!," 268–69.

News that the emperor and his cabinet had departed from Addis Ababa by train soon spread throughout the countryside. Communication with the interior was cut off. It was not long before lawlessness and bloodshed were rampant throughout the countryside, also. Former intertribal feuds were reignited, and deep-seated resentment against the Amhara overlords began to show its ugly face.

Eight months after they invaded Addis Ababa, the Italians arrived in Soddo and subsequently kept a vigilant eye on the expatriate missionaries.[12] On various stations in the south, SIM personnel experienced harassment from the local population as well as from the Italian military. Reporting from Addis Ababa, war correspondent Steer wrote, "The Reverend Harold Street and Mr. John Trewin, two missionaries in [Wolaitta], had been arrested by the local authorities [Italian soldiers] for moving about, they said, at forbidden hours. The Reverend Street was chained up with a dog's chain."[13] Eventually calm descended on Soddo. By February 1937 Soddo became the main gathering point for missionaries serving at SIM's southern stations such as Shama [Chencha], Bulki, Lambuda, and Duramei. Malcolm and Enid Forsberg were the last of the SIM missionaries to leave Bulki. Their story is similar to that of Norman and Flossie Couser and John and Peggy Phillips, who left Duramei and took shelter with Gudeilla believers at Lambuda, near Hosanna. Malcolm Forsberg recorded his family's secretive five-day trek from Bulki to Soddo, carried out nocturnally in an attempt to evade bandits.

> We resumed our journey as soon as darkness fell. Any bandits preying on the road would hardly expect travelers to pass at night. I had to lift Enid onto her mule. Her legs were swollen from the sunburn and from her condition [eight months pregnant], so she could do no more walking. Also the soles of her shoes were torn off. We finally reached the Demi River beyond which lay the last stretch of dangerous wilderness. . . . Midnight came and we began the gentle climb out of the lowlands to the Wolamo plain. . . . An open area suddenly appeared beside the road. "This is the [Wolaitta] Sunday market!" Alamo, our guide, exclaimed out loud. Our hearts leaped for joy, for now all our dangers were behind us and we were safe.[14]

---

12. Cotterell, *Born at Midnight*, 93.

13. Steer, *Caesar in Abyssinia*, 257.

14. Forsberg, *Land beyond the Nile*, 96.

Eventually, nineteen missionaries and seven of their children gathered in Soddo. From there they were transported to Addis Ababa by Italian trucks and an airplane on April 16, 1937.

On May 4, 1936, tragedy struck at Marako where two single SIM missionaries, Daisy McMillan and Freda Horn, were based. About fifty local people had arrived at the clinic claiming that one of their friends was sick and needed medical attention. Such a group was not unusual, for relatives and friends often accompanied a sick person. Lambie picks up the narrative:

> It was late in the afternoon. Miss Freda Horn who is a trained nurse was trying to get the particulars so as to do something, but it was a mere excuse, the Judas kiss as it were, for almost at once the crowd began to push them [the two nurses] about and force their way into the house, striving to get what they could as quickly as possible. The young women [Freda Horn and Daisy McMillan] were struck and kicked several times. . . . What hurt them most of all was not the pain of the blows inflicted upon their bodies, but to recognize amongst them several faces well known to them. . . . After taking almost everything in sight, the cruel band ran away and then somehow the Providence of our loving Lord was shown—*Ato* Dembel, an elderly neighbor, came to them and offered them the protection of his house and promised them that he and his servants would protect them.[15]

Well-known in the Marako area, Ato Dembel protected the two young missionary women for three weeks in a separate straw-roofed hut. Calm had not fully returned to the area, but Ato Dembel stealthily guided the two New Zealand women to Addis Ababa. Lambie continues, "*Ato* Dembel asked for no reward whatever but said, if we agreed, he would like us to baptize him. After careful questioning and prayer we came to the belief that he was indeed a born-again man and so we baptized him and he has gone back to his home."[16] When the British consul general heard the story of Ato Dembel's bravery, he gave him a reward of 200 Ethiopian dollars and escorted him around Addis Ababa in the embassy's fancy limousine.[17]

Significant unrest also broke out where SIM missionaries were based in the north at Lalibela and Debra Markos. In January 1936, just prior to the Italian soldiers taking control, Lambie recorded the following about the missionaries based in Debra Markos:

15. Lambie, "Record of Disaster," May 15, 1936, SIMIA, EA-1-82, File 2.

16. Lambie, "Record of Disaster," May 15, 1936, SIMIA, EA-1-82, File 2.

17. See Duff, *Cords of Love*, 318–20, for his full report of the Marako story.

At Debra Markos in the North was a brave little band of five—
Mr. Glen Cain (Deputy Field Director and his wife, Winnie),
Miss Jean Cable, Mr. Jack Starling, and Mr. Nick Simponis. The
story of their long siege . . . is something like this: Mr. Simponis
was already there. The others arrived there from Addis Ababa
the very last day of the old year [December 31, 1935]. They
were planning to make an extended trip, and with them we sent
nearly seventy mules to be turned over to the British Ambulance
No. 2 that was coming from Gondar, further in the north. They
only intended staying a short time in Debra Markos but the day
after they arrived, January 1st, 1936, a fearful revolution broke
out in Gojam province, where Debra Markos is located, and the
site of the Mission compound was the scene of several bloody
battles between soldiers loyal to the Ethiopian Government and
rebels determined to overthrow the Government. Many were
killed and many were wounded. . . . At about the same time the
Italian aeroplanes began coming over frequently and bombing
the town. The missionaries were busy treating wounded, and
without doctors and nurses or anything but a few simple medicines, yet they did a great work. . . . When bombers came over,
they crawled into a hole and when the bombers passed, they
crawled out of the hole and treated the victims of the bombs
and the rebels' bullets. . . . There was shooting every night and
alarms by day, but nothing touched them. They were worn out
physically and their provisions gave out. . . . The Governor went
with his men, and then at last the Italian army came in and their
physical dangers were over, all but for the return to Addis Ababa
which they undertook through a country bristling with rifles
and leaderless men.[18]

From January to late April 1936, Ken and Blanche Oglesby were the
only SIM missionaries based in Lalibela. Lambie writes: "All around Lalibella there was looting and murdering, but Lalibella itself was not touched.
Men looked with envious eyes at the missionaries, but God put a wall of fire
about them. . . . All roads had been cut for months and no [food] supplies
could be sent to them. A day or two later the [Italian] aeroplanes dropped
from the sky three large parcels of food for them."[19]

18. Lambie, "Record of Disaster," May 15, 1936," SIMIA, EA-1-82, File 2.

19. Lambie, "Record of Disaster," May 15, 1936," SIMIA, EA-1-82, File 2. Cotterell,
Born at Midnight, 92, reported, "On April 14 [1936], the Emperor arrived at the mission
station at Lalibella, together with *Ras* Kassa and his two sons." As mentioned earlier,
apparently the Oglesbys hosted the Emperor temporarily at the Lalibela SIM station, a
kindness Haile Sellassie I did not forget.

The Lambies left Addis Ababa on August 21, 1936.[20] Two years later the last SIM missionaries left Abyssinia of their own accord, on August 21, 1938. Months of living through the dark days of intertribal warfare and then Fascist rule placed a heavy strain on the missionaries. They were also grieving the deaths of their colleagues Tom Devers and Cliff Mitchell (see chapter 10) as well as Gertrude Pogue, who was engaged to Tom Devers. She died of appendicitis on January 10, 1937. SIM missionary Harry Glover also died soon after from an undiagnosed illness.

During this period of upheaval, the representative of the British and Foreign Bible Society in Addis Ababa was Thomas Percival Bevan, a British national. The Fascist regime served him with an expulsion order, but his wife's name was not included. When the train left Addis Ababa, Anne Marie Bevan was not a passenger, much to the chagrin of the Italians. She remained in Addis Ababa for some months and continued to facilitate the Scripture distribution ministry of the Bible Society. Regarding the brave and hardy missionaries who were being forced to leave, Mrs. Bevan stated, "God is not leaving Ethiopia. He is simply changing the workmen."[21] These words were prophetic as clusters of believers in Wolaitta, Hadiya, Gamo, Gofa, and Kambatta continued to multiply under gifted indigenous leadership.

---

20. Charlotte Lambie, letter to daughter Betty Rees, August 28, 1936, MHSC.
21. Cotterell, *Born at Midnight*, 96.

18

Furlough and Deputation, 1911–1946

*We realize that we are getting older and that the vigor
of youth has developed certain rheumatic twinges
which would bid us stay at home and sit by the fire.*

THOMAS LAMBIE AND CHARLOTTE LAMBIE,
LETTER TO SUPPORTERS, SEPTEMBER 1938

WHEN THE LAMBIES SERVED, the practice of most mission agencies was to allow their personnel to return to their sending countries after four or five years of service abroad for a year of furlough. Circumstances such as children's education or care for aging parents might disrupt the usual four- or five-year furlough cycle. Missionary furloughs provided rest and recuperation for weary missionaries serving cross-culturally, often in severe climates. For the Lambies, "home assignment," as it is now called, was also spent raising funds for hospitals as well as enrolling in medical schools for advanced specialization. And often the Lambies were personally in need of medical attention that could not be obtained in Abyssinia or the Anglo-Egyptian Sudan. This chapter details chronologically the Lambies' furlough periods from 1911 through 1946.

After serving four years at Doleib Hill on the Sobat River in what is now South Sudan, the Lambies, along with their sixteen-month-old son, Wallace, left in September 1911 for furlough. Their daughter, Betty, was born in Philadelphia, three days after their arrival in the United States.[1] After six months, Thomas Lambie returned to the Sudan in March 1912, while Charlotte and the children stayed with her parents, Albert and Elizabeth Claney, until September 1912. Lambie returned ahead of the family because he had been asked to assist Elbert McCreery, a fellow member of the United Presbyterian Mission, in launching a new mission station among the Nuer in southern Sudan at a spot called Nasir. Also on the Sobat River, Nasir was some 200 miles east of Doleib Hill.

For their next vacation (not a furlough), the Lambies spent the month of July 1914 in Alexandria.[2] For them the city was like a haven: they could spend time leisurely among other expatriates and enjoy spacious gardens in which to walk and relax. Soon, however, they were on their way back to southern Sudan and the recently established Nasir station. The Lambies spent a total of five lonely years there—Thomas and Charlotte were the only expatriates—working among the Nuer.

In traveling from their country of ministry to their homeland, missionaries are often exposed to exotic adventures. For their 1917 furlough (January to December), the Lambies decided to travel through the Orient and to disembark on the west coast of the United States because German submarines were active in the Mediterranean. Lambie wrote:

> How wonderful to see Penang and Singapore and Raffles Hotel and the Bund! How marvelous is the Botanic Garden, with its lawns and flowers and incense-bearing trees, such as Kubla Khan might have planted in Xanadu! Then on to Hong Kong, with its famous Peak and Kowloon across the water, where we went at night to admire the lighted city dominated by the pyramidal crag, up whose side crawled the funicular railway and the houses of the officers.[3]

In crossing the Pacific Ocean to San Francisco, the Lambies enjoyed all the amenities of a Canadian Pacific steamer's cuisine. They spent their 1917 furlough in the Philadelphia area and were involved with various speaking assignments in Presbyterian churches. They were especially blessed, Thomas wrote, "by our contact with Dr. Lewis Sperry Chafer at the New Wilmington Missionary Conference that summer. There were persuasive entreaties from close relatives to remain in America, but with glad hearts we turned whither He beckoned us to follow."[4]

1. Lambie, *Doctor without a Country*, 58.
2. Lambie, *Doctor without a Country*, 98.
3. Lambie, *Doctor without a Country*, 107.
4. Lambie, *Doctor without a Country*, 109.

When the Lambies returned to Khartoum, Sudan, in late 1917, they discovered that food supplies were severely rationed due to the European war. But at their southerly station of Nasir, God supplied food for them in other ways. Fish from the Sobat River and a plump goose shot on the river enhanced their daily larder. "Our trees were bearing fruit now. The bananas did well, and the guavas and the peanuts fairly surpassed themselves; there must have been more than twenty bushels of them."[5]

Their furlough in 1921 was fraught with unusual responsibilities for the Lambies. First, there was the agreement with Ras Tafari Makonnen, the future emperor of Abyssinia, to raise funds in order to build a modern hospital in Addis Ababa. Then there were the three Ethiopian young men, Bashawarad, Malakou, and Workou, whom the Lambies were responsible to enroll in a US college.[6] The Foreign Missions Board of the United Presbyterian Church greeted the Lambies warmly in Philadelphia, but broke disappointing news to them: due to financial limitations, the FMBUPC would not consider any new projects for five years. Funds for the proposed Addis Ababa hospital could be raised through interested individuals, but not by means of appeals made through United Presbyterian churches. In spite of that disappointment, the Lambies experienced God's special blessing on their efforts: a donor in Ohio gave $70,000 for the construction of the George Memorial Hospital in Addis Ababa (see the account of this unusual gift in chapter 4).[7] In 1922 when Dr. and Mrs. Lambie, with Wallace and Betty, returned to Abyssinia, they carried the gift of a photograph from President Harding to Ras Tafari Makonnen. At the request of Ras Tafari Makonnen, Lambie also arranged to have a threshing machine and tractor shipped from the United States to Abyssinia.[8]

Involvement with the construction and the eventual day-to-day running of the George Memorial Hospital took its toll on the Lambies. This work also limited their involvement in outreach to southern Abyssinia. Lambie later wrote, "Five years had elapsed [since 1922] and the hospital was a going concern; now it seemed to me we surely ought to get on with our work and open new stations in the south. But our church [United Presbyterian] was not ready to advance into new territory."[9]

5. Lambie, *Doctor without a Country*, 111.

6. The three Ethiopian young men were enrolled in Muskingum College, New Concord, Ohio. See Lambie, *Doctor without a Country*, 149, 157.

7. For this account, see Lambie, *Doctor without a Country*, 156–57.

8. Lambie, *Doctor without a Country*, 158.

9. Lambie, *Doctor without a Country*, 162.

On furlough in 1926 and into 1927, the Lambies faced a future of uncharted waters. The furlough proved to be a time of testing in several ways. First, should they resign from the Presbyterian Mission and relinquish the various benefits that had accrued to them after twenty years of missionary service? On March 6, 1927, they submitted their resignation. Second, their son Wallace was now seventeen years of age and ready to be enrolled in a US college. Third, 1927 saw the Lambies, the George Rhoads, and the Alfred Buxtons form the Abyssinian Frontiers Mission, which eventually—with the encouragement of Rowland Bingham, SIM's international director—amalgamated with SIM.[10] Of that period Lambie recorded: "There were plenty of discouragements that summer. Our family had very little money."[11] They returned to Abyssinia on December 25, 1927, with many challenges ahead of them.

Upon the Lambies' return to Abyssinia, the vicissitudes of life brought them health problems. In 1928, some six months after arriving back from furlough, Charlotte became ill. The diagnosis was that she needed to return to the United States for surgery. On April 2, 1929, Lambie escorted Charlotte and daughter Betty to Djibouti by train and arranged for their sea voyage to the United States.[12] In November 1929, after she had recovered from surgery performed by family friend Dr. Howard A. Kelly, Charlotte "gave an address at the annual meeting of the American Mission to Lepers in New York in which she presented the needs of the lepers of Abyssinia."[13] Her presentation sparked a generous gift of $5,000 annually for five years. This gift launched the building of the leprosarium at Furi, on the outskirts of Addis Ababa.[14]

Lambie's own furlough was delayed until May 25, 1930, because of his responsibilities related to Bingham's first visit to Abyssinia. During their furlough time together as a family, which lasted from May 1930 to November 1931, the Lambies felt a growing concern for Charlotte's aging parents who were residing at The Meadows in Owings Mills, Maryland. This property had been purchased by the Lambies early in their missionary career. Now the aged house was in constant need of repair, an expense that was too much for the elderly Claneys to bear. From Abyssinia Lambie wrote to Charlotte, "It does seem to me that we ought for their sakes if not for our own to sell

10. For the launching of the Abyssinian Frontiers Mission, see chapter 5.

11. Lambie, *Doctor without a Country*, 166.

12. Lambie, *Boot and Saddle*, 104.

13. Lambie, *Doctor without a Country*, 209. See Lambie, letter to Charlotte Lambie, late December 1929, MHSC.

14. Lambie, *Doctor without a Country*, 211.

the place and get [them] into town."[15] On November 20 of that year, with
the Lambies in attendance at the wedding celebration, nineteen-year-old
daughter Betty married Herbert Rees. Wallace, their son, was also able to
come from Medellin, Colombia, for the occasion.

The Lambies' letter of January 1932 to "Dear Friends" mentions that,
two months after their return to Ethiopia, negotiations regarding the location of the Furi Hospital as well as the site for SIM's headquarters at Akaki
were complete.[16]

In May 1935 the Lambies began a furlough in England and Scotland,
where Thomas was asked to speak in a number of churches regarding the
work in Abyssinia. The couple also visited their daughter Betty, her husband
Herbert, and their two grandchildren, by then residing near London. The
Lambies' furlough time in the United States lasted only three weeks, as Dr.
Lambie was suddenly summoned back to Abyssinia by Emperor Haile Sellassie to assume oversight of the Ethiopian Red Cross (see chapter 10). After
several months' delay in England dealing with the British Ambulance Service, the Lambies arrived back in Addis Ababa in September 1935, when he
was assigned by Emperor Haile Sellassie to be director general of the Ethiopian Red Cross.[17] Those five months away from Abyssinia hardly qualified
as "furlough" for the Lambies.

With the country's capital occupied by the Italian army, the Lambies
left Abyssinia on August 21, 1936, never to return. Their final departure
from Addis Ababa, now under the control of the Fascists, was a challenge.
"To receive permission for us to leave required many, many trips to that
same political bureau. Why they [the Fascists] wished to keep me or why
they suspected me of designs to harm them, I do not know. Eventually, [we]
were reluctantly given a permit to leave."[18]

It was three years before the Lambies would return to Africa, though
not to Ethiopia. Both of them were experiencing ill health. Lambie observed
that "more than thirty years in Africa spent under the most trying conditions had taken its toll. My wife had been in hospital for weeks with an
infected jaw that had weakened her permanently and [she] was suffering
from diabetes. . . . They had found me with a heart condition that seemed
to say, 'Slow down.'"[19] During this time, Lambie had been serving as SIM's
home director for the United States. Some voiced the opinion that the

15. Lambie, letter to Charlotte Lambie, September, 1929, MHSC.

16. Lambie, *Doctor without a Country*, 209.

17. Lambie, *Doctor without a Country*, 231.

18. Lambie, *A Bruised Reed*, 98.

19. Lambie, *A Doctor Carries On*, 15.

Lambies were needed more in the United States than they were in Africa. But it was a role, he admitted, in which he served "without conspicuous success. Someone else could do it far better."[20]

A significant reason why the Lambies remained in the United States until 1937 was so that he could regain his American citizenship. As he explained in an October 1939 letter, he had sacrificed his US citizenship for the furtherance of the gospel in Abyssinia. He wrote, "I had given up my country to become a citizen of Ethiopia in order to further mission efforts. Then, when Ethiopia folded [as a country] in 1936, I was indeed a man without a country. Due to my wife having retained her citizenship . . . I was able to take out first papers."[21]

A reasonable course of action under the circumstances was to go on a deputation trip, which the Lambies undertook from February 16 to April 16, 1938. They traveled by car from Baltimore, Maryland, south to Florida, west to California, then north to Seattle and Vancouver, Canada, and back east across the United States to Maryland. The trip was not a mere sightseeing excursion for the Lambies, nor were the US roads of the time multilane interstate highways. They traveled over 11,000 miles and spoke over one hundred times in various churches, colleges, and seminaries. The account the Lambies sent to their supporters and friends in September 1938 follows.

> [We] drove to Columbia, South Carolina, where we had meetings in the Columbia Bible College and had a fine visit with our sister, Marguerite Lambie McQuilkin and her husband, Robert, the head of Columbia Bible College. Meetings had been arranged for us in Spartanburg, N.C., [and] Augusta, Athens, and Atlanta, Georgia . . . and then to Orlando, Florida, to the Hampden Dubose Academy. . . . Then on to Eustis, Florida, . . . and from there a long three-days drive to Texas, via the Gulf Coast, New Orleans and Shreveport . . . we paid a visit to Carville, the American Leper Colony. . . . We wanted to get acquainted with some up-to-date methods. At Longview, Texas, we met our brother Charles S. Lambie, who had arranged meetings for us at Kilgore and Amarillo. We had four busy days at the Dallas Theological Seminary, where we met some splendid young men. One night we had the joy of speaking in the Scofield Church. Then, we went to Fort Worth, to be with our esteemed friends Dr. and Mrs. James Patterson, and to Weatherford, Texas. At Amarillo we had two big meetings; and then drove to Alamogordo, New

20. Lambie, *A Doctor Carries On*, 15.

21. Lambie, "Letter to Friends," October 10, 1939, MHSC. See chapter 9 for a fuller account of this portion of Lambie's life.

Mexico, where we spent four delightful days with Dr. and Mrs. Leo Gaddis. . . . Another day brought us to Tucson, Arizona, where we spent a long weekend and had a great time in the Baptist and Presbyterian churches; and then we went on to Phoenix, where we had meetings in the newly organized Bible School; and then on to Los Angeles, where we spent ten days with our life-long friends, the McCreerys, and nearly had a score of meetings in the Church of the Open Door and the Bible Institute of Los Angeles, the Congregational Church, Pasadena, and the United Presbyterian Church at Long Beach. From there we drove north, having helpful meetings at Lockeford and Chico, California; and then to Klamath Falls, Oregon, where our cousin, Aimee Lambie Smith's husband is pastor of the Presbyterian Church. At Tacoma, Portland, Seattle, and Bellingham we had more meetings and broadcasts, and then into Canada to Vancouver. Mr. Sam and Mrs. Esther Cassells, who are loyal deputational workers of the Sudan Interior Mission at Vancouver, had arranged ten days of meetings there. . . . They have made the best people of the Pacific north-west Sudan Interior Mission conscious. From Vancouver we drove to Toppenish, Washington, to our old friends the Fred Russells of Ethiopia; then on to Denver. . . . We had two big meetings at Denver at the Central Presbyterian [Church] and at Capital Heights; and then to our niece's ranch in Broken Bow, Nebraska; and then to Iowa to some of Mrs. Lambie's relatives and on to Detroit and Birmingham, where brother John Lambie is residing, and where we had a delightful time speaking at the first Baptist Church, Pontiac, where Dr. Robert H. Savage is pastor, and the Birmingham Presbyterian Church. . . . After seeing the family [in Pittsburgh] we drove back to Baltimore, arriving three months to the day after our departure. . . . God's gracious hand was over us.[22]

Soon after the Lambies returned from their transcontinental travels, Lambie wrote to his supporting friends, "Last week we went to Pittsburgh where I gave two lectures to the medical students on malaria and amoebic dysentery. They are appointing me as a research worker in tropical medicine connected with the University and this will help in Washington with my

22. Thomas and Charlotte Lambie, "Dear Friends—Letter to Supporters," September 1938, MHSC.

're-naturalization' and will allow me to stay abroad as long as necessary and will count the same as if I was in America."[23]

Lambie's appointment at the University of Pittsburgh was as "Special Lecturer in Tropical Medicine." The chancellor of the university, John G. Bowman, together with the dean of the medical school, made the appointment.[24] Lambie presented several extemporaneous lectures at the university on the topic of "Tropical Medicine," which were appreciated. By virtue of this special arrangement with the university, the Lambies were able in 1939 to return to the Sudan without a bona fide US passport. Then through the good offices of T. Roland Philips, pastor of the Baltimore Presbyterian Church, the intervention of Senator Radcliffe was obtained in the matter of Dr. Lambie's finally regaining his US citizenship. The Lambies returned to Sudan by ship, arriving in Alexandria on October 28, 1939. Because of the war, they were unfortunately unable to visit Betty and her children in England. During their extended stay in the United States, Lambie had been able to edit and publish *A Doctor without a Country*. He finally regained his American citizenship on July 11, 1940.

By August 1941, while he was serving as SIM's director in Sudan, the Lambies had become fatigued and needed recuperation. British physicians in Khartoum encouraged them to leave Sudan temporarily for medical reasons. They decided to take a vacation of several months in Palestine, where they were entertained by Christian friends, Mr. and Mrs. Alfred P. S. Clark. Alfred Clark, manager of the Palestinian branch of Barclays Bank and a longtime resident of Palestine, showed the Lambies great kindness to the extent of giving them an extended tour of the Holy Land in his private vehicle.[25] While on the tour, the Lambies met missionary friends they had known from both the United Kingdom and the United States. Afterward Lambie commented, "Our trip to Palestine did us a world of good and we returned to the Sudan feeling like getting to work in earnest."[26]

On July 9, 1942, the Lambies left Khartoum, Sudan, and returned to the United States for medical reasons.[27] Prior to leaving the Sudan, Lambie

---

23. Thomas and Charlotte Lambie, "Dear Friends—Letter to Supporters," September 1938, MHSC. See also Lambie, *Doctor's Great Commission*, 266: serving "as an apprentice T.B. specialist." Subsequent to his internship he was awarded an honorary Doctor of Science degree by the University of Pittsburgh. See also Cotterell, "Dr. T. A. Lambie: Some Biographical Notes," 43n1. "Dr. Thomas Lambie, M.D., Sc.D., F.R.G.S." appears on the title page of each of the five Lambie books published after 1942.

24. Lambie, *A Doctor Carries On*, 16.

25. See Lambie, *A Doctor Carries On*, 145–55, for an account of this tour.

26. Lambie, *A Doctor Carries On*, 157.

27. Roke, *They Went Forth*, 239–40.

wrote to E. Lester Whitaker, SIM home secretary in New York, "It is with mixed feelings that we turn our faces to America. Joy and Sorrow—joy at seeing friends—sorrow that we are leaving the work so dear to us and that which we may never see again."[28] From September 1942 to May 1943, they recuperated at the Houses of Fellowship, missionary rest homes in Ventnor, New Jersey, that were established in 1922 by Marguerite and Ida Doane (daughters of hymn writer William Howard Doane).[29]

While recuperating at Houses of Fellowship, the Lambies realized that the end might well have come to their thirty-five years of service in Africa. Medical tests revealed that they were in need of a lengthy recuperation. Around June 1943, while passing through Harrisburg, Pennsylvania, Lambie called on Dr. Alexander H. Stewart, a former classmate from his time in medical school in Pittsburgh forty years earlier. Dr. Stewart at the time was serving as the secretary of health for the State of Pennsylvania. Through his good graces, Lambie was invited to serve as an apprentice tuberculosis specialist at the Mont Alto State Sanatorium, located at South Mountain, which is some distance west of Gettysburg. At the sanatorium Lambie was placed under the tutelage of the director, Dr. Charles C. Custer. Lambie commented that Dr. Custer "was kindness itself and I learned to like the work very much, and of course when we like a thing, it becomes a pastime and a pleasure to us."[30] Dr. Custer so appreciated Lambie's professionalism that he was reluctant to see him leave and even arranged the promise of a wage increase if he would stay on.

In a letter to Alf Roke, Lester Whitaker confirms that Dr. Lambie's several activities from 1942 to 1946 were appreciated. "You will be interested to know that Dr. Lambie is taking a position in a Pennsylvania State Hospital for the time being. He still continues as a member of our U.S.A. Council, and is also acting this year as President and Managing Director of the New England Keswick at Monterey, Massachusetts."[31] At the same time, Lambie was in great demand as a Sunday speaker as far away as Washington, DC, Philadelphia, New York, and Boston.[32] Even while in training at the Mont Alto Sanatorium, Lambie did not stay idle during weekends. For example,

28. Lambie, letter to E. Lester Whitaker, home secretary for SIM in New York, June 26, 1942, SIMIA, KB-1-121, File 3.

29. Lambie, *Doctor's Great Commission*, 266. In 1967 Houses of Fellowship adopted the name "Overseas Ministries Study Center," and in 1987 it relocated to New Haven, Connecticut. See www.omsc.org/history.

30. Lambie, *Doctor's Great Commission*, 266–67.

31. E. Lester Whitaker, letter to Alf Roke, February 10, 1943, SIMIA, KB-1-121, File 3.

32. Lambie, *Doctor's Great Commission*, 267.

while he was serving as president and managing director of the New England Keswick organization (1944–46), he commented, "God gave gracious aid in getting new buildings and equipment for this splendid place in the Berkshire Hills of Massachusetts."[33]

Though the New England Keswick organization wanted him "to stay and perhaps give full time to its work," in January 1946 Dr. and Mrs. Lambie boarded ship to sail to Palestine, where they intended to serve under the Independent Board for Presbyterian Foreign Missions.[34] Unfortunately, Charlotte did not reach Palestine. The following chapter is a tribute to her life and ministry and also provides details related to her death during the voyage. Dr. Lambie continued the journey to Palestine alone, where he took up a new phase of his medical ministry. The story of his contribution in the Valley of Berachah, near Bethlehem, where he served out his final years of ministry, is presented in chapter 20.

33. Lambie, *Doctor's Great Commission*, 267.
34. Lambie, *Doctor's Great Commission*, 268.

The Keswick Convention was founded in 1875 in the United Kingdom by an Anglican and a Quaker. The views of John Wesley were influential in the formation of Keswick teaching. Throughout the history of the Keswick Convention, speakers from various denominations have been invited. Evangelical notables prominent in Keswick's early years included British Anglican Handley Moule, Reformed pastor from South Africa Andrew Murray, Baptist F. B. Meyer, and founder of the China Inland Mission Hudson Taylor. Amy Carmichael's decision to dedicate her life to missions was a response to Hudson Taylor's speaking. Billy Graham was impacted by Keswick teaching which he asserted in his autobiography *Just as I Am* came to him as a second blessing. John Stott gave the Bible expositions at the 1965 Keswick Convention, speaking on Romans 5–8. His presentation was a watershed, particularly on "death to sin," setting a new direction on the topic within Keswick. The Keswick Convention placed particular emphasis on the Lordship of Christ, personal holiness, discipleship, and promotion of missionary activity.

Rowland Bingham, international director of the Sudan Interior Mission, established the Canadian Keswick Conference Centre in the beautiful Muskoka Lakes area of Ontario in 1924. Many Canadian SIM candidates served guests at the Ferndale House/Muskoka conference center prior to their missionary placement in Africa. During Thomas Lambie's time away from ministry in Africa, he was often invited to speak at the later established New England Keswick, located in the Berkshire Hills of Massachusetts. His book *A Doctor Carries On* is dedicated to "Keswick—English, American, and Canadian—and to those 'who follow in their train.'" From 1944 to 1946, Lambie served as president of New England Keswick. During his leadership role at New England Keswick, he was able to acquire new buildings plus refurbishing the equipment and grounds. Lambie's rationale for Keswick was "Busy Christian workers certainly need to go apart and rest, to have quiet communion with God. Otherwise we are apt to become hot and tired, querulous and unreasoning."[35]

Because of his exemplary leadership at New England Keswick, which brought renewed dynamism to that ministry, Lambie was invited to continue in leadership there. Both he and his wife, Charlotte, struggled to know God's will. But as he preached and taught at Keswick on the need to be obedient to God's call, the Lambies became confident that God's calling for them was to launch a tuberculosis sanatorium in Palestine. While serving tuberculosis patients in Palestine, Lambie launched the annual Keswick Convention in the Middle East, which began in Jerusalem about 1950. It would appear that many of the 25 chapters of his book *A Bruised Reed* were sermons he had preached at Keswick Conventions. Although Lambie was a respected officer and gifted

---

35. Lambie, *A Bruised Reed*, 47.

speaker at Keswick Conventions in Massachusetts and Jerusalem, nowhere do we find in his writings that he was an advocate of "second blessing" theology propounded by many within that movement.

19

Tribute to Charlotte Claney Lambie: Her Life and Death

A wife of noble character who can find?
She is worth far more than rubies.
Her husband has full confidence in her
and lacks nothing of value.

PROVERBS 31:10–11 (NIV)

DR. THOMAS LAMBIE HAD only recently arrived in Egypt in 1907 when he first spotted Charlotte Claney as she was stepping out of Robinson Memorial Church, the large and beautiful Presbyterian house of worship located in Alexandria. Lambie acknowledged that "she was bright and vivacious; somehow I found her attractive."[1] Their romance flourished as best it could by letter—for Lambie, as a physician, was soon posted to Doleib Hill in the south of the Sudan—and communication was difficult. The Lambies were married in 1909 in Alexandria. A Presbyterian missionary friend of Charlotte's, Mrs. Nannie Finney (wife of Thomas J. Finney), made all the arrangements for the wedding. The ceremony took place in the Robinson Memorial Church, with tea served later at Mrs. Finney's home. The Lambies remained in Alexandria for their honeymoon and called on various missionaries to share their joy and delight as newlyweds. Later Lambie rhapso-

1. Lambie, *Doctor without a Country*, 16.

208

dized: "Was there ever such a place to spend a honeymoon as Alexandria! Especially when one has come from the hot Sudan, where every breath seems like one drawn from a furnace. We went mooning about to the huge amusement of the missionary colony. Too swiftly the days sped."[2]

Soon after the wedding, the Lambies were stationed in Khartoum, in charge of directing the American Presbyterian Mission clinic there. Later they were assigned to Doleib Hill on the Sobat River, a rather isolated mission station far to the south. Their son, Wallace, was born in Khartoum in 1910. In 1911 the Lambies traveled to the United States by ship. "Three days after we reached America," Lambie reported, "Anne Elizabeth [fondly known as Betty] appeared on the scene."[3]

PIONEERING AT NASIR ON THE SOBAT RIVER

In 1912 the Lambies were back in southern Sudan. While Thomas Lambie was assisting Rev. Elbert McCreery in building a home for the Lambie family and a clinic at Nasir, Charlotte and the children remained at Doleib Hill. There, some 200 miles downriver from Nasir, they resided in their former mission house. Mrs. Hannah McCreery was the only other expatriate present at the station at that time. When Lambie arrived by boat at Doleib Hill, he anticipated a joyous welcome from Charlotte and his two children. But when he climbed up the bank of the Sobat River and looked toward the house where Charlotte and the children should have been, he was startled. What met his eyes was "the burned out shell of our house, the ruins still smoking! Were they all dead—my dear wife and my precious babes? I had an agonizing moment that seemed to last hours."[4] When he drew closer he found that his wife and the two children, Wallace and Betty, were all well, though they had experienced a narrow escape from death several days before. The fire began when son Wallace, not quite three years old, had gotten into a box of matches and struck one. Soon the mosquito net ignited. Charlotte, with a mother's heart full of compassion, rushed in and snatched the children to safety. All their possessions—clothing and food supplies—were consumed, but the Lambies praised God that no lives were lost.

2. Lambie, *Doctor without a Country*, 47.
3. Lambie, *Doctor without a Country*, 58.
4. Lambie, *Doctor without a Country*, 78.

Gardening and Orchards

Charlotte loved gardening. In Nasir (1912–18) she planted carrots, cabbage, peanuts, sweet potatoes, and peas. In an orchard she grew oranges, guavas, papaya, mangos, and bananas. Adequate vegetables and fruit sustained the family in good health. Charlotte also had a brood of Rhode Island Red chickens which another missionary had given to the Lambies. The chickens supplied the family with eggs and delicious chicken meat, foods almost unknown to the Nuer in southern Sudan.[5] Peanuts, which grew very well in the sandy soil of Nasir, were used to make nourishing soup. Charlotte also kept several cows that produced adequate milk for young Wallace and Betty. Within a few years, the guava, banana, and papaya trees were producing in abundance. When the Lambies relocated in 1919 to Sayo (Dembi Dollo), in western Abyssinia, Charlotte once again planted a garden, finding that sweet potatoes grew very well in the highlands. She hired a gardener to plant hundreds of banana, fig, peach, and guava seedlings. Howard Kelly paid tribute to her, "Mrs. Lambie, who had followed [her husband] from the homeland, managed to enlarge the monotonous diet, sometimes almost verging on starvation, by introducing such welcome fruits as guavas and limes in abundance, and useful vegetables, such as tomatoes and sweet potatoes. In due course, too, came chickens, eggs, and milk."[6] Lambie himself wrote: "I have found my wife to be so wise in counsel and advice and not shirking any hardship."[7]

Suffering and Illness

Charlotte struggled from debilitating diabetes during most of her missionary career in Sudan and Abyssinia. She was dependent on regular insulin shots injected by Dr. Lambie. She had various operations that meant boat travel down the Nile to medical facilities in Khartoum or Cairo. Always an avid reader and a good letter writer to family and friends in the United States, she also loved sewing. But her diabetes led to a gradual decline in her eyesight, and eventually she had to give up these pursuits one by one. On December 19, 1941, she wrote to her daughter, Betty, "I am praying to God to restore my sight or else to make me a blessing with my blindness . . . wish

5. Lambie, *Doctor without a Country*, 87, 97.

6. Howard A. Kelly, "Introduction," in Lambie, *Doctor without a Country*, 4.

7. Lambie, *Boot and Saddle in Africa*, 25.

I had faith in Him to restore my sight."[8] Lambie would spend hours reading aloud to her from books she loved.[9] Her favorites were Christian classics such as the sermons of the Scottish preacher Robert Murray McCheyne of Dundee.

In 1929, she also went to the United States for rather complicated medical treatment. From Lambie's letter to Charlotte on September 29 that year, sent from Abyssinia, we learn that their intimacy in marriage was diminished by her medical situation, and he pled with her to proceed with necessary surgery. He wrote, "Tell [Dr. Howard Kelly] . . . and follow through what he advises." He continued, "If you are going to be strong for riding around Abyssinia with me, on some of the trips at least, you will have to be stronger than you are, and to be stronger you must have the repair operation done."[10]

APPRECIATION OF BEAUTY

Charlotte had a beautiful singing voice. Lambie recalled nearing their home after a successful hunting trip along the Sobat River. "As I approached our little home after dark . . . I saw light streaming from the open window and heard Charlotte singing at the little organ:

> O sing ye hallelujah!
> 'Tis good our God to praise.
> 'Tis pleasant and becoming
> To Him our songs to raise.[11]

Charlotte brought beauty into the Lambie home not only by singing, but also in selecting an excellent location at Sayo for the new mission station in Wellega, Abyssinia.

> My wife had an eye for beauty and practicality; she saw a rounded hilltop half a mile from Sayo, where there would be ample space for a garden and grazing as well as for all ordinary Mission activities. It had a delightful outlook in all directions, and

---

8. Charlotte Lambie, letter to daughter Betty Rees, December 19, 1941, MHSC. Until 1944 Charlotte continued writing to Betty as best she could. Toward the end of 1944, her writing became nearly illegible. After 1944 there are no more letters by Charlotte in the MHSC.

9. Lambie, *Doctor's Great Commission*, 267.

10. Lambie, letter to Charlotte, September 29, 1929, MHSC.

11. Lambie, *Doctor without a Country*, 91–92.

was far enough away from the squalid town of Sayo . . . and we
would have a much greater freedom in developing our work.[12]

ORGANIZATIONAL ABILITY

On the many long treks that the Lambies took within Abyssinia—in total as
much as 6,000 miles on mules and horses—Charlotte took full responsibility for the food supplies. She juggled a number of factors: the limitations of
their finances, the number of travelers in the group, the time they would
be away, and to what extent the trekkers would be able to live off locally
acquired supplies. On the Lambies' three-month trek to Lalibela, Charlotte
"did not fail," Lambie wrote, "to provide us with a good meal three times a
day."[13] She was his "constant companion and comfort who kept the domestic
side of our camp in order with daily hot baths [in make-shift canvas tubs]
for our often tired bodies and then delicious food on our tables."[14] Lambie
was aware that it was usual for vast quantities of food to be consumed while
on trek and that to have adequate daily provisions required careful fore-
thought. He paid his wife this compliment:

> Mrs. Lambie had perhaps the largest and most thankless task,
> for she was our commissary department. What careful planning
> those trips took! There were so many factors to take into con-
> sideration, how much we could spend for stores, and then the
> number of mouths to feed, and the length of time we expected
> to be away from our base, and the availability of supplies that
> would carry well [on donkeys], be nourishing, and give us suf-
> ficient calories and vitamins for those hard journeys. So far as
> possible, she tried to make us live off the country, husbanding
> our precious stores very carefully for emergencies. . . . To my
> wife's careful planning and daily provision these journeys owed
> much of their success.[15]

When it was thought that the Lambies would accompany the Abyssinian government into exile in Gorei in May 1936, Charlotte was the one who
organized the effort to acquire food supplies for six months (see chapter
12).[16]

---

12. Lambie, *Doctor without a Country*, 131.
13. Lambie, *Doctor without a Country*, 217.
14. Lambie, *Boot and Saddle in Africa*, 147.
15. Lambie, *Boot and Saddle in Africa*, 115.
16. Lambie, *Doctor without a Country*, 245.

Strong Faith in God Regarding Open Doors for Ministry

In 1922, believing that God was about to open a new door for ministry among the unreached ethnic groups of southern Abyssinia, the Lambies arrived in Addis Ababa. They made the trip from Sayo, western Abyssinia, by mule. On arrival Lambie requested an appointment with the regent, Ras Tafari Makonnen. Before leaving his room at Taitu Hotel, Lambie wrote, "my wife and I knelt beside the great ornate brass bedstead that once, we had been told, had been Empress Taitou's [wife of Menelik II], and sought guidance and direction from heaven's king. After that, the prospect of a visit to an earthly king did not seem quite so terrifying."[17] Their prayer was answered, for soon afterward they returned to the United States and miraculously raised over $70,000 for the "Lambie Hospital" which was completed at Guleili in 1924 (see details in chapter 4).[18]

In 1930, when Charlotte was in the United States with daughter Betty, "they had been passing through a hard time with repeated operations and very little money. Reduced to two dollars one Sunday, she and Betty were given the verse, 'Seek first the kingdom of God and his righteousness and all these things shall be added unto you' [Matt. 6:33]. They went to church and put the two dollars into the offering, then went home ready to seek God first and let Him do what seemed best. . . . In a few days' time cash and checks came in from many unknown and unexpected sources."[19] Several weeks later when Charlotte was asked to speak of the needs of Abyssinia, "she gave an address at the annual meeting of the American Mission to Lepers [in New York], in which she presented the needs of lepers in Abyssinia. God used her message to create interest in Abyssinia, with the result that they agreed to give five thousand dollars a year for five years to build a leprosarium there."[20] This leprosy ministry launched in Addis Ababa in 1932 eventually developed into the All Africa Leprosy and Tuberculosis Rehabilitation Training Centre and continues in an expanded form to this day. All glory to God for the faith of Charlotte Lambie.

17. Lambie, *Boot and Saddle in Africa*, 61–62.
18. Lambie, *Doctor without a Country*, 155–59.
19. Lambie, *Doctor without a Country*, 208.
20. Lambie, *Doctor without a Country*, 209.

INTREPID TRAVELER, ENDURING WEARINESS,
SICKNESS, AND SADNESS

Lambie wrote the following in April 1934, after a mule journey to Lalibela in the north,

> In all these long journeys, with one exception [a journey to Moyale, on the Kenyan border], my wife has been my constant companion. Has any other missionary woman trekking in Africa covered one-fourth of the miles she has, often with pain and weariness? On some high plateaus it would be too cold to sleep, even with four blankets to cover one. By day we [might] go through some low valley and be scorched with the heat. We struggled on together.[21]

For the several thousand wearisome miles of trekking that Charlotte endured in East Africa accompanying her husband, she was elected to the Royal Geographical Society of Great Britain on February 21, 1938. She was recommended by Thomas Lambie and Henry Balfour on the basis of personal knowledge.[22] Henry Balfour, an intrepid traveler, including in countries in East Africa, was a past president of the Royal Geographical Society.

Then in November 1934, while the Lambies were returning from their second trek north to Lalibela, a postman met them on the road with a sackful of letters. Lambie described what followed.

> On opening the letters on that bare hillside, we received the stunning news that our only son, Wallace, had met instant death in South America over a month before. The news got to Addis Ababa the next day, but took over a month to get to us. Weary from the exertions of two months of hard trekking . . . the blow came upon us with fierce impact. Our Heavenly Father alone supplied the strength to enable us to accept this as from His dear hand. What it meant to my wife only those can appreciate who have had similar experience. Somehow, we stumbled back to Addis Ababa after another three weeks of hard going.[23]

---

21. Lambie, *Doctor without a Country*, 213.

22. For this information, I am indebted to Miss Julie Carrington of the Royal Geographical Society and to archival information on http://discovery.nationalarchives.gov.uk.

23. Lambie, *Doctor without a Country*, 229. See chapter 9 for details of Wallace's death.

Family Relationships

Throughout the Lambies' missionary career in Abyssinia and Sudan, Charlotte wrote many letters by hand to their daughter, Betty. Not all of these letters have survived, but Betty's daughter, Margaret Hall, has kindly made twenty hand-written letters available to me. Their dates span from November 20, 1935, to May 23, 1944.[24] Writing in uncertain times during the Italo-Ethiopian war, Charlotte addressed Betty, her only daughter, now married just over five years, in endearing terms: "Darling 'wee Betty,'" "My darling sweet precious 'wee Betty,'" "My own darling 'wee Betty,'" "My precious 'wee Betty,'" and "Dearest Betty."

On November 20, 1935, Charlotte wrote to Betty, "Everything is very normal. . . . What a darling bride you were five years ago. I love you so much darling and long to see you." In a letter dated December 9, 1935, she wrote, "We love you so much. Don't worry about us for there is really no danger here in Addis Ababa. I know you have written but where are the letters?" In late December (date missing), 1935, Charlotte wrote, "They say the Italians have a 'white nigger' list [of those] whom they plan to shoot as soon as they arrive. A Dr. Hamer and Dad and one journalist are on the list! Of course, we do not believe they would actually do this. . . . I believe Dad is too well-known internationally, don't you?" Her letter of March 8, 1936, reflected war-related pressures: "Poor Dad and Mr. Everet Colson [financial advisor to Haile Sellassie] are working far too hard these days. I was at tea at Colsons yesterday . . . and when Mr. Colson came home he could hardly get his breath. He is suffering from high blood pressure—he looks so white and worn."

Charlotte wrote on April 17, 1936 (six years after Betty and Herbert's marriage), in a more domestic vein, but the letter still is tinged by the uncertainties of war: "I'm busy making Margaret Mary [Betty's firstborn] a little flowered yellow dress. . . . I finished a suit for David [born 1934]. I wonder if things would get through on the trains now. We are all calm and happy at the mission [headquarters at Akaki]." Two days later, on April 19, Charlotte added, "Just a short line to tell you we got your sweet letter and the photos, they are so splendid and satisfying. . . . I am so happy to have the photos—you are all looking well, isn't Margaret Mary getting fat? Herbert looks fine and isn't David a darling? . . . If anything should happen to us out here 'The Meadows' [the property in Maryland purchased in 1930 for Charlotte's parents] is yours, and the deed and legal papers are in Judge Waxter's office in Baltimore."

24. The letters are part of the MHSC.

The Italian military entered Addis Ababa on May 5, 1936. On May 13, Charlotte wrote, "It's so peaceful since the Italians came, they have been very nice to Dad. . . . Dad has been in bed four days with 'flu'. I hope he's soon better, for I'm tired of all the nervous strain of the riots and now Dad being ill." On July 5 she lamented, "And to think wee David is two years old and we didn't send him a present. It's awful to be so far separated." Her letter of August 27, written aboard the SS *Tennessee* later that summer while sailing on the Red Sea, states: "Djibouti is full of spies and other Italians but we were taken to the top of the Continental Hotel and had lovely rooms. . . . This ship is going to Antwerp, so we are doing a 'new thing'. We shall probably arrive in England about the middle of September. I wish you'd hurry up and have the new baby before we go on to America." Charlotte signed off, "Kiss Margaret Mary and David for me. With fondest love to you all from Mother."

Some years later, after the Lambies had settled in Pennsylvania and Dr. Lambie was an apprentice tuberculosis specialist, Charlotte wrote, with a sense of humor, to Betty on May 23, 1944, "You will be shocked [at] the way we have aged. I look like a gargoyle." This letter is the last one we have from Charlotte.

Unexpected Death and Legacy

In early 1946, the Lambies were on their way by ship from Liverpool to Palestine to build a tuberculosis sanatorium in Bethlehem. As a couple, the Lambies were not in robust health and should not have been undertaking a new missionary venture for the Independent Board for Presbyterian Foreign Missions, but nevertheless they went. While en route, they had spent Christmas 1945 in England with their daughter Betty and their three grandchildren.[25] Thomas Lambie wrote, "Apparently the fatigue and poor food [on the ship from Liverpool] had disturbed her [Charlotte's] sugar tolerance, and although we kept up the established routine of her insulin . . . something was evidently wrong."[26] While in Port Said, Egypt, the Lambies were resting in a hotel and had prayer together. When Charlotte was served a second cup of tea she said,

> "I feel so funny" as she handed me back the cup, and those were her last words. She lay back in bed and in two seconds she was gone to be with the Lord. We had no friends in Port Said

---

25. Lambie, *Doctor's Great Commission*, 269.
26. Lambie, *Doctor's Great Commission*, 269.

excepting the agent of the Bible Society, so there by the seaside I laid her body to rest in the British cemetery.[27]

A short telegram cabled to the office of the Independent Board for Presbyterian Foreign Missions, dated January 25, 1946, bore the brief message, "Mrs. Lambie died cerebral hemorrhage 5:30 this afternoon."[28] On January 30 Lambie wrote, rather brokenhearted, to friends from SIM days, supporters, and IBPFM staff, "My Jesus doeth all things well."[29] These words were no doubt difficult for him to express. He and Charlotte had pioneered mission enterprises in Africa together for nearly thirty-five years.

Charlotte Claney, born in 1883, died on January 25, 1946, in Port Said, Egypt. The only friend that Dr. Lambie had in Port Said was the Canadian agent of the British and Foreign Bible Society, Rev. Leonard Francis Geary.[30] Together with that Christian brother, Thomas Lambie laid his wife of thirty-seven years to rest in the Port Said British cemetery. There were no other friends present to cheer or comfort him through this hard experience.[31] After two more days of travel on the Mediterranean, the ship docked at Tel Aviv, and Lambie arrived by train in Jerusalem alone. Former friends, the Alfred Clarks and the Frank Cupples, met him at the station and took him to their homes, where, he wrote, "their tender compassion and loving care for me meant more than I can ever tell."[32]

Charlotte's life certainly epitomized the qualities of "the wife of noble character" portrayed in Proverbs 31:26–29 (NIV):

She speaks with wisdom,
and faithful instruction is on her tongue.
She watches over the affairs of her household
and does not eat the bread of idleness.
Her children arise and call her blessed;

27. Lambie, *Doctor's Great Commission*, 270.

28. Holdcroft, "Supplement Copy," 1. This special issue of *Biblical Missions* consisted of a single page, telling of Charlotte's death. The periodical *Biblical Missions* was a monthly publication of the Independent Board for Presbyterian Foreign Missions.

29. Holdcroft, "Field News," 5.

30. I thank Dr. Onesimus Ngundu, assistant librarian, Bible Society's Library, Cambridge University Library, England, for this information.

31. See Holdcroft, "Supplement Copy," 1.

32. Lambie, *Doctor's Great Commission*, 269–70. Mr. and Mrs. Frank Cupples were head of the Todd Osborne House as well as being members of the Mission to Mediterranean Garrisons, located in the Arab quarters of Jerusalem. See Carlson, *Cairo to Damascus*, 172.

her husband also, and he praises her:
"Many women do noble things,
but you surpass them all."

20

Establishing the Tuberculosis Sanatorium
near Bethlehem

Wait until you are sure of God's Will.
Waiting does not mean lolling about in an easy chair
waiting for the bell to ring, but it means seeking His face.

THOMAS A. LAMBIE, *A DOCTOR'S GREAT COMMISSION*, 267

THE SEED OF THE vision that animated Thomas Lambie's ministry at a tuberculosis sanatorium near Bethlehem was planted while he was still a missionary in the Sudan. Beginning in 1939, while serving as SIM director in
Sudan, Lambie went through various kinds of stress and strain. Physically,
he reached a low ebb, and in late 1941 the British doctors in Khartoum
advised him to take a two-month rest in a cooler climate. Heeding their
advice, the Lambies chose to visit Palestine, a place where they had not been
before. Later Lambie recalled, "What strong emotions filled our hearts as we
saw the highlands of Judea and as our train chugged into the Jerusalem rail-
way station. We finally arrived at the city of the great King, where our Lord
was crucified."[1] The Lambies' two months in Palestine as guests of Alfred
Clark and his wife helped him to regain strength. An extensive tour of the
country with the Clarks also enabled them to see the need among the Arab

---

1. Lambie, *Doctor's Great Commission*, 262.

population for a sanatorium to treat tuberculosis patients.[2] As they returned to Sudan, they carried this new vision in their hearts.

To recapitulate, in July 1942 when the Lambies departed from Khartoum, they were weary of soul as well as weak of body, discouraged by criticism levied against them by some in the Sudan SIM family. At that time their future appeared very uncertain. Upon arriving in the United States, they went to Houses of Fellowship in Ventnor, New Jersey, to recoup.[3] At this point no family obligations weighed upon them. As reported in chapter 9, Wallace, their only son, had died in an accident seven years earlier and was buried in Medellin, Colombia. Their daughter, Betty, now married for twelve years, was residing with her husband, Herbert Rees, and their four children in London. Though the way was unimpeded, their path forward was not clear. In 1942 Lambie came to realize that his alienation from Emperor Haile Sellassie was seemingly irreversible, foreclosing his return to serve in any capacity in Ethiopia. For health reasons, also, it appeared that further service in the Sudan was out of the picture, and the Lambies spent the next several years in the United States.

During this season of his life, Lambie struggled with how people were to determine God's will. He wrestled with questions such as: "Has He led you to indelible Scripture verses that you cannot escape? Has He influenced godly friends of yours to agree with you? Has He made the providential fit? Has He shut you up to this? If so—alright, then go ahead. He will never fail you."[4] Ever the entrepreneur in mission, Lambie's attention was caught when he heard that the Independent Board for Presbyterian Foreign Missions (IBPFM) was considering an expansion of its ministry into Palestine.[5] The Lambies sensed the beginning of a definite call to serve tuberculosis patients in Palestine and began exploring plans to launch a tuberculosis sanatorium there. In 1945 he "wrote to ask J. Gordon Holdcroft [the IBPFM's director] if they would be interested in a sanatorium in the Holy Land, and in my [Dr. Lambie's] going out to start one."[6]

The Lambies subsequently joined the IBPFM, and in December 1945 began the journey to the Holy Land.[7] En route they were able to spend a happy Christmas with daughter Betty Rees and her four children in England.

2. Lambie, *Doctor's Great Commission*, 262–63.

3. Lambie, *Doctor's Great Commission*, 266.

4. Lambie, *Doctor's Great Commission*, 267–68.

5. The IBPFM was a separate mission agency from the Foreign Missions Board of the United Presbyterian Church of North America under which Thomas and Charlotte Lambie initially served in the Sudan and Abyssinia from 1907 to 1927.

6. Lambie, *Doctor's Great Commission*, 268.

7. See Lambie, "Dr. and Mrs. T. A. Lambie Sail for Palestine," 12–13.

On January 12, 1946, they sailed from Liverpool full of enthusiasm for a new ministry in Palestine.

The trip from Liverpool to Port Said, Egypt, was very trying, regarding both sanitation and food. When they docked at Port Said on January 22, many of the passengers onboard ship had been affected by food poisoning. Charlotte Lambie had become very ill. Apparently, fatigue as well as food poisoning was interfering with her insulin intake. Three days later a short telegram to the IBPFM office bore this sad message: "Mrs. Lambie died cerebral hemorrhage 5:30 this afternoon."[8] The date was January 25, 1946. Lambie buried his wife in Port Said and continued on the journey to Palestine (see chapter 19 for details and Lambie's tribute to Charlotte). In a three-page letter in mid-1946 he wrote to supporters, "Pray for me. I feel so weak and lonely and helpless. I miss you and need you more than ever. Today I went to Bethlehem with some soldiers and beside Christ's birthplace and manger I prayed for strength."[9]

When Dr. Lambie, bowed down in sorrow, arrived in Jerusalem, he was met by Rev. Weston Stewart, the Anglican bishop of Jerusalem, who asked him to take responsibility for the Church of England hospital at Hebron. It was to be a temporary six-month assignment as Lambie was keen to make progress on building the IBPFM's tuberculosis sanatorium.

During the initial months of 1946, Lambie's first goal was to obtain land on which the proposed sanatorium could be constructed. He wrote, "In many ways I seemed to be wasting my time, for I was not getting forward in getting the land for the sanatorium. I gave myself to much earnest prayer and He seemed to give assurance that the answer was near, as it indeed was."[10] Soon after, the property of an Egyptian medical doctor, who was about to retire and return to his homeland, became available near Bethlehem. After land negotiations were finalized and payment made by the IBPFM, Lambie moved into an old stone house on the property. He was joined there by an Arab carpenter and mason by the name of Ijmail, who slowly made repairs on the dilapidated house.

Missionary friends showed various kindnesses to the bereaved Dr. Lambie, though he desperately missed the culinary skills of his departed wife, Charlotte. One incident deserves quoting:

> One day Mrs. Frank Cupples sent me a large jar of delicious soup. I heated it up and served Ijmail and myself for supper. I

8. Lambie, *Doctor's Great Commission*, 273–74. See, also, Holdcroft, "Supplement Copy," 1.

9. Lambie, letter to supporters, June 30, 1946, MHSC.

10. Lambie, *Doctor's Great Commission*, 171.

say delicious, and I am sure it was, although for four or five years
I had been unable to taste or smell anything. We only used half
the soup. We had no ice and the weather was hot. The next night
I served the same soup. I finished my bowl but Ijmail did not
touch his. A few days later he said to me, "Doctor, you know that
soup you served me several days ago?" "Yes." "Well, it smelled
something terrible. I could not eat it and tried it on my dog and
even he wouldn't eat it!"[11]

The land purchased for the sanatorium overlooked the Valley of Berachah, south of Bethlehem. Life was very lonely for a bereft husband, but
soon Lambie began to think of a cure.

> There was one person whom I could not forget, a former [SIM]
> missionary associate in Abyssinia [who] had also been in Nige-
> ria for some years, and whose courage and loyalty had filled me
> with admiration, Miss Irma Schneck. She agreed to come and
> help me to plan for the sanatorium, flying from Kano. I suppose
> I was guilty of duplicity and guile, for I needed help for more
> things than the sanatorium, but anyhow after much thought and
> prayer it seemed to both of us that we should be married, and it
> was one of those best decisions.[12]

The wedding of Thomas and Irma took place on October 1, 1947, in
the Alfred Clarks' beautiful Jerusalem home and garden with many notable guests present. The newly married couple spent their honeymoon in
Nazareth. But all was not peaceful in and around Jerusalem in 1947–48. The
returning Jews were terrorizing the local Palestinian population. Jerusalem
was cordoned off into various zones, with murder, violence, and terrorism
throughout the city and surrounding areas. As the unrest continued, the
IBPFM encouraged the Lambies to return to the United States to share the
financial needs of the proposed tuberculosis sanatorium.

Some potential US donors thought that conditions in Palestine were
too unstable for moving ahead with a project as large as the one envisioned
by Lambie. Reports of terrorism, bombings, and shooting in and around
Jerusalem continued, and train service to and from the city was curtailed
for a period. Sincere Christians in the United States were concerned about
the country's future stability. From friends in Palestine, the Lambies were
hearing discouraging news:

11. Lambie, *Doctor's Great Commission*, 273–74
12. Lambie, *Doctor's Great Commission*, 274.

We have lost all our belongings in Palestine and some would think this to be guidance for us not to go back, but in all ages the Gospel of Christ has meant sacrifice and loss and what poor missionaries we should be if we permitted this to prevent us from going on his errands and doing his will.[13]

In an article submitted to *Biblical Missions*, the IBPFM's journal, Lambie stated that in any great work for God, prayer must have priority. Before leaving for the United States to publicize the proposed tuberculosis sanatorium, he acknowledged that it was only God who would bring success to that particular enterprise. At the same time, Lambie knew that one had to work with all one's strength as if the whole enterprise depended on human initiative. Together with Irma, Lambie set out on this venture of faith, asking others to join them in believing that God would provide finances, personnel, and strength day by day. He concluded the article with a strong plea: "We have to believe and perhaps this is the hardest of all."[14]

Once in the United States, Thomas Lambie and his new wife, Irma, set off in February 1948 on an extended tour of the country, "letting people know" of the needs of the proposed sanatorium in Palestine. In a new Dodge that was given to them, they began a transcontinental trek that followed nearly the same route that Thomas and Charlotte had traveled ten years earlier (see chapter 18). They left from Philadelphia in mid-February—not an ideal time for travel in North America! They headed down to Columbia Bible College in Columbia, South Carolina, where the husband of Lambie's sister Marguerite, Robert McQuilkin, served as president. From there they traveled south to Augusta, Georgia, and then on down to Florida. Journeying next north by northwest, they arrived in Ohio to visit Irma's family roots. In Ohio the Lambies had the moving experience of visiting the home of a family who had recently lost two daughters to tuberculosis. These parents sacrificially gave $1,500 in memory of their daughters for the proposed sanatorium in Palestine. The Lambies' crossing of the great expanse of the US Midwest elicited the comment: "Fog, ice and cold pursued us until we reached Albuquerque [New Mexico], where things improved."[15]

Lambie's creative abilities came alive when he realized that the hymn composer and pianist, Robert Harkness, and his gifted soloist wife would be attending a meeting at the Glendale Presbyterian Church in California. Since Lambie would be showing slides of the Holy Land, he made a request of Harkness, who had composed the music for the hymn *Draw Near, O*

---

13. Lambie, "Return to Palestine," 18.
14. Lambie, "Let Us Rise Up and Build," 13.
15. Lambie, *Doctor's Great Commission*, 277.

Lord! "Robert, I have one slide depicting Cleopas and his friend on their walk to Emmaus. When we get to that place with the pictures would you be willing to play [the hymn], and would Mrs. [Ruth] Harkness be willing to sing it? I would so much appreciate it."[16] To this the couple agreed. The first of the hymn's four stanzas reads:

> Jesus himself drew near,
> And joined them as they walked,
> And soon their hearts began to burn,
> As of Himself He talked:
> Draw near, O Lord! Draw near, O Lord!

After two weeks of fruitful meetings in the Los Angeles area, the Lambies headed up the California coast, speaking in various churches. Soon after they began a leg of their journey up into the high Sierra Mountains, they experienced an unusual challenge, very unlike anything on an African safari. "Up, up we mounted, everything white with snow, and snow falling rapidly, and apparently no traffic at all on the road. If we stopped I felt we should never get started again. The mountain [road] seemed endless, but at last, praise God, we made it."[17] In Seattle, Washington, they were welcomed by the pastor of the First United Presbyterian Church, who had been a missionary colleague of Lambie's in the Sudan. Throughout their lengthy journey they were able to widely present the plans for the sanatorium to be built near Bethlehem.

After arriving safely back in Pennsylvania, the Lambies fulfilled several more weeks of speaking engagements in various churches as well as at the New England Keswick conference. Then early in October 1948, Lambie, ever the learner, joined a small group of thirty-five postgraduate tuberculosis students at Saranac Lake, New York, for several weeks of intensive lectures on recent advances in tuberculosis cure. He found the material helpful, but at age 63 admitted, "Most of the students were very much younger than I, approximately half my age. . . . It was hard for me to keep up to their quick young minds."[18]

In May 1948 Lambie had made an unexpected trip to England to visit his daughter, Betty, and four grandchildren: "A kind friend, the same one who had given me the Dodge, now offered to pay a round trip flight to

---

16. Lambie, *Doctor's Great Commission*, 277. While we were enrolled at Fuller Theological Seminary in Pasadena, California, during our 1971–72 study leave, my wife Lila and I attended Glendale Presbyterian Church.

17. Lambie, *Doctor's Great Commission*, 278.

18. Lambie, *Doctor's Great Commission*, 279.

England to see my daughter and grandchildren. They were in some hard trouble, so I was glad to be able to go. We had a wonderful reunion."[19] Betty and Herbert, who had struggled in their marriage relationship, eventually separated in 1948.[20]

Soon after that trip to England, Lambie became seriously ill and returned to Philadelphia. His condition was so serious that family members were notified. His brother John arrived from Detroit, and the Lambie family began making preparations for a funeral and burial place. Lambie wrote:

> I had one bad fifteen minutes, very low in vitality, and the devil whispered in my ear, "You are a great sinner." "Yes," I said, "I am." "There is no hope for you." "Yes, I admit all you say, but Our Lord Jesus has died for me. My sins are sunk in the depths of the deepest sea, as far as the east is from the west: Jesus has died for me." Through weakness and delirium, He sustained me, and through major surgery when my spleen was removed, I continued to praise Him. I lingered on the brink for days, but God brought me back.[21]

Lambie's recovery progressed slowly. Together he and Irma flew from Philadelphia to Miami, Florida, where they spent several months with Irma's sister. Because of his health history, friends and family advised the Lambies to abandon all plans of returning to Palestine. But Lambie was not to be dissuaded, and at the beginning of August 1949, he and Irma sailed from New York for the Middle East on the SS *Excalibur*, landing in Beirut. Clearing customs for the Dodge they had been given took days of hard work as they went from one office to another. Irma Lambie wrote of those days:

> We stopped at St. George's Hostel in Arab Jerusalem. The day we arrived, August 29 [1949], the American Consulate opened a branch office in Arab Jerusalem. We were invited to the reception and met a good many interesting people. We stayed at the hostel for two days, but spent our time getting the Dodge car licensed, and Doctor and I both got our driver's licenses. Then, too, we made a couple of trips to the Customs office, Arab bank, and to the Consulate. We also visited the Garden Tomb and met some of our old friends. It all seemed strange and especially odd

19. Lambie, *Doctor's Great Commission*, 278.

20. Margaret Hall, letter to Paul Balisky, January 28, 2018, PBSC.

21. Lambie, *Doctor's Great Commission*, 280.

not to see our friends, missionaries, on the other side of the line. There is a no-man's land which separates the city.[22]

Upon their arrival in Palestine this second time, the Lambies experienced several setbacks. Their personal goods, which they had stored with an Arab friend in Jerusalem, had been looted.[23] Also, while they were away, their former makeshift residence in Bethlehem had been occupied by the local Jewish police, so in early 1950 they moved into a house with missionary colleagues.

> LaVerne and Louise Donaldson [with their three children] secured a house in Bethlehem big enough to hold us all, but not too big. In fact, it was a tight fit, and [during] the winter [it] proved very unsuitable. The walls dripped with water. There were no modern conveniences. It was a cold winter with much snow, and in our cramped, practically slum conditions, it was very uncomfortable, but we had only to think of the One Who was born not more than a stone's throw away, to feel that our position was so much better than His, that we took shame to ourselves for having even a complaining thought.[24]

It was not long before the Lambies were back at the Palestinian location called Ain Arroub in Arabic. Lying a dozen or so miles south of Bethlehem in the vicinity of Hebron, the area was totally Muslim. Lambie began a clinic in temporary quarters and began treating tuberculosis patients, up to as many 200 each day. Construction also began on the new sanatorium. Gaining government permission for building met with several rebuffs. But through a drawn-out process, permission was finally obtained not only for the sanatorium but also for the Lambie residence. The latter building would also serve as a rest home for vacationing missionaries. During the process of gaining permission from the Jordanian government in Amman, Lambie established genuine friendships with various of the officials.[25]

---

22. Irma Lambie, letter to supporters, September 23, 1949, cited in Holdcroft, "Mission to the Holy Land," 15.

23. See the account by Donald James MacKay, "Introduction," in Lambie, *A Bruised Reed*, 14–15.

24. Lambie, *Doctor's Great Commission*, 281.

25. Lambie, "Annual Report," 13.

Tuberculosis sanatorium in Ain Arroub, Palestine

By May 1950 the Lambies were able to begin building a home of their own on the property they had initially purchased from the retired Egyptian doctor.[26] Construction of the large sanatorium near Bethlehem was also initiated under the skilled supervision of Bill Mooring, a builder from the United States. Lambie later wrote:

> Our finances were a daily miracle. Sometimes the barrel was nearly dry, but never completely so. We had no debts, and the building rose to the glory of God. Its foundations were upon the solid rock. It was constructed of lovely gray stone with many re-enforced concrete pillars to withstand earthquake shocks. Slight earth tremors are often experienced in the Holy Land.[27]

26. Lambie, *A Bride for His Son*, 172.

27. Lambie, *Doctor's Great Commission*, 282. See also Lambie, *A Bride for His Son*, 173–74.

As construction moved ahead on the new sanatorium, Lambie received encouragement in his determination to serve the Arab population from Dr. Chaim Yassky, head of the Jewish Hadassah Hospital in Hadera (located on the coast between Tel Aviv and Haifa). Dr. Yassky wrote to him:

> Dr. Lambie, what we do for tuberculosis is almost laughable, it is so little, so inadequate, a mere 100 bed hospital at Hadera. This is for Jewish people, and is a mere drop in the bucket. The Arab's need is even more absolute. Nothing whatever is provided for him, and unless nature effects a cure, which sometimes happens, he is doomed.[28]

The Balfour Declaration of 1917 was a statement, issued as a letter from the British foreign secretary, of support for the establishment within Palestine of a national home for the Jewish people. This promise of a homeland was not implemented until 1947, when the Jews were given back some of the Palestinian homeland that they had lost nearly 2,000 years earlier. The Arabs in 1947 reluctantly agreed that the Jews then in Palestine should be tolerated but that their number should not increase. At that time neither the Palestinians nor the Jewish settlers were willing to accept partitioning of Palestine into Jewish and Arab states. Intransigence on both sides continues to fuel the conflict even to the present.

In 1952 the Lambies were overwhelmed by the sheer number of Arab refugees camping next to the newly constructed Berachah Sanatorium. "Our hearts went out to those thousands of refugees, our next door neighbours who are living in miserable tents with no 'refuge from the storm' and our hearts really wept for them."[29] Such scenes caused Lambie to question whether biblical prophecy regarding the Jews reclaiming the land should be fulfilled in this unjust and unfair manner.

> Now, two-thirds of the Arabs have been dispossessed of their holdings. Their farms, their orchards, their vineyards, their orange groves by which they lived, are all in possession of the Jews. It is no good to say that they [Arabs] have wasted the land, for I have seen many beautiful farms they have had. Here is a great population of nearly one million souls dispossessed of all they had, and no recompense is made to them nor probably will be.[30]

28. Chaim Yassky, to Lambie, cited in Lambie, "Palestine, Focal Point of the World," 25.

29. Lambie, "News from the Holy Land," 9.

30. Lambie, *Doctor's Great Commission*, 286.

In May 1953, the Lambies flew to England for a much needed vacation. Again, they enjoyed visiting with his daughter, Betty, and the four grandchildren.

> Our daughter lives in the country, forty minutes from London, in an ancient cottage dating back to 1422, with thatched roof and quaint diamond panes in the windows. She had modernized it, and for the first few days the four grandchildren were all there. What a happy time. My namesake, six years old, having no father to caress him, regarded me something like an angel from heaven, and would kiss me over and over saying, "Oh grandfather you are so lovely."[31]

The Lambies found their short stay in England refreshing. The sound of birds, the beauty of the countryside, and the view of the distant mountains of Wales were a source of solace and encouragement. A special pleasure of their time in London was to attend the coronation of young Queen Elizabeth II. A London doctor friend procured two wonderful seats for them from which they were able to view the grand proceedings.[32]

Returning once more to the Valley of Berachah, south of Bethlehem, Lambie made a significant contribution to the attempt to treat and curb infectious tuberculosis. The 130-bed sanatorium, for which the Lambies had traveled extensively while raising funds in the United States, was finally dedicated in 1952.

> At last the building was completed, or about as nearly completed as any hospital ever is, for there is always something needing to be done, and in August 1952 we held a dedicatory service when many notables came from the Holy Land and the members of the Middle East Bible Conference from America, via Beirut, and many local friends and consular agents. Many kind words were said. The main speaker was our beloved Dr. J. Gordon Holdcroft, head of our mission [IBPFM]. The hospital was inspected and refreshments served. God had wrought a miracle for us and we praise Him.[33]

In his response to Rev. Gordon Holdcroft's address, Lambie stated:

> Five years ago I had a vision for a tuberculosis sanatorium for the people of Palestine. I was then on the staff of Pennsylvania

---

31. Lambie, *Doctor's Great Commission*, 284.

32. As a girl of twelve, my wife, Lila Propst Balisky, was also in London with her Africa Inland Mission family, which likewise attended the gala 1953 coronation.

33. Lambie, *Doctor's Great Commission*, 282–83.

Hospital Number One for tuberculosis. I had a generous salary, but the need of the Holy Land seemed very great with no tuberculosis hospital at all. One could not expect to duplicate that wonderful structure in Palestine, but surely something should be done for all the people of Palestine. After prayer, much prayer, the vision deepened and as a result I left my well-paying job and turned to the Holy Land to try to help in healing bodies and souls and pointing them to the Saviour.[34]

By early 1953 the men's and women's wards were complete and patients had begun to be admitted. Then there was the need for a nurses' residence as they were at that point being housed in a section of the sanatorium, which was medically unsafe. Building of the nursing complex began, even though funds were lacking. "We began to pray for this and God again has been answering our need, and the walls are going up and we trust that it will be built and paid for. . . . We still need much money to finish it."[35]

Training student nurses was a high priority for Berachah Sanatorium. Without local Arab nurses who understood the language and culture, the medical work would flounder.

Thus our training school was started, and it has, it seems to me, already accomplished great things. A number of young sweet women have now had a year's training in nursing in both theory and practice, and are proving invaluable. Perhaps the good done to these young people is the most important thing we have done.[36]

In April of 1953 the sanatorium celebrated the capping ceremony for the first group of young women who successfully passed their exams. The graduating class consisted mainly of nurses from the Greek Orthodox Church. A large crowd of parents and friends gathered at the sanatorium to celebrate the occasion.[37]

The year 1953 also saw two talented medical colleagues join the ministry at the Berachah Sanatorium. They were Dr. George P. Dillard, Jr., from Draper, North Carolina, and Dr. Henry Backhouse, from London, England. Several qualified nurses who specialized in teaching joined the staff as well.[38] Among these dedicated nurses were Mrs. Dorothy Dillard (doctor's

---

34. Lambie, "Christian Sanatorium in the Holy Land," 9.

35. Lambie, *Doctor's Great Commission*, 283–84.

36. Lambie, *Doctor's Great Commission*, 283.

37. Lambie, "Christmas Service on the Shepherds' Fields," 5.

38. Lambie, "Swords Drawn Up to the Gates of Heaven," 30.

wife), Miss Pauline Frederick, and Mrs. May Podbregger.[39] But Lambie felt the need also to train young Arab nurses to assist in ministry. This ambition became a priority of the sanatorium.

> So often on the mission field the good work done by the Christian doctors and nurses is nullified by unconverted helpers. A good philanthropic work is done, but without spiritual content. We thought it best to get some nurses trained not only as nurses, but as spiritual helpers with us, even if it delayed the care of the sick. A single godless nurse of strong personality can undo the work of many others who are seeking not only to heal but to save the patients. . . . Thus our training school [as mentioned] was started, and has, it seems to me, already accomplished great things. A number of sweet young women have now had a year's training in both theory and practice, and are proving invaluable.[40]

Lambie lived a wholesome life, albeit by now in a frail and weakened body because of years of physical exertion in harsh climates. Still, toward the end of his life, not all was peace and bliss in Lambie's mind. He expressed his concern just one year before his death on April 14, 1954.

> One thing has troubled me, and that was the matter of the continuance of the work, for manifestly our Independent Board for Presbyterian Foreign Missions with its worldwide commitments is in no position to maintain such a great work at a tremendous upkeep. "What happens when Lambie dies?" was what people were saying and what Lambie himself was thinking. Is there no one who could carry on, not only medically or even administratively, but who could carry the prayer burden and really believe God for its upkeep and maintenance?[41]

In 1952 Gordon Holdcroft, IBPFM's director, had expressed this same concern. He wrote then that "one of the greatest needs we face is to find a properly qualified physician, a tuberculosis specialist, for the sanatorium. Such a man would have a life work of the very highest possibilities before him."[42]

But God did answer prayer and the needs were met as the work at the sanatorium developed. Young qualified medical staff were gradually

---

39. Irma Lambie, circular letter, "Dearly Beloved," May 1, 1954, IBPFM Archives (Plymouth Meeting, PA), File, "Missionary Correspondence."

40. Lambie, *Doctor's Great Commission*, 283.

41. Lambie, *Doctor's Great Commission*, 284.

42. Holdcroft, "Progress and Problems in Palestine," 22.

recruited from both the United States and England. During these developments, Lambie commented, "All these young people, so fresh and clean and highly educated filled us with thanksgiving, and I almost felt like saying, 'Now God let thy servant depart in peace for I have seen the Lord's salvation.'"[43]

43. Lambie, *Doctor's Great Commission*, 283.

21

The Death of Dr. Thomas A. Lambie

As far as we know that glad event may take place at any time.
What a glorious sight that will be! All labours and trials over now.

THOMAS A. LAMBIE, *A BRIDE FOR HIS SON*, 188

DR. THOMAS A. LAMBIE died at the Garden Tomb in Jerusalem on Wednesday, April 14, 1954, while he was preparing for the following Sunday's Easter sunrise service. His second wife, Mrs. Irma Schneck Lambie, wrote the following account of his death.

> The afternoon of April 14, 1954, we went to the Jerusalem airport to meet a friend. The doctor usually carried a writing board as he was working on [the manuscript of his final book] *A Bride for His Son*. The last thing he wrote was about King David, in Chapter 7: "David had his picked men. King Jesus has His. We cannot get into the first class under David but we can get into the present warfare under our great Captain. . . ." On our way back from the airport he suggested that we stop by the Garden Tomb. We went into the home of the warden [Mr. S. J. Mattar] and the doctor lay down on a couch to rest. A number of us were talking about the Easter Sunrise [service] to be held at the Tomb, where the doctor was to bring the message. He told us that he was going to talk about the appearances of our Lord after the Resurrection. He started to name them and finished giving us six. He said, "Seven..." and then there was silence. He entered

233

the Celestial City without having to bid us good-by. It was fitting that he should be talking about the Lord whom he loved dearly and then the next instant to be with Him. A glorious entrance into Heaven! He loved the Garden Tomb. God chose the perfect place from which to call him Home.[1]

On April 15 Dr. Lambie was buried in Bethlehem, near the birthplace of his Lord and Savior. Ten or a dozen miles south of Bethlehem stands the seventy-five-bed Berachah Tuberculosis Sanatorium. A bronze plaque at the entrance to that building reads:

To the glory of God

Thomas Alexander Lambie, M.D., D.Sc.

1885–1954

Built This, His Seventh Hospital

In His Last Years

Author and Pioneer Doctor

1907–1954

In Egypt, the Sudan, Ethiopia

And the Holy Land

Beloved for His Selfless Life

And Steadfast Service

Man of Faith and Prayer

For the Word of God

And the Testimony of Jesus Christ[2]

A statement written by Dr. Lambie about a year before his death might well serve as his epitaph:

And so, dear reader, we have come to the end at last, but I would like my last word to be of praise to God and our Lord Jesus Christ. For anything of value that has been done in my poor life, may all glory be His. All the mistakes and failures are mine. I lay down my pen, leaving the future of this great work to God and to you. "Let everything that hath breath praise the Lord. Praise ye the Lord."[3]

In his final years, Dr. Lambie, an ever-willing volunteer, served as chairperson of the committee that oversaw the Shepherd's Field where

1. Irma Lambie, "Preface," in Lambie, *A Bride for His Son*, 16.

2. Irma Lambie, "Preface," in Lambie, *A Bride for His Son*, 9.

3. Lambie, *Doctor's Great Commission*, 287–88.

biblical scholars think that the angels appeared, announcing the birth of Christ. He is reported to have conducted Christmas Eve services for the hundreds of tourists gathered there. He was also one of the volunteer custodians of the Garden Tomb and often addressed the many visitors who attended the Easter sunrise service at the Tomb.

Two days following his death, the *Philadelphia Inquirer* reported: "Dr. Thomas A. Lambie, widely known medical missionary who served as personal physician to Emperor Haile Selassie of Ethiopia for a time, died Wednesday at Ain Arroub, Jordan. He was 69."[4]

In its periodical *Biblical Missions*, the Independent Board for Presbyterian Foreign Missions gave details regarding Thomas Lambie's funeral service.

> The main funeral service was held in the Church of England Cathedral in Jerusalem. The Anglican Bishop, Mr. Weston Stewart, graciously offered the Cathedral for the funeral for his friend. The Rev. LaVerne Donaldson and the Rev. Robert G. Hamilton of the Holy Land Mission of The Independent Board for Presbyterian Foreign Missions conducted the funeral service. The pallbearers were Dr. George Dillard, Berachah Sanatorium; Dr. Henry Backhouse, Berachah Sanatorium; Mr. Robert Dawson, British Vice Consul; Mr. S. J. Mattar, Warden, Garden Tomb; Dr. M. Dajani, Arab National Hospital; Mr. Najib Khoury, United Nations Works and Relief. The service was held the following day, April 15, at three pm. After the service the funeral procession drove to Bethlehem where the body was laid to rest at the new church property of The Independent Board for Presbyterian Foreign Missions. On the hillside facing west under the shade of two olive trees, the body found rest.[5]

Dr. Lambie's earthly journey was complete. He had fought the good fight and finished his course. The following words appear on his grave stone in Bethlehem.

IN LOVING MEMORY

OF

THOMAS ALEXANDER LAMBIE

1885–1954

WITH CHRIST

WHICH IS FAR BETTER

4. "Dr. Lambie Dies; Missionary Aide," *Philadelphia Inquirer*, April 16, 1954.

5. Holdcroft, "Dr. Lambie Called Home," 5–6.

22

Thomas A. Lambie:
An Assessment of His Life and Ministry

"Do you see a man skilled in his work?
He will serve before kings:
he will not serve before obscure men.

PROVERBS 22:29 (NIV)

WHEN THOMAS LAMBIE BEGAN his missionary career in Sudan in 1907 with the Foreign Missions Board of the United Presbyterian Church of North America, his missionary colleagues dubbed him a "loose cannon."[1] His unconstrained enthusiasm for life, his devotion to Christ, and his skill as a physician opened doors for him to serve in Sudan, Abyssinia, and Palestine. Pioneer conditions—which involved travel by boat on the Nile, trekking by horse and mule throughout mountainous Abyssinia, and suffering debilitating sicknesses—and even old age did not deter him from his obedience to the Great Commission. This final chapter utilizes twelve lenses to summarize Lambie's life and ministry.

---

1. Partee, *Story of Don McClure*, 445.

Lifelong Christian Commitment

Lambie was raised in a strong evangelical home and nurtured in the Eighth Presbyterian Church of Pittsburgh, Pennsylvania, pastored by Dr. James M. Wallace. At the young age of eleven, Thomas had a vision of Christ that he never forgot. His commitment to lifetime service in mission was made while attending a New Wilmington Mission Conference. At that time he was enrolled at the Western Pennsylvania Medical School in Pittsburgh and soon made application to the Foreign Missions Board of the United Presbyterian Church of North America.[2] His commitment to missionary service proved to be steadfast and lifelong (for his early life, see chapter 1).

Role as Missionary Doctor

Lambie's perception of a "missionary doctor" was that this profession would open doors for mission outreach.[3] As a pragmatic person, he soon found that serving as a medical doctor did open many opportunities for verbal witness. His medical credentials allowed him to pioneer missionary activity in western Abyssinia in 1919.[4] These credentials also brought Lambie into favor with the future emperor of Abyssinia, Haile Sellassie I, under whose direction he eventually established four hospitals. In 1935 Lambie enthused, "Medicine was once again the spear point of the camel's nose."[5] Lambie's remarkable medical career culminated near Bethlehem, Jordan, where he built a large tuberculosis sanatorium which served the needy Palestinian population. At one stage in his career, he was tempted to remain in the United States and join his brother-in-law's medical practice. God kindly assisted him, however, in overcoming that temptation by an unusual dream that took him back to Sudan (see chapter 3).

---

2. Lambie, *Doctor without a Country*, 14.

3. Lambie, *Doctor without a Country*, 15.

4. Donald Crummey, "The Politics of Modernization: Protestant and Catholic Missionaries in Modern Ethiopia," in *Missionary Factor in Ethiopia*, ed. Getachew Haile et al.; see p. 91, "Lambie and his colleagues owed their being in Ethiopia to their command of the medical and educational dimensions [of] modernity and to the modernizing vision of Haile Sellassie."

5. Lambie, "Conquest by Healing in Ethiopia," 73.

GIFT OF ESTABLISHING TRUSTING RELATIONSHIPS
WITH THOSE IN AUTHORITY

Lambie found it easy to develop trusting relationships with individuals of various economic levels and social standing. While serving in Abyssinia, he developed a special relationship with Emperor Haile Sellassie as well as with the governors of several Abyssinian provinces. The George Memorial Hospital in Addis Ababa gave professional medical service to all who entered, including those in official government positions. Lambie became a personal advisor to the emperor on some official matters. For example, he developed a correspondence with a Mr. J. Loder Park, American consul based in Aden, who was attempting to develop American-sponsored agriculture and trading in Ethiopia as well as to negotiate concessions for the Anglo-American Oil Company for oil exploration in the Ogaden. Loder Park complimented Lambie, "You are a real American, in whom I would place every confidence. . . . You are the one man in that country personally acquainted with Him [Emperor Haile Sellassie] that I can trust absolutely."[6] Lambie responded with a bold recommendation that "the Anglo-American Oil Company . . . appoint me to act as their agent for them."[7]

In a separate role, Lambie was asked by the emperor to accompany three Abyssinian scholars to the United States and to help enroll them in a US college. While in the United States, he conveyed a special letter of greeting to President Harding from Emperor Haile Sellassie. President Harding reciprocated by sending a large photograph of himself to the emperor via Lambie.[8] Lambie was also respected and honored by former medical colleagues who were in positions of authority in Pennsylvania. These colleagues assisted him in his enrollment in a tuberculosis training program which qualified him for his ministry in Palestine.[9]

TRUSTING RELATIONSHIP WITH SIM's
INTERNATIONAL DIRECTOR

Lambie and Rowland Bingham, SIM's international director, developed mutual respect in furthering the cause of mission. Bingham trusted Lambie and his two associates, George Rhoad and Alfred Buxton, with the launching

6. J. Loder Park, letter to Lambie, November 12, 1925, MHSC, "Sundries, 1925."

7. See chapter 4 and also Lambie, letter to J. Loder Park, November 29, 1925, MHSC, "Sundries, 1925."

8. Lambie, *Doctor without a Country*, 158.

9. Lambie, *Doctor's Great Commission*, 287.

of a new mission venture into Abyssinia. Lambie, a younger man but with years of mission experience in both Sudan and Ethiopia, looked to Bingham as a son to a father. He valued Bingham's wisdom as SIM Ethiopia anticipated expanding its ministry into northern Abyssinia, the heart of the Ethiopian Orthodox Church. When Lambie struggled with interpersonal relationships with SIM colleagues in Sudan, he accepted Bingham's fatherly advice and confessed his shortcomings (see chapter 15).

RELATIONSHIP WITH HIS FAMILY

Missionary pioneering was not conducive to a comfortable family life, but Lambie did his best as husband and father to care for his family. His two children, Wallace and Betty, born in the Sudan in 1910 and 1911, often suffered from malaria and heat rash. He took all precautions in screening his Sudanese residences to make them mosquito proof. When Charlotte experienced appendicitis in southern Sudan, far from professional medical help, Lambie's prayer was answered when a large riverboat appeared. "The captain was going to make a quick trip to Khartoum."[10] He took the family down the Sobat River and eventually the Nile to a hospital in Khartoum. When Charlotte accompanied him and others on treks of hundreds of miles by mule and horse to open new mission stations, he depended on her to provide daily food. She proved to be a true spiritual "soul-friend" to her husband through vicissitudes such as setbacks from government officials, lack of finances in Ethiopia during the years of the Great Depression in the 1930s, and misunderstandings with fellow missionaries.

Leaving their seventeen-year-old son Wallace, in Maryland with Charlotte's parents was not easy for Lambie or his wife. Later, learning by mail of Wallace's accidental death in Medellin, Colombia, where he was employed by the US National Bank, became a heavy burden to bear. Lambie struggled in his relationship with Herbert Rees, a Cambridge don, who was his daughter Betty's suitor and became his son-in-law. But he dearly loved his daughter and the four grandchildren. After Charlotte's unexpected death and burial in Port Said, Egypt, in 1946, Lambie carried on, alone in his sorrow, for over a year in a medical practice in Jordan. He then married Irma Schneck, a former SIM missionary, whom he respected and loved until his death in 1954. Irma proved to be an ideal helpmeet for Lambie in his loneliness and sorrow. During the strenuous latter years of his life when he was launching the tuberculous sanatorium near Bethlehem, Lambie depended

---

10. Lambie, *Doctor without a Country*, 100.

on Irma who proved to be an ideal companion and capable secretary, especially in the many demands of communicating with donors.

Passion to Reach Non-Christians with the Gospel

When Lambie's former mission society, the FMBUPC, proved unable to expand into southern Abyssinia, Lambie felt compelled, with a few others, to launch an independent organization, the Abyssinian Frontiers Mission. In God's providence, this new organization soon amalgamated with the previously existing Sudan Interior Mission, and eventually, sixteen mission stations were established in Abyssinia. But this desire to expand the sphere of gospel witness meant thousands of miles of trekking by horse or mule in order to locate and finally establish mission stations. Lambie did not experience the reward of missionary outreach in seeing many converts baptized. By 1936, when the Lambies departed Ethiopia, the baptized believers meeting weekly in three small churches numbered only twenty-six. But the seed had been planted. Through the decades, this small beginning has yielded fruit which today numbers over nine million baptized believers in the Kale Heywet Church of Ethiopia.

Effective Speaker and Writer

Lambie as a speaker:

Speaking to raise funds for the Addis Ababa Hospital, 1922 (*A Doctor without a Country*, 155–58)

Speaking in churches in the United Kingdom (*A Doctor without a Country*, 230)

Extended speaking tour in the United States (*A Doctor's Great Commission*, 277)

Speaking at New England Keswick (*A Doctor's Great Commission*, 278)

Annual speaker at Easter Sunrise Services, Jerusalem (*A Bride for His Son*, 16)

Books by Lambie:

Abayte! or, Ethiopia's Plea (1935)

A Doctor without a Country (1939)

A Doctor Carries On (1942)

Boot and Saddle in Africa (1943)

A Bruised Reed: Light from Bible Lands on Bible Illustrations (1952)

A Doctor's Great Commission (1954; chaps. 17–20, pp. 253–88, added more recently)

A Bride for His Son: More Light from Bible Lands on Bible Illustrations (1957)

Articles in journals:

"The Importance of Abyssinia," *World Dominion* (September 1926)

"Evangelism in Ethiopia—Leaves from the Diary of Dr. T. A. Lambie," *United Presbyterian Journal* (October 4–December 27, 1928), thirteen articles

"Conquest by Healing in Ethiopia," *Conquest by Healing* [publication of the Medical Missionary Association] (September 1935)

"I Have Begun to Give You Possession," *Evangelical Christian*, August 25, 1937

"A New Challenge to the Sudan Interior Mission, or, 'A Way Out' Which Is 'A Way Into,'" *Evangelical Christian*, May 30, 1937

"Our New Task," *Evangelical Christian*, June 28, 1937

Personal correspondence to Charlotte, Wallace, and Betty:

Over 1,000 pages of endearing handwritten letters to Charlotte are extant. The majority were written in tents by lantern light while Lambie was on trek in southern Abyssinia.

Several short letters written to Wallace while he was employed in Medellin, Colombia, have survived.

After Charlotte's death in 1946, Lambie wrote loving fatherly letters to his daughter, Betty, who was residing with her four children in England.

FRIENDS WITH INDIVIDUALS OF SIGNIFICANT INFLUENCE

Throughout his missionary career Lambie had a unique ability to develop sincere friendship with individuals in high places who assisted him in his missionary endeavors. While serving in Sudan, he befriended Sir Steward Symnes, governor general of Sudan, and also Captain Chauncey Hugh

Stigand, British Inspector of Nasir District.[11] In Abyssinia Lambie sought the patronage of a number of government officials; of special significance were Haile Sellassie, emperor of Abyssinia, and Ras Birru Walda Gabriel, Abyssinian minister of war.[12] In Palestine Lambie befriended Alfred P. Clark, director of the Barclays Bank branches in Palestine, as well as King Abdulah of Jordan.[13]

Peter Cotterell proposed to explain Dr. Lambie's ability to befriend officials in high positions in the following manner: "This intercourse with the highest officials is in part explained by Lambie's patrician background. . . . His grandfather had apparently held some position in the White House in Washington."[14]

CREATIVE BENT AND AESTHETIC SENSIBILITY

While the Lambies were on a journey to southern Sudan on the Nile River in 1913, the wood burning steamer malfunctioned. Along with the other passengers, the Lambies appeared to be stranded far from help. Lambie was able to locate the mechanical problem and provide a remedy so that the journey could continue.

In the Sudan, when the British military experienced leaking benzene because their tin containers were being bounced in the back of trucks on rough roads, Lambie invented special chests or "coverings" for the fuel containers. These were constructed from bamboo carefully wired to mahogany slats. Over time more than 2,000 of these protective fuel container coverings were manufactured in the British military's Khartoum shop. Lambie was informed that they enabled thousands of liters of fuel to be delivered safely to their destination with minimal spillage.

Lambie placed value on the aesthetic appearance of the facilities he developed. The George Memorial Hospital in Addis Ababa was well-constructed with lovely cedar trees planted around the circumference of the facility and flower beds decorating the main entrance. Many flowering plants

---

11. Lambie, "Report of the Interview between Governor General of the Anglo-Egyptian Sudan, Sir S. Symnes, and Drs. R. V. Bingham and T. A. Lambie at Khartoum, Anglo-Egyptian Sudan, on March 14, 1937," SIMIA, Box KB-121, File 1. For Chauncey Hugh Stigand, see Lambie, *Doctor without a Country*, 122.

12. See, respectively, Lambie, *Doctor without a Country*, 146 and 245.

13. Lambie mentions Clark in *A Doctor Carries On*, 144–45, and King Abdulah in his "Annual Report of the Holy Land Branch," 13.

14. Cotterell, "Dr. T. A. Lambie: Some Biographical Notes," 45fn9. Cotterell's explanation seems inadequate, since Jean Pierre Sioussat, one of Lambie's great-grandfathers, was not a White House official, but a doorman, one of the staff.

and trees beautified the property of the large sanatorium he constructed near Bethlehem, Jordan. Even when water was scarce, Lambie insisted that all plants and trees were to be sufficiently watered. He had a love of God's creation, especially the highlands of Ethiopia with their diverse flora and fauna. He was also a great lover of animals. When his bulldog, "Bill," went missing near Lake Abaye, he wrote that he "felt deprived of a real friend."[15] *Boot and Saddle in Africa*, some claim, is Lambie's best written book. Its title is taken from Robert Browning's poem, "Boot and Saddle," the first line of which reads, "Boot, saddle, to horse, and away!" Lambie loved riding his favorite horse, an Arabian gelding named "Birru." He wrote, "There is something about a good horse that brings a response out of all who love the outdoor life, something that nothing else ever does."[16] Lambie respected his riding horses and his mules. He never used spurs or a whip but guided them with reins and his voice.

COMMENDATIONS IN FOREWORDS AND INTRODUCTIONS TO HIS BOOKS

Dr. Howard A. Kelly, of Johns Hopkins University wrote in the Introduction to *A Doctor without a Country*: "It has appeared to me more and more, as the subject has opened up in its delightful natural fashion, expressing the personality of the writer, that I was following one who walked closely in the footsteps of our great David Livingstone, exploring the vast interior of Southern Africa" (p. 3).

Remarks by newcaster Lowell Thomas given in his broadcast across the United States on January 15, 1941, were included in the Foreword he wrote for *A Doctor Carries On*: "Dr. Lambie, 'The Doctor Without a Country,' believes that the push is on now, the campaign, that will, as he puts it, 'Change Benito Mussolini into Finito Mussolini'" (p. 8).

Robert C. McQuilkin, president of Columbia Bible College, Columbia, South Carolina, and also brother-in-law to Thomas Lambie, wrote in his Introduction to *Boot and Saddle in Africa*: "As a pioneer in Africa Dr. Lambie is in the succession of Doctor Livingstone, with the same indifference to hardships and with a tender, affectionate love for the peoples of Africa. . . . In all these fellowships there has been the message of the Lord that was so manifest in Livingstone's life, that he who would be chief among you must be servant of all" (p. 5).

---

15. Lambie, *Doctor without a Country*, 184.
16. Lambie, *Boot and Saddle in Africa*, 7.

Donald James MacKay, from Philadelphia, wrote in the Introduction to *A Bruised Reed: Light from Bible Lands on Bible Illustrations*: "With a vision, inspired of the Lord of the Harvest, he has led advances into the Anglo-Egyptian Sudan and Ethiopia. Undismayed by pioneer conditions or discouraging problems, he has had a long and useful missionary career" (p. 10).

William Culbertson, president of Moody Bible Institute, Chicago, wrote in his Introduction to *A Bride for His Son*: "He was the kind of Christian who did one good just to be with. The simplicity of his life, the contagion of his enthusiasm, the fullness of his surrender, and the depth of his devotion to Christ heartened everyone who knew him" (p. 19).

V. Raymond Edman, president of Wheaton College, Wheaton, Illinois, paid tribute to Lambie in his Foreword to *A Doctor's Great Commission*: "Every now and then, not very frequently, one meets a man who is deeply taught of God, who is filled with the Spirit of God, who is in reality, 'a man of God.' One makes that discovery not by what he says or does, so much as by what he *is*" (p. 7).

Personable Hospitality to All

Lambie's welcoming spirit was evident wherever he traveled or made his abode. When he settled in Palestine, his home at Berachah Sanatorium quickly became a hub for many Holy Land tourists. An annual group of tourists, supervised by archaeologist Joseph P. Free of Wheaton College, Wheaton, Illinois, would visit the sanatorium and then enjoy the hospitality of the Lambie home. His door was always open to Arab refugees, Jewish settlers, and US diplomats. Lambie himself wrote:

> Frequently Christian tourists came to see us, often in large groups. Dr. Free of Wheaton College brings out a special group every year. Dr. John Huffman of Winona Lake [Indiana] School of Theology does likewise. These parties bring inspiration and help to us, and we praise God for them. We cannot take them all in as staying guests as they are too many, but love to have them come at least one day and have coffee and doughnuts with us.[17]

Contributions to the Geographic Study of East Africa

Lambie was elected a Fellow of Great Britain's Royal Geographical Society (RGS) in 1923. Apparently around 1914 he had given a paper to the RGS

17. Lambie, *Doctor's Great Commission*, 287.

describing the rivers and tributaries flowing from Abyssinia into the Sudan. A handwritten copy of this paper, presented to a meeting of the RGS, is held in the Margaret Hall Special Collection.[18] According to RGS protocol, potential candidates for membership in the society must be recommended by an RGS member who is conversant with the contribution that the candidate has made to geography. The missionary educator Robert Hall Glover was the person who recommended Thomas Lambie for election as a Fellow of the Royal Geographical Society.[19]

Shortcomings and Weaknesses

In his letters and books, Dr. Lambie confessed ways in which his relationships with his mission colleagues fell short. Also, during his period as executive director of the Ethiopian Red Cross, he often felt frustrated in dealing with Abyssinian officialdom as well as with volunteers from Geneva who were serving on the International Committee of the Red Cross. As seen in chapter 12, Lambie's vacillating stance regarding the Fascists definitely invited misunderstanding and rebuke. For example, in early 1934 Lambie had written that the Fascists would not condone evangelical missions if they were to conquer Abyssinia. He cited the case of Eritrea, where evangelical mission work had been shut down. SIM colleague Malcolm Forsberg no doubt expressed the sentiments of others also who found it difficult to excuse Lambie's so-called "surrender" to the Italians in the mistaken hope that the Fascists might allow SIM to continue serving in Abyssinia. Forsberg insightfully wrote, "I deny that the Lord has to depend on disloyalty and inconsistency to maintain his work."[20]

Alfred Roke was also somewhat critical of Lambie's practice of Scripture "proof-texting" as a mode of leadership while he was SIM director in Abyssinia. Lambie based his decision (to "surrender" to the Italians) on proof-texting such verses as Romans 13:1. Roke concluded that "this kind of theology seems to need a lot of luck."[21] Clarence Duff, another long-serving and well respected SIM colleague who was in addition Lambie's deputy in

18. Lambie, "Speech on Sudan, 1914," MHSC.

19. In obtaining archival information related to Thomas Lambie, I am indebted to Julie Carrington of the Royal Geographical Society and to information found on http://discovery.nationalarchives.gov.uk.

20. Forsberg, letter to Bingham, January 16, 1942, SIMIA, Forsberg, Malcolm and Enid, Box 09, File 4.

21. Roke, *They Went Forth*, 180.

Abyssinia, sharply disagreed with Lambie for compromising SIM as an organization by surrendering to the Italian junta.[22]

Various other expatriates in Addis Ababa at that time were disappointed in Lambie's surrender to the Fascists. John Spencer, adviser to the Abyssinian government in international law, stated that it was "a defection to the Italians."[23] British Minister Sidney Barton condemned Lambie's collusion with the Italians as "a pusillanimous attempt to curry favour with the Italians."[24] Finally, Marcel Junod, an International Committee Red Cross member, called Lambie's attitude "a shameful manoeuvre."[25] Some years later, as Lambie reflected on the past, he thought differently of his actions, stating, "The appeasement policy will never work with . . . [the] Italians, and I should have known better and acted differently. I hope I shall never do it again"[26]

In spite of Lambie's weaknesses, his dealings with various authorities in Haile Sellassie's government (1919–36) and his interfacing with British officials in the Sudan (1939–42) lead one to assume that he was skilled in diplomacy. Donald Donham wrote that Lambie was a "flexible politician, able to play the game of give-and-take with Ethiopian nobility."[27] But his vacillating appeasement policy in his dealings with the Italians during his final days in Abyssinia was his undoing.

FINAL APPRAISAL

To summarize the illustrious life and ministry of Dr. Thomas A. Lambie succinctly is a challenge. How, one might ask, was Lambie able to sustain his resilience as a pioneer missionary for over four decades despite the challenging and varied situations he faced in Sudan, Abyssinia, and Palestine? As his writings attest, his perseverance can be attributed to his daily immersion in scripture and consistent prayer life. He certainly had faults, as did other pioneer missionaries. Clarence Duff, an SIM missionary colleague in Abyssinia, gave this assessment of Lambie: "I regard Dr. Lambie as one of the best and greatest men it has been my privilege to know. If sometimes his judgement or his actions proved to be unwise, he rose above his faults, outlived

22. See Roke, *They Went Forth*, 211–12.

23. Spencer, *Ethiopia at Bay*, 85.

24. Cited in Baudendistel, *Between Bombs and Good Intentions*, 43.

25. Baudendistel, *Between Bombs and Good Intentions*, 43.

26. Lambie, "Statement" to Bingham, March 16, 1942, SIMIA, KB-21, File. See, also, SIMIA, Forsberg, Malcolm and Enid, Box 09, File 4.

27. Donham, *Marxist Modern*, 87.

them and the criticisms incurred, and went on to fresh achievements."[28] In his numerous books, articles, and letters, Lambie himself referred to David Livingstone, who was, perhaps, his missionary hero in Africa. What was said of David Livingstone may be written of Lambie as well: "Judgement of the man should be based, not on the thoughts of particular days or situations, but on his whole life and service."[29]

For Thomas A. Lambie a fitting and final accolade may be composed by adapting the simple but profound statement found in 2 Timothy 4:7: "He fought the good fight, finished the course, and kept the faith."

28. Duff, *Cords of Love*, 334.

29. Roy Bridges, "David Livingston's Journal Entry for 26 March 1866," in *Essays in Religious Studies for Andrew Walls*, ed. Thrower, 60.

Appendix 1

"Abyssinia" versus "Ethiopia"

THROUGHOUT THIS BIOGRAPHY OF Thomas A. Lambie, the name "Abyssinia" appears more often than does "Ethiopia." The reason for the former name's prominence comes from the country's history.

The name "Ethiopia" originates from Greek "*itoopis*," meaning "the land of burnt faces" (Jeremiah 13:23 refers to dark-skinned Ethiopians). The first known application of *itoopis* to Ethiopia is found in the Greek version of a mid-fourth-century trilingual inscription. The inscription is found on a stele that dates from the time of Ezana, the Aksumite king who introduced Christianity into Ethiopia.[1] In translating various references in the Bible, the ancient Ethiopian literary language of Ge'ez used the term "*Etyopiyam*." Following the Ge'ez translation, the Ethiopian Bible Society's Amharic translation (1973) uses "*Etyopiyam*" in Job 28:19; Psalm 68:31; Isaiah 43:3, 45:14; and Acts 8:27. Subsequent translations by the Ethiopian Bible Society have retained *Etyopiyam* in these verses. It can be assumed that the designation "*Etyopiyam*" is of ancient standing.

Historically, the word "Abyssinia" comes from Arabic "*habesha*," which refers to the peoples of northern present-day Ethiopia. These peoples formed as an amalgamation, over the course of several centuries, of tribes from southern Arabia with the people already present within the Horn of Africa. The process produced a dark-skinned people group, who resided in their own domain that was called "Abyssinia."[2] Portuguese explorers in the sixteenth century followed the lead already set by Arabic speakers and

1. Trimingham, *Islam and the Bible*, 38–40.
2. Ullendorff, *The Ethiopians*, 50–57.

writers, who used "Abyssinia" to designate the Horn of Africa as an overall region. This designation continued down the centuries through the Italian occupation of 1936–1941. Even today, it is not uncommon for Ethiopians, when speaking colloquially, to refer to themselves as *"habesha"* (Abyssinians). And Ethiopians have complimented some SIM colleagues who have mastered the Ethiopian language and culture especially well by stating, "He (or she) is a *habesha.*"

On June 29, 1936, Emperor Haile Sellassie I addressed the League of Nations in Geneva. He began his historic speech with the words, "I, Haile Sellassie, Emperor of Ethiopia, am here today to claim justice that is due to my people."[3] Five years later, on May 5, 1941, when he victoriously returned to his throne in Addis Abba, the country became officially known as "Ethiopia."

---

3. Haile Sellassie, *My Life and Ethiopia's Progress,* 300.

Appendix 2

Act of US Congress Authorizing
the Naturalization of Thomas A. Lambie

SENATOR GEORGE L. RADCLIFFE of Maryland introduced a special bill into the United States Congress that authorized the restoration of Thomas A. Lambie's US citizenship through the process of naturalization. It read:

[Private–No. 472—76th Congress]
[Chapter 591–3rd Session]
[S. 2768]

AN ACT
Authorizing the naturalization of
Thomas A. Lambie

Be it enacted by the Senate and House of Representatives of the United States of America in Congress assembled, That, notwithstanding any other provision of law, at any time within one year after the date of enactment of this Act, Thomas A. Lambie, of Owings Mills, Maryland, may be naturalized as a citizen of the United States by taking the naturalization oath of allegiance before any court having jurisdiction of the naturalization of aliens.

This special bill was approved on July 11, 1940, and apparently aroused unusual comment in local newspapers. The *Baltimore Sun* reported, "Dr. Thomas Lambie, a resident of Owings Mills but a citizen of Emperor Haile Selassie's pre-Italian Ethiopia, appeared on the road to obtaining his second citizenship when the Senate passed and sent to the House a bill allowing him to resume his status as an American citizen."[1]

Lambie expressed gratitude for the help Pastor Roland Philips, Arlington (Virginia) Presbyterian Church, extended by introducing him to Senator Radcliffe.

1. See Lambie, *A Doctor Carries On*, 18.

Appendix 3

"Remembering Dr. Lambie,"
Lowell Thomas, Radio Newscaster

ON JANUARY 13, 1941, newscaster Lowell Thomas spoke of Thomas Lambie on his radio program. Two days later William R. Barbour, editor in chief of Fleming H. Revell Company, publisher of some of Lambie's books, sent Lambie a transcript of the broadcast.

> Remember Dr. Lambie, the American who was Haile Sellassie's chief advisor, in the days before the King of Kings was obliged to take it on the lam (escape). Well, Dr. Lambie is back on the Abyssinia border again. He recently wrote a book entitled *A Doctor without a Country*. When he became a sort of Grand Vizier to the King of Kings he was obliged to give up his American citizenship. But a bill has passed the Senate which is intended to restore those rights.
>
> I have just had a long message from Dr. Lambie. He sends it to me from deep in the Sudan. In one telegram he describes the death of Dr. Robert Grieve, a young American from Seattle, and his wife, who were bombed at Doro, on the Abyssinia border, an unimportant village where there was no reason at all for the Italians to drop bombs. Dr. Lambie says that Bob Grieve was attempting to signal the Italian planes with an American flag and actually fell with the flag enveloping him.
>
> But what is more to the point at present, Dr. Lambie says that a few months ago the Sudan was almost unprotected and now all that has changed. He believes that the British are ready for a big push, and says John Bull's war machine in Africa is now

going in full gear, with the trailer car of Haile Selassie fastened on behind. He says that large numbers of Abyssinians have been living in the Sudan since the Italo-Ethiopian war. And they are yearning for their cool Abyssinian mountains. Their cry at present, said Dr. Lambie is: "Addis Ababa! Only a month away! On to Addis Ababa."

Dr. Lambie, "the doctor without a country," believes that the push is on now, the campaign that will, as he put it, "Change Benito Mussolini into Finito Mussolini."

Lowell Thomas, who died in 1976, was a newscaster for four decades over both the CBS and NBC radio networks.[1]

1. For the above transcript, see Lambie, *A Doctor Carries On*, 7–8.

Appendix 4

Dr. Thomas A. Lambie's Membership in the Royal Geographical Society

THE FOLLOWING EMAIL ACKNOWLEDGES that Dr. Thomas A. Lambie was indeed a Fellow of the Royal Geographical Society.

> Dear Dr. Balisky,
>
> Thank you for your email. I am sorry for the delay in reply. We have been extremely busy lately. We hold candidate for election certificates for both Rev'd Thomas Lambie, M.D., and Mrs. T.A. Lambie.
>
> With kind regards,
>
> Julie[1]

Thomas Lambie was elected a Fellow of the Royal Geographical Society on April 23, 1923. He resigned in February 1931, but rejoined in 1936, after which he remained a Fellow until his death in 1954. He was recommended on the basis of personal knowledge by Robert Hall Glover.

Charlotte Lambie was elected a Fellow of the Royal Geographical Society on February 21, 1938, and resigned in December 1940. She was recommended by Thomas A. Lambie and, on the basis of personal knowledge, by Henry Balfour.

---

1. Julie Carrington, Royal Geographical Society, email to Paul Balisky, April 27, 2016.

Appendix 5

Official Permit for Lambie's Guns

የኢትዮጵያ: መንግሥት.

እልግ:ወራሽ:ተፈሪ: n:

የኢትዮጵያ: መንግሥት. እልግ: ወራሽ ተፈሪ መኰንን.
ይደረሳ: ስንቡር: መሴ. ሎሬ. የጅቡግዋ.ቶኔ. የጅቡቲ:አገር: ገዥዥ
ስ ሳም: ስርስዋ: ይሁን.—
የ ዳንፕር: ሳም ቤ. ስስታ. መመገኛ. ስዬስት. ኺህ: ፲ይቶ ዐጿ.
ኢትዮጵያ ስገግባ ሳፎ: እናስታ ወቅ ፖያስግ. የገተቱ. ኗቅ ግ—
፲፱፻፲ ፱ መ ተ: ምስረቱ ተ ዴሬ. ስጿ ስ: እበገ. በተ መ—

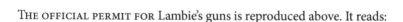

THE OFFICIAL PERMIT FOR Lambie's guns is reproduced above. It reads:

Tafari Makonnen, Regent and heir to the throne of the Ethiopian Government,

Dear Moise Lauret, Governor of Djibouti, in the French Colony,

Peace to you.

We inform you [of] the approval of the importation of Doctor Lambie's three rifles and six thousand [rounds] of ammunition.

Written on February 8, 1924 a.d., in the city of Addis Ababa.

Two seals appear on the permit. At the bottom it is stamped with the official seal of the Imperial Ethiopian Government. The official seal (with a lion) of Tafari Makonnen, Regent of Ethiopian Government, appears at the upper left.

Zenebe Gebrehana, manager of SIM Publication and Distribution, Addis Ababa, kindly translated Lambie's gun permit from Amharic to English.

Appendix 6

Letter from Ras Tafari Makonnen to Thomas A. Lambie, May 30, 1922

የኢትዮጵያ፡ መንግሥት፡

አልጋ፡ወራሽ፡ተፈሪ፡ስ፡

Adis. Ababa, Abyssinia.
30th May 1922.

Dr. T. A. Lambie,
200 north Fifteenth Street.
Philadelphia
U. S. A.

Dear Dr. Lambie

Since you left this country I have not received any letter from you untill the present moment. I hope that yourself with all the members of your family, and also the three Ethiopian youngmen, who had accompanied you, are in good health.

Please inform me, in detail, about the traction-engine and the Ethiopian Type-writer. I hope that it will be possible to improve the said Type-writer to make it as perfect as possible.

At the same time, please, write me about the hospital and the result of your enterprise in relative with it. Awaiting for your letter and your early return, I remain,

yours faithfully,

THE LETTER ON THE preceding page, dated May 30, 1922, shows that Ras Tafari Makonnen, ruler of Abyssinia, felt he had ready access to American education and technology through his new acquaintance, Dr. Thomas Lambie. The three Ethiopian students whom the Lambies escorted to the United States were Bashawarad, Workou, and Malaku (photograph courtesy of MHSC).

Chronology of Thomas A. Lambie, 1885–1954

1885	February 8: Thomas A. Lambie is born, Pittsburgh, Pennsylvania
1901	September: Lambie matriculates, University of Pittsburgh Medical School
1905	He is deeply motivated by John R. Mott, "The Evangelization of the World in This Generation"
1906	June: Lambie graduates with MD degree, University of Pittsburgh Medical School
1907	He is appointed to the Anglo-Egyptian Sudan by Foreign Missions Board of the United Presbyterian Church to serve as medical doctor at Doleib Hill on Sobat River
1909	April 6: Thomas marries Charlotte Claney, US missionary teacher, in Alexandria, Egypt
1910	April 26: Son Wallace is born, in Tanta, Egypt
1911–12	September to September: Lambie family on furlough in the United States. Lambie returns to Sudan March 1912
1911	September 12: Daughter Elizabeth Anne (Betty) is born, in Philadelphia, Pennsylvania
1912	Lambie family pioneers ministry among the Nuer, based at Nasir on the Sobat River
1914	July: Lambie family takes a one-month vacation in Alexandria, Egypt
1917	January to December: Lambie family on furlough in the United States

1918	Lambie family returns to ministry among the Nuer, based at Nasir station on the Sobat River
1919	Lambie is invited to Sayo (Dembi Dollo) by Ras Birru to launch medical work in Abyssinia
1921	Lambie family travels by mule from Sayo to Addis Ababa, where they meet Ras Tafari Makonnen
1921–22	January to January: Lambie family on furlough in the United States to raise funds for proposed hospital in Addis Ababa
1923–26	Lambie builds George Memorial Hospital; then serves as its surgeon-general
1923	April 23: He is elected a fellow of the Royal Geographical Society
1925	June: Lambie is mentioned in *National Geographic Magazine*
1926	July: Lambie family arrives in the United States for furlough
1927	March 6: Thomas and Charlotte Lambie resign from United Presbyterian Mission
1927	The Lambies, George Rhoads, and Alfred Buxtons launch Abyssinian Frontiers Mission
1927	Abyssinian Frontiers Mission amalgamates with Sudan Interior Mission (SIM)
1927	December 25: Lambie and SIM party arrive in Addis Ababa
1928	March 7: Lambie and the nine new missionaries leave Addis Ababa and head south
1928	March–April: Lambie and party are welcomed by Mosheshe in Hosanna, Yigezu in Soddo, and Birru in Agere Selam
1928	October 28: Lambies celebrate Ras Tafari's elevation to throne as king
1928	November: SIM missionaries at Hosanna, Soddo, and Agere Selam receive eviction notice
1929	March: SIM receives permission to locate at Marako, Lambuda, Soddo, Homatcho, and Yirga Alem
1929	April 2: For medical reasons, Charlotte Lambie returns to the United States with daughter Betty; they remain there until Lambie joins them in May 1930.
1929	Lambie serves as medical doctor in Soddo

1930	January 24: He leaves with Rhoad family for Moyale to await Rowland Bingham
1930	March 1: Lambie, with Rhoad family, meets Bingham at Moyale
1930	April 1: Empress Zauditu succumbs to diabetes
1930	April 2: Ras Tafari Makonnen is proclaimed emperor with the name Haile Sellassie I
1930	April 16: Lambie, Rhoad family, and Bingham reach Homatcho from Moyale
1930	April 21: Lambie and Bingham share in landmark SIM conference in Soddo
1930	May 12: Lambie and Bingham are welcomed in Addis Ababa by government officials
1930	May 24: Lambie and Bingham present two Persian cats (brought by Miss Marcella Scholl) to Emperor Haile Sellassie
1930	May 25: Lambie accompanies Bingham to the United States for furlough (which extends to November 1931)
1930	November 2: SIM members are invited to Haile Sellassie's coronation in St. George's Cathedral, Addis Ababa
1930	November 20: Wedding of daughter Betty to Herbert Rees; Lambies and son Wallace attend ceremony
1931	November: Thomas and Charlotte Lambie return to Abyssinia
1932	February 2: Lambie receives notification that 180 acres have been granted for leprosarium and SIM headquarters property
1932	April 19: Lambie and Rhoad receive letter from Cain, Duff, and Lewis asking, "Why delay baptism?"
1932	May 5: Lambie writes to Bingham asking for clarification on establishing native church
1932	May 16: Lambie chairs second significant SIM Ethiopia council meeting held at Soddo
1932	June 1: He writes to Bingham complaining of compatibility issues with Rhoad
1932	June 19: Rhoad relocates to the United States to serve as SIM deputy general director
1932	July 17: Lambie asks that Glen Cain, who is ill, be flown from Sidamo to Addis Ababa in Haile Sellassie's plane

1932	July 19: Lambie reports to Rhoad that the roof is now on the SIM headquarters building
1932	September 15: Thomas Lambie and Miss E. W. Robertson escort Oswald J. Smith from Addis Ababa to Marako; then, due to his ill health, they bring him back to Addis Ababa
1932	November: Construction is well underway for leprosarium at Furi
1932	December 25: First SIM baptisms; Lambie and Glen Cain baptize four Sidamo in Homacho
1932	December 28: Lambie negotiates with Ras Desta; receives permission for SIM station in Yerga Alem
1933	January–March: Lambies travel south from Soddo to expedite expanding number of stations in the south
1933	March 18: While with Duff and John Phillips at Durami, Lambies share that they are weary from travel
1933	December 1–6: Lambie visits Soddo for significant SIM council meetings
1933	December 10: Baptism of ten candidates at Soddo; Lambie does not attend the baptism
1934	February 6: Lambie returns from southern Abyssinia to Addis Ababa to meet Bingham, who has just arrived
1934	February 8–12: Lambie co-chairs, with Bingham, SIM council meeting at Soddo
1934	February 12: Bingham informs SIM council that George Rhoad has resigned from SIM
1934	February 23: Lambies and Bingham leave Addis Ababa on mule trek to northern Ethiopia
1934	March 15: Lambies and Bingham arrive at Lalibela to explore possibilities for SIM station there
1934	April 5: Charlotte Lambie ill; she, Thomas, and Bingham are flown from Debra Markos to Addis Ababa
1934	April 28–30: Lambie goes with Bingham to Soddo to meet with SIM personnel from surrounding areas
1934	April 30: Mission personnel strongly affirm Lambie as SIM director in Ethiopia

1934	May 14: Mr. and Mrs. Oglesby, Dr. Harriet Skemp, and Miss Blair set off to serve in Lalibela
1934	December 5: Italians annex part of Ethiopia into Italian Somaliland after the Wal Wal incident
1934	December 26: Lambies return to Lalibela to finalize matter of land for SIM station
1935	January 28: Lambies receive telegram on the trail about the sudden death of their son Wallace
1935	April: Lambie becomes an Abyssinian citizen in order to legally procure mission station property
1935	May–September: Lambies fly to England and the United States to represent the ministry of SIM
1935	Lambie publishes *Abayte! Or Ethiopia's Plea for Help*
1935	September 20: Lambies return to Addis Ababa; Lambie is appointed executive secretary of Ethiopian Red Cross
1935	October 3: Italian forces under the command of General de Bono invade Ethiopia
1935	October 11: Lambie officiates at wedding of the Duffs with the emperor in attendance
1935	November 5: SIM launches Ethiopian Red Cross Unit #4, staffed by Dr. Hooper, Smith, and Webb
1936	February–May: Chaos in countryside; SIM personnel advised to remain on their stations
1936	April 1–4: Lambie chairs final SIM field council in Addis Ababa
1936	April: Sixteen SIM stations are functioning in Abyssinia
1936	April 14: Haile Sellassie takes refuge with the Oglesbys at SIM station at Lalibela
1936	April 26–30: Lambie organizes, with others, feeding of over 3,500 soldiers destitute from the war
1936	May 2: Haile Sellassie and his cabinet leave Addis Ababa by train for Djibouti, going then to Europe
1936	May 6: Armed bandits attack Daisy McMillan and Freda Horn in Marako
1936	May–June: Ato Dembel escorts Daisy McMillan and Freda Horn from Marako to Addis Ababa

1936	May 9: Cliff Mitchell and Tom Devers are speared to death in Arsi Desert
1936	May 10: Lambie writes letter to General Graziani, submitting to Italian forces; his action is viewed by Abyssinians as "surrender"
1936	June–August: Lambies occasionally entertain Italian personnel in their Akaki home
1936	August 21: Lambies leave for England, then the United States, never to return to Ethiopia
1937	March 14–25: Lambie and Bingham investigate SIM opportunities in Sudan
1938	February 21: Charlotte Lambie is elected a fellow of the Royal Geographical Society
1938	August 21: Clarence Duff is the last SIM missionary to leave Abyssinia
1939	Lambie publishes *A Doctor without a Country*
1939	November: Lambies return to Sudan; Lambie appointed as director of SIM in Sudan; serves until 1942
1940	July 11: Lambie regains his US citizenship by act of US Congress
1941	March–April: Lambie serves as a British propaganda agent supporting Ethiopian patriot fighters, working from a base in Malakal
1941	August–October: Lambies take short medical leave in Palestine; are hosted by the Alfred Clarks
1942	July 9: Lambies, rather exhausted and with health care needs, leave Sudan via Nigeria for the United States
1942–43	Lambies take leave of absence from SIM, stay at Houses of Fellowship, Ventnor, New Jersey (now Overseas Ministries Study Center, New Haven, Connecticut)
1942	Lambie is awarded honorary ScD degree by University of Pittsburgh
1942	He publishes *A Doctor Carries On*
1943–46	Lambie trains at tuberculosis sanatorium near Gettysburg, Pennsylvania
1943–46	He becomes involved part-time with New England Keswick, Massachusetts
1943	Lambie publishes *Boot and Saddle in Africa*

1944-46	He serves as president of New England Keswick, with various speaking engagements
1945	May 23: Thomas and Charlotte Lambie join the Independent Board for Presbyterian Foreign Missions (IBPFM) to serve in Palestine
1946	January 25: En route via England to Palestine, Charlotte Lambie dies suddenly at Port Said, Egypt
1946-47	Lambie serves as medical doctor at the British Hospital in Hebron
1947	October 1: Thomas Lambie marries Irma Schneck, former SIM missionary in Jimma, Abyssinia, but at that time serving in Nigeria
1947	October 3: Lambies leave for the United States to raise funds for the proposed tuberculosis sanatorium to be built near Bethlehem
1948	May: Lambie flies from the United States to England to visit his daughter Betty as she and her husband Herbert have now separated
1948	October: Seriously ill in the United States, Lambie has his spleen removed
1949	Lambies return to Palestine and begin construction of tuberculosis sanatorium
1952	August: Dedication of the Berachah Tuberculosis Sanatorium, with J. Gordon Holdcroft, director of IBPFM, participating
1952	Lambie publishes *A Bruised Reed*
1953	May-June: Lambies fly to England for a short vacation with daughter Betty Rees and her four children
1953	President Raymond V. Edman and Professor Joseph Free, Wheaton College, Wheaton, Illinois, probably around Easter time, visit the Lambies at the Berachah Tuberculosis Sanatorium
1954	April 14: Thomas Lambie dies at the Garden Tomb while preparing a sermon for Easter sunrise service
1954	April 16: Lambie is buried at the Baraka Bible Presbyterian Church, Bethlehem, Jordan
1954	Lambie publishes (posthumously) *A Doctor's Great Commission*
1957	Lambie publishes (posthumously) *A Bride for His Son*

Glossary of Ethiopian Titles

Abuna (Abun.)	Metropolitan of the Ethiopian Orthodox Tewahido Church
Alaqa	Ecclesiastical title referring to the chief priest
Ato	Equivalent to "Mr."
Balabat	Indigenous official in southern Ethiopia who provided the chief administrative link between his own ethnic population and the central government
Bajirond	Treasurer
Bitwadid	A senior advisor to the imperial court
Blattengeta (Blatta.)	Title given to learned men and scholars
Dajazmatch (Dajjaz. or Dej.)	Literally "commander of the gate"; a title of nobility
Echage	Administrative head of the Ethiopian Orthodox Tewahido Church
Fitawrare (Fit.)	Literally "leader of the vanguard"; a title of nobility
Grazmatch (Graz.)	Literally "commander of the left"; a title of nobility
Lij	Literally "child"; a title reserved for the children of high-ranking nobility
L'ul	Literally "prince"; a title borne by sons of the royal family

L'elt (or *Li'ilt*)	Literally "princess"; a title borne by daughters of the royal family
Naftanya	A northern soldier allocated a piece of land in the south as a reward for military service to the imperial government
Nagadras (*Nag.*)	Literally "chief of the merchants"; with authority to collect taxes
Nigus	Amharic word for king; used of Tafari Makonnen after 1928
Nigusa Nagast	Emperor; literally "king of kings"; title given to Haile Sellassie after 1930
Qinyazmatch (*Qinyaz.*)	Military title, now of lesser rank; literally "commander of the right"; a title of nobility
Ras	Literally "head;" a title of high nobility; positioned in battle next to the king
Tsahafe t'ezas	Minister of the Pen, head of the royal scribes, keeper of the royal seals
Weizero	Equivalent to "Mrs."

Glossary of Amharic Words

Amba	Flat-topped mountain often used as a fortress
Anjera	Flat bread made of a small grain indigenous to Abyssinia
Ensette	False banana tree grown for food in southern Abyssinia
Ferenj	A European, a white man
Kale Heywet (Church)	Word of Life Church, a large Ethiopian evangelical denomination
Santim	Smallest value coin, similar to a penny
Shifta	An outlaw, a brigand, a bandit
Sila nefas	Literally, "because of the wind" (i.e., take an excursion for a holiday or for one's health)
Teff	Small brown grain used to make flat bread
Y'hidar beshita	Influenza epidemic that ravaged Abyssinia in November 1918

Archives and Special Collections

MATERIALS WRITTEN BY THOMAS A. Lambie or written to him or relevant to his life and his entrepreneurial missionary career are housed in archives and personal special collections located around the world. These materials consist of letters, reports, manuscripts, texts of speeches, addresses, diaries, and journals among other items. I have utilized materials from the archives and special collections listed below in preparing this book. My thanks for the help provided by the staff of each. Abbreviations or acronyms, if used, are also shown below.

Archival materials such as correspondence, reports, and manuscripts are not listed in the bibliography. These materials vary in length from a single page to thirty pages and more; without them this biography of Thomas Lambie could not have been written. Descriptions of the materials and aids for locating them appear in the footnotes.

Abbreviation	Archive or Private Special Collection
	Bethel Synod Archives, Addis Ababa, Ethiopia
	Foreign Missions Board of the United Presbyterian Church of North America, located in Presbyterian Historical Society, National Archives of the PC(USA), Philadelphia, Pennsylvania
IBPFM	Independent Board for Presbyterian Foreign Missions Archives, Plymouth Meeting, Pennsylvania
MHSC	Margaret Rees Hall Special Collection, Kerry (near Newtown), Wales, United Kingdom
	Stephen Roke Special Collection (Alfred Roke materials), New Zealand; see also www.rokefamily.org

PBSC	Paul Balisky Special Collection, Grande Prairie, Alberta, Canada
SIMIA	SIM International Archives, Charlotte, North Carolina
SSNA	South Sudan National Archives, Juba, South Sudan

Bibliography

Anderson, David M., and Douglas H. Johnson, eds. *Revealing Prophets: Prophecy in Eastern African History*. London: Currey, 1995.

Anderson, Gerald H., ed. *Biographical Dictionary of Christian Missions*. Grand Rapids: Eerdmans, 1998.

Aren, Gustav. *Envoys of the Gospel in Ethiopia*. Stockholm/Addis Ababa: Evangelical Church Mekane Yesus, 1999.

Artin, Yacoub Pasha. *England in the Sudan*. London: Macmillan, 1911.

Bahru Zewde. *A History of Modern Ethiopia, 1855-1991*. Addis Ababa: Addis Ababa Univ. Press, 2002.

Balisky, E. Paul. "Esa Lale, a Prophet of Religious Innovation in Southern Ethiopia." In *Proceedings of the 14th International Conference of Ethiopian Studies, November 6-11, 2000, Addis Ababa*, 568-81. Addis Ababa: Addis Ababa University, 2002.

———. *Wolaitta Evangelists: A Study of Religious Innovation in Southern Ethiopia, 1937-1975*. Eugene, OR: Pickwick, 2009.

Baudendistel, Rainer. *Between Bombs and Good Intentions: The Red Cross and the Italo-Ethiopian War, 1935-1936*. New York: Berghahn, 2006.

Baye Yimam, ed. *Ethiopian Studies at the End of the Second Millennium*, vol. 1, *Proceedings of the XIVth International Conference of Ethiopian Studies, November 6-11, 2000, Addis Ababa*. Addis Ababa, 2002.

Bingham, Rowland V. "Across Africa by Mule and Motor." *Evangelical Christian* (July 1936) 260-61, 266, 282.

———. "The Editor Safely Home." *Evangelical Christian* (August 1934) 303-4.

———. "Entering into Ethiopia with Christ." *Evangelical Christian* (June 1936) 226, 241.

———. "Ethiopia and the Mission Red Cross." *Evangelical Christian* (October 1935) 382.

———. "From Aden to Addis Ababa and Beyond." *Evangelical Christian* (August 1934) 193-94.

———. "Italy and Ethiopia." *Evangelical Christian* (June 1936) 219-20.

———. "The Lure of Lalibella, Ethiopia." *Evangelical Christian* (August 1934) 300-2, 328.

———. "A New Call to a New Land." *Evangelical Christian* (October 1927) 399.

———. "On Ethiopia's Frontiers." *Evangelical Christian* (June 1937) 308-9.

———. "Our Mission: Red Cross for Ethiopia." *Evangelical Christian* (December 1935) 507-10.

———. *Seven Sevens of Years and a Jubilee: The Story of the Sudan Interior Mission.* Toronto: Evangelical, 1943.

———. "The Situation in Ethiopia." *Evangelical Christian* (July 1936) 257–58.

Bryan, Jack. "Is the World's Next Missions Movement in Ethiopia?" *Christianity Today,* June 21, 2019. www.christianitytoday.com/ct/2019/july-august/ethiopia-missions.html.

Carlson, Roy. *Cairo to Damascus.* New York: Knopf, 1951.

Cooper, Barbara M., et al., eds. *Transforming Africa's Religious Landscapes: The Sudan Interior Mission (SIM), Past and Present.* Trenton, NJ: Africa World, 2018.

Cotterell, F. Peter. *Born at Midnight.* Chicago: Moody, 1973.

———. "Dr. T. A. Lambie: Some Biographical Notes." *Journal of Ethiopian Studies* 10, no.1 (January 1972) 43–53.

Debela Birri. *Divine Plan Unfolding: The Story of Ethiopian Evangelical Church Bethel.* Minneapolis: Lutheran Univ. Press, 2014.

———. "History of the Evangelical Church Bethel, 1919 to 1947." ThD diss., Chicago: Lutheran School of Theology, 1995.

Donham, Donald L. *Marxist Modern: An Ethnographic History of the Ethiopian Revolution.* Los Angeles: Univ. of California Press, 1999.

Duff, Clarence W. *Cords of Love: A Testimony to God's Grace in Pre-Italian Ethiopia.* Phillipsburg, NJ: Presbyterian and Reformed, 1980.

Ethiopian Red Cross Society: 1935–1985. Addis Ababa: Ethiopian Red Cross Society, 1985.

Fargher, Brian L. *The Origins of the New Churches Movement in Southern Ethiopia, 1927–1944.* Leiden: Brill, 1996.

Forsberg, Malcolm. *Land beyond the Nile.* New York: Harper & Brothers, 1958.

———. *Last Days on the Nile.* Philadelphia: Lippincott, 1966.

Getachew Haile, et al., eds. *The Missionary Factor in Ethiopia.* Frankfurt: Lang, 1998.

Gidada Solon. *The Other Side of Darkness.* New York: Friendship, 1972.

Girma Bekele. *The In-Between People: A Reading of David Bosch through the Lens of Mission History and Contemporary Challenges in Ethiopia.* Eugene, OR: Pickwick, 2011.

Grubb, Norman. *Alfred Buxton of Abyssinia and Congo.* London: Lutterworth, 1942.

Haile Sellassie. *My Life and Ethiopia's Progress: Autobiography of Emperor Haile Sellassie I.* Translated and annotated by Edward Ullendorff. London: Oxford Univ. Press, 1999.

Holdcroft, J. Gordon. "Dr. Lambie Called Home." *Biblical Missions* (June/July 1954) 5–6.

———. "Field News." *Biblical Missions* (March 1946) 5.

———. "Mission to the Holy Land." *Biblical Missions* (October–November 1949) 14–16.

———. "Progress and Problems in Palestine." *Biblical Missions* (February 1952) 22.

———. "Supplement Copy" [describing Charlotte Lambie's death]. *Biblical Missions* (February 1946) 1.

Kwarteng, Kwasi. *Ghosts of Empire: Britain's Legacies in the Modern World.* New York: Public Affairs, 2011.

Lambie, Thomas A. "Abyssinia: Sokota and the Word of God." *Evangelical Christian* (May 1935) 213–14.

———. "Abyssinia: The Road of the King's Son." *Evangelical Christian* (May 1934) 290.

———. "Annual Report of the Holy Land Branch." *Biblical Missions* (March 1950) 12–14.

———. *Boot and Saddle in Africa.* New York: Fleming H. Revell, 1943.

———. *A Bride for His Son: More Light from the Bible Lands on Bible Illustrations.* New York: Loizeaux, 1957.

———. *A Bruised Reed: Light from Bible Lands on Bible Illustrations.* New York: Loizeaux, 1952.

———. "Christian Sanatorium in the Holy Land." *Biblical Missions* (November 1950) 9–10.

———. "Christmas Service on the Shepherds' Fields." *Biblical Missions* (April 1953) 5–6.

———. "Conquest by Healing in Ethiopia." *Officers' Christian Union Quarterly Missionary Letter* (September 1935) 70–72.

———. *A Doctor Carries On.* New York: Fleming H. Revell, 1942.

———. *A Doctor without a Country.* New York: Fleming H. Revell, 1939.

———. *A Doctor's Great Commission.* Wheaton, IL: Van Kampen, 1954.

———. "Dr. and Mrs. T. A. Lambie Sail for Palestine." *Biblical Missions* (August–September 1948) 12–13.

———. "Evangelism in Ethiopia—Leaves from the Diary of Dr. T. A. Lambie" [thirteen articles]. *United Presbyterian Journal* (October 4–December 27, 1928).

———. "God's Guidance in War's Alarm." *Evangelical Christian* (September 1936) 332–33, 347–48.

———. "I Have Begun to Give . . . Begin to Possess." *Evangelical Christian* (August 1937) 387.

———. "The Importance of Abyssinia." *World Dominion* (September 1926) 192–98.

———. "Let Us Rise Up and Build." *Biblical Missions* (December 1947) 12–13.

———. "A New Challenge to the Sudan Interior Mission, or, 'A Way Out' Which Is 'A Way Into.'" *Evangelical Christian* (March 1937) 133.

———. "News from the Holy Land." *Biblical Missions* (June–July 1952) 9.

———. "Our New Task." *Evangelical Christian* (June 1937) 292.

———. "Palestine, Focal Point of the World." *Biblical Missions* (June–July 1948) 23–26.

———. "Return to Palestine." *Biblical Missions* (October 1948) 17–19.

———. "Swords Drawn Up to the Gates of Heaven." *Biblical Missions* (May 1954) 24–31.

———. "When Addis Ababa Fell. . . ! Experiences and the Carnage of War." *Evangelical Christian* (July 1936) 268–69.

Marcus, Harold G. *Haile Sellassie I: The Formative Years, 1892–1936.* Lawrenceville, NJ: Red Sea, 1998.

———. *The Life and Times of Menelik II: Ethiopia, 1844–1913.* Lawrenceville, NJ: Red Sea, 1995.

"Medical Missionary Heroes: Malaku Bayen, Robert Hockman, and Winifred (nee Thompson) Hockman." *Muskingum: The Magazine for Alumni and Friends* 93, no. 1 (Fall 2002) 4.

Mesele Terecha Kebede. *Leprosy, Leprosaria, and Society in Ethiopia: A Historical Study of Selected Sites, 1901–2001.* Addis Ababa: AHRI/ALERT, 2005.

Mikre-Sellassie G/Ammanuel. *Church and Mission in Ethiopia during the Italian Occupation.* Addis Ababa: Mikre-Sellassie G/Ammanuel/Artistic Printing Enterprise, 2014.

Mockler, Anthony. *Haile Selassie's War*. Oxford: Signal, 2003.

Nelson, Kathleen, and Alan Sullivan, eds. *John Melly of Ethiopia*. London: Faber and Faber, 1937.

Pankhurst, Richard, ed. *The Ethiopian Royal Chronicles*. Addis Ababa: Oxford Univ. Press, 1967.

―――. "The Hedar Beshita of 1918." *Journal of Ethiopian Studies* 13, no. 2 (July 1975) 103–31.

―――. *An Introduction to the Medical History of Ethiopia*. Trenton, NJ: Red Sea, 1990.

Partee, Charles. *The Story of Don McClure: Adventure in Africa; From Khartoum to Addis Ababa in Five Decades*. Lanham, MD: University Press of America, 2000.

Pierli, Francesco, et al., eds. *Gateway to the Heart of Africa: Missionary Pioneers in Sudan*. Nairobi: Paulines Publications Africa, 1998.

Playfair, Guy W. *Our Trip across Africa*. Jos, Nigeria: Niger Press, 1930.

Pollock, John. *Kitchener: The Road to Omdurman*. London: Constable & Robinson, 1999.

Roke, Alfred G. *They Went Forth: Trials and Triumphs of a Pioneer S.I.M. Missionary in Ethiopia*. Auckland: Alf Roke, 2003.

Roke, Don. *Gordon of Bajang: The Short Life of Gordon Clifford Roke, 13th October 1939–27th June 1942*. Auckland: Don Roke, 2011.

Sharkey, Heather J. *Living with Colonialism: Nationalism and Culture in the Anglo-Egyptian Sudan*. Berkeley: Univ. of California Press, 2003.

Snow, Peter. *When Britain Burned the White House: The 1814 Invasion of Washington*. New York: St. Martin's, 2013.

Spencer, John H. *Ethiopia at Bay: A Personal Account of the Haile Sellassie Years*. Algonac, MI: Reference, 1984.

Steer, George L. *Caesar in Abyssinia*. London: Hodder & Stoughton, 1936.

Ullendorff, Edward. *The Ethiopians: An Introduction to Country and People*. London: Oxford Univ. Press, 1967.

Thrower, James, ed. *Essays in Religious Studies for Andrew Walls*. Aberdeen: Aberdeen Univ. Press, 1986.

Tibebe Eshete. *The Evangelical Movement in Ethiopia: Resistance and Resilience*. Waco, TX: Baylor Univ. Press, 2017.

―――. "The SIM in Ethiopia, 1927–1970: A Preliminary Note." Unpublished paper, Michigan State University, May 17, 2001.

Trimingham, J. Spencer. *The Christian Church and Missions in Ethiopia*. London: World Dominion, 1950.

Turaki, Yusufu. *An Introduction to the History of SIM/ECWA in Nigeria: 1893–1993*. Jos, Nigeria: Yusufu Turaki, 1993.

Walker, C. H. [Craven Howell]. *The Abyssinian at Home*. London: Sheldon, 1933.

Index

Page numbers in *italics* refer to illustrations.

CPSIA information can be obtained
at www.ICGtesting.com
Printed in the USA
BVHW042101260320
576144BV00013B/289